# The Positive Obligations of the State under the European Convention of Human Rights

The system of the European Convention of Human Rights imposes posit- ive obligations on the state to guarantee human rights in circumstances where state agents do not directly interfere. In addition to the traditional/ liberal negative obligation of non-interference, the state must actively protect the human rights of individuals residing within its jurisdiction. The liability of the state in terms of positive obligations induces a free- standing imperative of human rights that changes fundamentally the per- ception of the role of the state and the participatory ability of the individual, who can now assert their human rights in all circumstances in which they are relevant. In that regard, positive obligations herald the most advanced review of the state's business ever attempted in interna- tional law.

The book undertakes a comprehensive study of positive obligations: from establishing the legitimacy of positive obligations within the system of the Convention to their practical implementation at the national level. Analysing in-depth legal principles that pervade the whole system of the Convention, a coherent methodological framework of critical stages and parameters is provided to determine the content of positive obligations in a consistent, predictable and realistic manner.

This study of the Convention explains and critically analyses the state's positive obligations, as imposed by the European Court of Human Rights, and sets out original proposals for their future development. The book will be of interest to those who study, research or practice public law, civil rights and liberties or international/European human rights law.

**Dimitris Xenos** is a Research Fellow at the European Public Law Organisa- tion, Athens. He also acts as a legal consultant on issues of human rights law.

# Routledge research in human rights law

**The Positive Obligations of the State under the European Convention of Human Rights**
*Dimitris Xenos*

*Forthcoming titles in this series include:*

**The European Court of Human Rights in the Post-Cold War Era**
Universality in transition
*James A. Sweeney*

**Children and International Human Rights Law**
The right of the child to be heard
*Aisling Parkes*

**Ensuring and Enforcing Economic, Social and Cultural Rights**
The jurisprudence of the UN committee on economic, social and cultural rights
*Marco Odello and Francesco Seatzu*

**The EU as a 'Global Player' in Human Rights?**
*Jan Wetzel*

**Vindicating Socio-Economic Rights**
International standards and comparative experiences
*Paul O'Connell*

**Corporate Human Rights Violations**
Overcoming regulatory hurdles
*Surya Deva*

**Jurisdiction, Immunity and Transnational Human Rights Litigation**
*Xiaodong Yang*

# The Positive Obligations of the State under the European Convention of Human Rights

## Dimitris Xenos

Routledge
Taylor & Francis Group

LONDON AND NEW YORK

First published 2012
by Routledge
2 Park Square, Milton Park, Abingdon, Oxon OX14 4RN

Simultaneously published in the USA and Canada
by Routledge
711 Third Avenue, New York, NY 10017

*Routledge is an imprint of the Taylor & Francis Group, an informa business*

First issued in paperback 2013

*British Library Cataloguing in Publication Data*
A catalogue record for this book is available from the British Library

*Library of Congress Cataloging in Publication Data*
Xenos, Dimitris.
The positive obligations of the state under the European Convention
of Human Rights/Dimitris Xenos.
p. cm.
Includes bibliographical references.
1. Convention for the Protection of Human Rights and Fundamental
Freedoms (1950) 2. Human rights–Europe. 3. International and
municipal law–Europe. I. Title.
KJC5132.X46 2011
341.4'8094–dc22

2011003141

ISBN: 978-0-415-66812-5 (hbk)
ISBN: 978-0-203-80781-1 (ebk)
ISBN: 978-0-415-87024-5 (pbk)

Typeset in Baskerville
by Wearset Ltd, Boldon, Tyne and Wear

For Athena and her mother

# Contents

# Table of cases

# Legal instruments

# Foreword

To what extent should the state be responsible for protecting those under its jurisdiction from violations of their human rights by private parties, and from possible breaches arising from circumstances which, although it may not itself have created, it may nevertheless be said to have an obligation to remedy? This sophisticated, erudite and detailed study considers the legitimacy and limits of such 'positive obligations' in the context of the European Convention on Human Rights. Seeking to find a comprehensive methodological framework, it focuses on the technical expertise required of the European Court of Human Rights, and the most appropriate form of judicial reasoning, given both the goals and objectives of the Convention and the responsibilities and capacities of state parties.

While the study of positive obligations under the Convention has interested other commentators, Dr Xenos's contribution is particularly stimulating, thorough, thought-provoking, nuanced, and conscious of both theoretical and practical dimensions. As he fully acknowledges, the potentially open-ended scope of positive obligations creates both problems and opportunities. A key question is whether principled limits can be found or if it is simply a matter of pragmatic balancing, subject to elastic national margins of appreciation. Over the past thirty years or so the Court has, for the most part in the complainants brought to its attention, addressed the issue simply by conducting a series of ad hoc balancing exercises with other competing interests loosely derived from the limitation clauses attached to specific Convention provisions. Dr Xenos powerfully and convincingly argues that this has resulted in a jurisprudence without adequate theoretical foundations which undermines the potential impact of positive obligations. As he says: 'positive obligations are often used as a buzzword for every measure of compliance with human rights standards, a fact that leads gradually to their dilution.'

According to Dr Xenos, with respect to active third-party violations, the state's core positive obligation is to provide adequate legal and administrative systems that offer both minimum preventive protection and adequate remedies in cases of violation. But, inevitably, these will vary according to context and will also be subject to national margins of appreciation reflecting the state's many other responsibilities. As Dr Xenos maintains, procedural safeguards, the participation of complainants in the implementation and enforcement of positive obligations at the domestic level, and effective processes of investigation, are of particular importance. In his excellent and highly original chapter on vulnerable individuals, Dr Xenos argues that the key issues for the Court here are whether it can coherently justify its intervention and whether recognising a particular positive obligation will impose a disproportionate burden on public resources.

Dr Xenos's study makes a major contribution, not only to the debate about positive obligations, but also to our understanding of the relationship between civil and political rights, on the one hand, and social and economic rights on the other, and to how the European Convention on Human Rights can and ought to be interpreted. It should, therefore be required reading for students, scholars and policy-makers interested in these fields.

Steven Greer
Professor of Human Rights
University of Bristol

# Preface

Human rights are not simply safeguards against state interference but must be enjoyed in a wide range of circumstances. The system of the European Convention of Human Rights guarantees this by imposing positive obligations on the contracting state to actively protect human rights. As a consequence, a profound and permanent change has been brought about in the understanding and assertion of human rights.

A great number of activities that may be addressed in other legal areas (e.g. of national, supranational or international law systems) can engage the responsibility of the state under the Convention when protection of human rights has not been guaranteed. In some recent analyses, the co-existence or interaction of various legal systems is placed within a complex combination of international law and political intergovernmental arrangements that also prescribe a form of transnational governance characterised by an abstract polycentric model.

The Convention, however, is an independent and autonomous legal authority that creates and guarantees individual human rights under international law. It does not compromise when the protection of human rights is at stake. It does not answer to subjective proposals and convenient politico-legal rhetoric, but deals with real complaints by real victims of human rights violations. Accordingly, what we are mostly interested in with this study is the voice of the ordinary individual, and most importantly, the very possibility of the expression of that voice that has been made possible by the application and development of positive obligations within the system of the Convention.

In the department of law, we make things possible with legal rules. Because the art of a lawyer is law, our job here is to show how positive obligations work or can work in legally binding terms. We deal with legal questions and propose legal answers that aim to prove a manageable application of positive obligations. A methodological framework is provided to determine a realistic and tangible content of positive obligations.

The current study is an updated and slightly revised version of my doctoral thesis that was completed under the supervision of Holly Cullen and Roger Masterman at Durham University. I am indebted to both for their professionalism, the dialectics and the care that they have shown all these years with their constructive comments. I thank also the examiners, Kevin Boyle and Gavin Phillipson, for their useful suggestions.

I wish to thank the judge and former president of the Inter-American Court of Human Rights, Antonio Augusto Cançado Trinidade, for useful discussion on various occasions in the European Court's library and after the end of some seminars in Strasbourg, and for his general advice: 'concentrate on the [legal] science' which I have taken seriously. I owe great gratitude to Steven Greer and Spyridon Flogaitis for valuable advice and discussion. Special thanks to Maria for intellectual conversations and, in particular, on the importance of taking risks.

In this work, Chapter 3 is based on the article entitled 'The human rights of the vulnerable', which was published in the *International Journal of Human Rights*, Vol. 13 (4) in 2009 (copyright Taylor & Francis). For some of the cases discussed in the main text and footnotes, their official English translation had not been available in HUDOC's database (the Court's case-law electronic portal) when the final manuscript was submitted. Translations of primary and secondary sources not in English are my own, unless otherwise noted.

D.X.

January 2011

# Abbreviations

| | |
|---|---|
| *AJIL* | American Journal of International Law |
| *Camb Q Healthc Ethics* | Cambridge Quarterly of Healthcare Ethics |
| *CrimLR* | Criminal Law Review |
| *ΔτΑ* | Δικαιώματα του Ανθρώπου |
| *EEEυρΔ* | Ελληνική Επιθεώρηση Ευρωπαϊκού Δικαίου |
| *ECLR* | European Constitutional Law Review |
| *EHRLR* | European Human Rights Law Review |
| *EJIL* | European Journal of International Law |
| *ELJ* | European Law Journal |
| *ELR* | European Law Review |
| *ER* | European Review |
| *ERPL* | European Review of Public Law |
| *HRLJ* | Human Rights Law Journal |
| *HRLR* | Human Rights Law Review |
| *HRR* | Human Rights Review |
| *GLJ* | German Law Journal |
| *ICLQ* | International and Comparative Law Quarterly |
| *I·CON* | International Journal of Constitutional Law |
| *IFLJ* | International Family Law Journal |
| *IJHR* | International Journal of Human Rights |
| *ILJ* | Industrial Law Journal |
| *JCP* | Juris Classeur Periodique, La Semaine Juridique |
| *JLS* | Journal of Law and Society |
| *LLR* | Liverpool Law Review |
| *MJ* | Maastricht Journal of European and Comparative Law |
| *MLR* | Modern Law Review |
| *NILR* | Netherlands International Law Review |
| *NQHR* | Netherlands Quarterly of Human Rights |
| *N-SAIL* | Non-State Actors and International Law |
| *OJLS* | Oxford Journal of Legal Studies |
| *RDI* | Rivista di Diritto Internazionale |
| *RGDIP* | Revue Générale de Droit International Public |

| | |
|---|---|
| *RHDI* | Revue Hellénique de Droit International |
| *RIDC* | Revue Internationale de Droit Comparé |
| *RIDU* | Rivista Internazionale dei Diritti dell'Uomo |
| *RLR* | Ritsumeikan Law Review |
| *RTDH* | Revue Trimestrielle des Droits de l'Homme |
| *STL* | Scots Law Times |
| *ToΣ* | Το Σύνταγμα |
| *ΧρΙΔΕ* | Χρονικά Ιδιωτικού Δικαίου |
| *YbkEL* | Yearbook of European Law |
| *YLJ* | Yale Law Journal |

There really is no such thing as art, there are only artists.

Ernst Gombrich

# 1 The working base

## 1.1 What's right and what's wrong with positive obligations

The discourse of the protection of human rights sixty-one years after the signing of the European Convention of Human Rights (hereinafter, the Convention)[1] is now placed within a normalised era of European history in which the state acts as their principal protector and guarantor. These are the times in which human rights are increasingly advertised in political manifestos and their established status is reflected in university study packages and job opportunities both linked to the growing supermarket of governmental, intergovernmental, international or non-governmental human rights organisations.[2] In this mainstream climate, the obvious and fundamental functions of the state, and by extension, of law, are re-discussed, rediscovered and restated in order to secure a normal starting point. As Phedon Vegleris recalled in the early 1970s:

> [i]t is also undeniable that the protection of the individual from attacks on his liberties by other private individuals constitutes one of the normal functions of the law, particularly civil and criminal law, and an essential task of the executive and judicial authorities. And it is a historical fact that this function of the law was in operation and had reached a certain degree of stability even before the rights of the individual vis-à-vis the State were proclaimed, or means

1 Convention for the Protection of Human Rights and Fundamental Freedoms signed in Rome, 4 November 1950, E.T.S. 5, 213 U.N.T.S. 221 (as amended by Protocols No. 11 and No. 14).
2 Some tensions are currently observed with the franchising of non-governmental organisations. See, e.g., *Moscow Branch of the Salvation Army* v. *Russia* [2006] no. 72881/01; *Church of Scientology Moscow* v. *Russia* [2007] no. 18147/02. A. Giddens, 'Foreword', in M. Glasius *et al.* (eds), *Global Civil Society* (Oxford: Oxford University Press, 2002), p. iii: 'NGOs are no more elected than big corporations are, and substituting orthodox democratic politics with a world run by NGOs is therefore problematic.'

of defence against agents acting on behalf of the State were instituted.[3]

Viewed from the neutral and normal point of a genuine democracy, human rights violations by the state are the exception rather than the rule, and therefore the time has come to reverse the perspective from which the human rights discourse is made, namely the classical liberal view of the state's non-interference (negative obligation).[4]

In response to a new generation of human rights claims pushed forward by a new generation of Europeans, who have been brought up free from the complexes of the past, the Convention has passed to its complete phase under which entitlement to human rights means entitlement to enjoy human rights and not merely an entitlement to their non-violation by state agents. States are perceived as having 'inherent' positive obligations to protect and guarantee human rights within their territory. The Convention imposes positive obligations on the state to actively protect the human rights of individuals against acts of interference from other private parties. To the extent that it is the state which has the sovereign power and ability to regulate all activities operating within its jurisdiction, its indirect responsibility can reasonably be raised when human rights are violated by private parties.

Departing from the point that it is 'a historical fact' that the active protection of individuals from acts of interference of other individuals constitutes one of the normal and classic functions defining the state,[5] the subject matter of positive obligations appears basic at a first glance. There are, however, important questions on important details. Moving from general to specific issues, it is asked whether protection exists in the particular context of private interactions or whether protection is effective through regulation and procedural safeguards. Of importance, also, is the question of when human rights protection is provided and on whom the initiative of protection depends. If protection in a given context has been provided by the state, it pays to see the background/history of how

3  P. Vegleris, ' "Twenty Years" Experience of the Convention and Future Prospects', in A.H. Robertson (ed.), *Privacy and Human Rights* (Manchester: Manchester University Press, 1973), pp. 341–412, p. 382; from the same book, see also, J. De Meyer, 'The Right to Respect for Private and Family Life, Home and Communications in Relations Between Individuals, and the Resulting Obligations for States Parties to the Convention', pp. 255–275, p. 273.

4  G. Malinverni, 'Les Fonctions des Droits Fondamentaux dans la Jurisprudence de la Commission et la Cour Européennes des Droits de l'Homme', in W. Haller *et al.* (eds), *Im Dienst an der Gemeinschaft* (Basel: Helbing & Lichtenhahn, 1989), pp. 539–560, p. 539: 'In recent years, this concept appears to be insufficient, because of its purely negative character. Indeed, it does not allow fundamental rights to assume the function that is expected of them in a modern society. Therefore, to the traditional concept a constitutive concept of liberties is contrasted.', (translation).

5  P. Vegleris, in A.H. Robertson (ed.), *Privacy and Human Rights*.

protection of human rights was pressed by social forces and how long it took to acquire its current legal status.

By contrast, the uniqueness of positive obligations is that the active protection of human rights is demanded *right now* or should have *already* been provided for by the state's mechanism in circumstances in which there are known human rights issues. More importantly, the initiator of this demand is not the elected member of the Parliament, but the ordinary individual. In this account, positive obligations impose real constitutional priorities on the state's business in the form of the active protection of human rights. Other means of asserting protection of human rights, such as street-level pressure, collective actions, campaigns of civil society groups, lobbying work and modern institutionalised monitoring systems, remain usual and helpful avenues. But the emergence of the ordinary individual, the atomic unit, as the initiator of the constitutional claim (in legally binding terms) of the protection of human rights in contexts in which private individuals interact, has no precedent in the political history of humankind.

To illustrate this point, we can look at those cases from the jurisprudence of European Court of Human Rights (hereinafter, the Court) in which states have been found in breach of their positive obligation to regulate and effectively implement health and safety standards for industrial activities, whose operation violated the human rights of some individuals.[6] The message, therefore, is that an industrial activity (set up by private or public funds) must operate under health and safety standards. This issue, however, is basic, for the debate and campaign for safety standards in industrial sites is not new. Rather, the novelty of the message of positive obligations is the one single individual who is able to pursue their grievance within the system of the Convention and oblige a whole state, this most powerful and structured organisation, to prioritise its work and guarantee the protection of human rights in the various contexts in which private individuals interact.

Positive obligations exist because the binding system of the Convention exists. Therefore, the participatory ability of the ordinary individual to initiate the constitutional claim exists only because of the Convention. The current study covers the state of law on positive obligations, as has developed in the system of the European Convention of Human Rights. Previous major studies on positive obligations have covered the jurisprudence until the year of 2002, but there have been many and important developments since that time. A number of these developments concern positive obligations in circumstances where various individuals claim assistance from the state because they cannot enjoy human rights due to their own circumstances of personal vulnerability (physical and

6 See, e.g., *Guerra and Others* v. *Italy* [1998] no. 14967/89; *Oneryildiz* v. *Turkey* [2004] no. 48939/99; *Tatar* v. *Romania* [2009] no. 6702_/01 (available in French only).

psychological condition). This is an important and considerable extension
of the scope of positive obligations, and that of the Convention, which can
only be explained by the fact that the ordinary individual has become
increasingly aware of their participatory ability to initiate the constitutional claim of human rights protection at the supranational level of the
Convention. As, generally speaking, the protection of human rights is not
only restricted to acts of interference, positive obligations are now debated
and asserted across the board.

However, the problem with positive obligations is that their scope
appears open-ended. As the study of the case-law will show, the Court does
not set general conceptual limitations for its intervention to review the
manner by which human rights standards are safeguarded in private interactions, other than those linked to the conceptual scope of the Convention rights which are often described and interpreted in equally broad
terms. In principle, positive obligations can be claimed everywhere, a fact
that creates problems as well as opportunities. Where positive obligations
concern direct assistance to vulnerable individuals (i.e. an act of interference from a given source is absent), limitations are considered in relation
to the state's margin of appreciation, whose evaluation is not always clear.
The list of problems with positive obligations is long, if one takes a close
look at how they have developed in the jurisprudence. Often, problems do
not exist separately but come as a result of a previous problem that arises
in relation to a legal test or principle. In this regard, our study has to give
due weight to the most important and preliminary questions. Problems
may also arise from lack of focus on what is really at stake.

The underlying interests of this study lie in the wider effects of positive
obligations, whose application in the system of the Convention produces
two consecutive results. In particular:

1    Positive obligations secure the participatory position of the ordinary
     individual to initiate the constitutional question of the active protec-
     tion of human rights in all areas in which they are relevant (i.e.
     beyond direct interference by state actors), thereby changing funda-
     mentally the structure of democratic governance.

And, as a consequence of the first result:

2    They expand the intensity of review of the states' system at lengths not
     previously imagined or attempted by any national or international law
     institution, through the empowerment of their nationals who are now
     able, for the first time, to be personally engaged in a continuous vigi-
     lance and re-discussion of the standards of human rights protection.

It should be noted, however, that the open discussion on positive obligations is not made over the above-stated results. European judges are

renowned for their low profile and cautiousness with states' sensitivities about the ever-decreasing national sovereignty that unavoidably results from the interaction of national legal systems with European human rights law. It is to their credit that they have always managed to sense carefully the international climate and the changing social dynamics in various corners of Europe before moving to modify steadily and progressively the intensity of their review on the states' legal system. There are numerous statements by the Court on the state's margin of appreciation and on the optional choice of the domestic incorporation of the Convention but, in reality, what is actually observed is a considerable expansion of positive obligations and numerous rulings against the states that we present and discuss in the following chapters.

The whole debate on positive obligations over the last thirty years is being held in the neutral technical language of European human rights law. If the scope of positive obligations has to be curtailed or expanded, it has to be made in technical terms, because their wider effects are not openly stated so that there can be any meaningful elaboration or challenge. It is important, however, for the reader of this study to appreciate the significance of the issue with which we deal here from an early stage.

The current study of positive obligations concentrates on the technical points of law, save for a brief discussion of the object and purpose of the *Aims* Convention in a sub-section of this introductory chapter. We have set two principal aims: first, to explain the content of positive obligations in ① accordance with their potential to extend and further improve the protection of human rights in a wide range of circumstances in which the state does not directly interfere; second, to transpose the content of positive ② obligations at the domestic level through procedural safeguards and institutional access for the participation of the ordinary individual so as to guarantee the implementation of protection and the continuous debate of human rights.

The principal condition for achieving these aims regards the practical realisation of positive obligations. The content of positive obligations has to be sought over a scope of human rights protection that can realistically be handled at both national and supranational level so as to emerge as a pan-European minimum standard. Accordingly, the challenge is that the open-ended scope of positive obligations, as has ambitiously been set by the Convention, has to be brought under a manageable level and be secured by a coherent methodological framework to provide certainty and predictability in the planning of the application and development of positive obligations. — *does this apply?*.

All aims and challenges discussed above are addressed in the rest of the chapters, whose overview is detailed in the following section that sets out the route-map for the rest of study.

## 1.2  Overview of chapters

The current study is interested in the real and practical results of positive obligations that can be achieved or reasonably expected by the articulation of a doctrine in technical terms. The system of the Convention produces such results and, therefore, our exclusive area of study is its jurisprudence that is related or connected to the development of positive obligations.

Before moving to address the aims and challenges of this study in the following chapters, various essential starting points have to be secured as a working base in the introductory chapter. It has to be noted that there has been a substantial body of jurisprudence on positive obligations in the last thirty years without a connection being made to any theoretical base. Of course, the Court responds to individual petitions and senses the changes in civil society dynamics across its jurisdiction so as to develop accordingly the state's positive obligations.

There are, however, two reasons why we need some theoretical input: first, because in the volumes of European human rights law literature, positive obligations are at times ignored and scholarly commentary still debates the legitimacy of their subject matter or the conceptual limits of the Court's intervention in private relationships; we need to include discussion of the object and purpose of the Convention, the influential scholarly contributions preceding the first application of positive obligations in the late 1970s, an analysis of the early case-law on positive obligations, and the current national and international debate on the protection of human rights in private interactions. Second, a theoretical discussion provides useful background knowledge that can help explain the ever-increasing expansion of positive obligations in the Court's jurisprudence.

However, in view of the fact that the jurisprudence on positive obligations has continuously progressed for the last thirty years through an internal development of various technical principles, rather than the subjectivity of theory, the theoretical discussion in this study cannot move beyond its introduction. It should also be noted that when there is a theoretical debate on the conceptual limits of positive obligations, it is the practical issue of the reasonable management and control of positive obligations (i.e. the technical legal issue) that prompts and ultimately justifies a given theoretical position.

There are additional basic issues of context and subject matter that determine crucial perspectives and conceptual parameters about the scope and structure of the Convention rights, which have to be secured early in the study, as they affect considerably the technical discussion in the following chapters.

This chapter also provides an analysis of the Court's internal debate on the manner and intensity of its review of the state's legal system that aim to improve the quality of the European judges' decisions and the management of the ever-growing caseload. From this ongoing debate, various trends and shifts in focus have emerged that reflect the current evaluation of the capabilities, objectives and function of the Court which guide the discussion of positive obligations in subsequent chapters.

Having covered the essential starting points for the study of positive obligations, we arrange the plan of chapters to cover the substantive content of positive obligations in Chapters 2 and 3, before moving, in Chapter 4, to discuss the procedural framework that guarantees the implementation of positive obligations at the domestic level.

Chapter 2 covers the application and development of positive obligations in the system of the Convention. Positive obligations are determined through a coherent framework that accords due weight to contextual differences. With reference to the Court's internal debate, the chapter relies on current case-law developments to assert the distinctiveness of positive obligations which establishes their potential and guides accordingly the determination of their content. The critical condition, against which the state's international liability can be engaged when human rights are  violated by non-state actors, is identified and placed at the centre of the proposed framework. Since the question of international liability arises first, the content of positive obligations, at whichever stage and level is examined, is determined in conformity with the conditions engaging the state's liability under the Convention.

The more detailed discussion of positive obligations is sub-divided according to the nature and structure of the Convention rights and the practical limitations of the cost of human rights protection. Critical conditions and parameters that affect the judicial examination are addressed in order of their respective importance. The length of this chapter exceeds that of any other chapter due to the large number of critical details that all have to be identified and be known before determining positive obligations in the wide range of circumstances in which human rights can be threatened in private interactions.

Chapter 3 continues the discussion on the substantive content of positive obligations that extends to the protection of vulnerable individuals who cannot enjoy human rights due to their own personal (physical and/or mental) condition. Before a content of positive obligations can be described, limits of legitimacy and practicality of protection are identified. The chapter recognises (the possibility of) positive obligations through well-defined limits, given that protection of human rights is claimed in the very wide range of circumstances in which the causal element of a prior interference from a private or public actor is absent. Limits that relate to the scope of the Convention rights have already been introduced and discussed in the preceding chapters, as they concern basic and preliminary questions of the content of positive obligations whose application transcends context. Their discussion in this chapter is particularly valuable for the whole thesis of this study that aims to establish a manageable scope of

positive obligations through a methodological framework of critical principles and parameters and procedural guarantees. In that regard, the
content of positive obligations is not only examined as a personal form of
protection but as the very framework through which any given content of
protection can be asserted and finally emerge.

Chapter 4 completes the study by addressing the question of the
domestic implementation of the substantive content of positive obligations
that is covered in the previous chapters. It discusses procedural rights and
legal principles by which the Court reviews procedural safeguards and
structures that are crucial for the enforcement of positive obligations in
the state's legal order. The analysis of the procedural framework extends
to the procedural aspects of the substantive content of positive obligations
(as is discussed in previous chapters) which target both the private parties
that directly violate human rights and the public officials who discharge
the state's positive obligations in relation to the acts of the former. Procedural safeguards are marked as access points for the participation of the
ordinary individual in the implementation and enforcement of the substantive content of positive obligations at the domestic level. The underlying aim is to manage positive obligations at the European level through
an intensified review of the domestic procedural infrastructure in the
critical stages (and sub-stages) of the decision-making process of public
administration.

## 1.3  Basic issues of context and subject matter

### 1.3.1  *The distinctiveness of human rights*

Stating the most basic point, the protective role of the state is examined
over 'human rights'. The trademark term 'human rights' that is recognisa-
ble universally was launched with the Universal Declaration of Human
Rights by the General Assembly of the United Nations in 1948.[7] Closely
connected to human rights are the so-called fundamental freedoms (e.g.
freedom of expression), which have both an individual and collective/
political dimension. Being mutually inclusive, human rights and fundamental freedoms form one interconnected whole, with the term 'human
rights' encompassing fundamental freedoms. Also, under the strict liberal
understanding, the rights of individuals are freedoms from acts of interference and, therefore, human rights can be seen as synonymous to
fundamental freedoms. However, the use of the term 'rights' instead of

---

7  For a detailed analysis of the Universal Declaration of Human Rights, see P. Drost, *Human
   Rights as Legal Rights: The Realization of Individual Human Rights in Positive International Law*
   (Leyden: A.W. Sijthoff, 2nd edn, 1965). The membership of the United Nations has
   expanded since its foundation in 1945, with Switzerland becoming the 190th member and,
   thus, a member of the General Assembly in 2002.

'freedoms' has a great significance, in that the 'rights' term connotes a natural law imperative that induces an open-ended negotiation of the relationship between the state and the individual citizen, as well as the full and continuous arrangement of constitutional balances of rights and freedoms between the citizens themselves. This position is further influenced by the concurring existence of international law that aims at the rights of *everyone* in order to prescribe universal values, rather than to simply preserve the state of citizens and their individual interests, for which purpose human rights had originally developed and accordingly declared. In this connection, human rights gradually emerge, in addition or otherwise, as a special and distinguishable category of rights that revolve around intrinsic elements of one's personhood to define indispensable anthropocentric values of universal standing.

Other alternative or concurring terminology exists, such as 'fundamental rights' which is more expansive and does not automatically reveal the exact nature of the rights referred to.[8] Examples from the wording used in national constitutions include: *Droits de l'Homme et du Citoyen* (the Rights of Man and of the Citizen); *Grundrechte/Grondrechten* (Basic Rights); Human Rights Act; *Ατομικά και Κοινωνικά Δικαιώματα* (Individual and Social Rights); *Diritti e Doveri dei Cittadini* (Rights and Duties of Citizens); *Drepturile, Libertăţile Şi Îndatoririle Fundamentale* (Fundamental Rights, Liberties, and Duties); *Temel Haklar ve Ödevler/Direitos e Deveres Fundamentales/De los Derechos y Derebes Fundamentales* (Fundamental Rights and Duties); *Основни Права и Задължения на Гражданите* (Fundamental Rights and Duties of Citizens).

However, it is not the label given to a category or set of rights that is important, but rather their nature and exact content. For the purposes of the current study, which is exclusively made on the European Convention of Human Rights, human rights include fundamental freedoms that apply to every individual (citizens and non-citizens, including those from non-member states) within its territorial jurisdiction.[9] The content of human rights and fundamental freedoms that are covered in this study are those of Section I that lists the so-called substantive rights of the Convention. Further rights of concurring or supplementary nature have been added to its text, such as the proprietary right under Article 1 of Protocol 1. However, despite being undeniably important, this right

8 See, e.g., Article 30: 'Protection in the event of unjustified dismissal', Charter of Fundamental Rights of the European Union (*Official Journal of the European Communities*, C 364/1; C 303/1).

9 In some circumstances, the states are also accountable for extraterritorial violations, see, e.g., *Loizidou* v. *Turkey* [1995] no. 15318/89 *Xenides-Arestis* v. *Turkey* [2005] no. 46347/99; *Al-Saadoon and Mufdhi* v. *the United Kingdom* [2010] no. 61498/08. See, further, B. Simpson, *Human Rights and the End of the Empire* (Oxford: Oxford University Press, 2001); S. Helaoui, 'Respecting Human Rights Abroad? On the Extraterritorial Application of the European Convention on Human Rights' (Mphil, University of Lund, 2005).

can be compromised relatively easily by way of monetary compensation due to the wide discretion accorded to the state to pursue general socio-economic policies.[10] Thus, different evaluative standards require separate studies.

### 1.3.2 International responsibility and the general scope of human rights protection

The general scope of human rights protection, against which the international liability of the contracting state is arranged, is indicated in the title of the Convention and its first provision (Article 1). Both the title and the first Article are worded in broad terms allowing the Court to self-assert its autonomy[11] and interpret the Convention as a 'living instrument'.[12]

### 1.3.2.1 Article 1

The first Article is cited immediately before Section I and sets out the terms of the state's international responsibility as follows:

> The High Contracting Parties shall secure to everyone within their jurisdiction the rights and freedoms defined in Section I of this Convention./Les Hautes Parties contractantes reconnaissent à toute personne relevant de leur juridiction les droits et libertés définis au titre I de la présente Convention.

Although both the English and the French text are official, it is widely accepted that it is the English version of 'shall secure' rather than the lighter wording of 'reconnaissent' ('recognise') that expresses the real scope and potential of the Convention.[13] The Court had the opportunity in an early case to clarify that

10 See, e.g., *James and Others* v. *the United Kingdom* [1986] no. 8793/79, para. 46: 'The Court, finding it natural that the margin of appreciation available to the legislature in implementing social and economic policies should be a wide one, will respect the legislature's judgment as to what is "in the public interest" unless that judgment be manifestly without reasonable foundation.' *Association of General Practitioners* v. *Denmark* (dec.) [1989] no. 12947/87; *Andersson and Others* v. *Sweden* (dec.) [1991] no. 14083/88, para. 128: *The Former King of Greece and Others* v. *Greece* [2000] no. 25701/94, para 87; *Jahn and Others* v. *Germany* [2002] nos. 46720/99,…, 72552/01, para. 91; *Walker* v. *the United Kingdom* [2006] no. 37212/02, para. 33; *Poznanski and Others* v. *Germany* (dec.) [2007] no. 25101/05.
11 *Al-Saadoon & Mufdhi* v. *the United Kingdom* [2010] no. 61498/08, para. 128: 'a Contracting Party is responsible under Article 1 of the Convention for all acts and omissions of its organs regardless of whether the act or omission in question was a consequence of domestic law or of the necessity to comply with international legal obligations.'
12 *Tyrer* v. *the United Kingdom* [1978] no. 5856/72, para. 31; *Pretty* v. *the United Kingdom* [2002] no. 2346/02, para. 54.
13 J. De Meyer, in A.H. Robertson (ed.), *Privacy and Human Rights*, p. 259.

Unlike international treaties of the classic kind, the Convention comprises more than mere reciprocal engagements between contracting States. It creates, over and above a network of mutual, bilateral undertakings, objective obligations which, in the words of the Preamble, benefit from a "collective enforcement"... By substituting the words "shall secure" for the words "undertake to secure" in the text of Article 1 (art. 1), the drafters of the Convention also intended to make it clear that the rights and freedoms set out in Section I would be directly secured to anyone within the jurisdiction of the Contracting States.... The Convention does not merely oblige the higher authorities of the Contracting States to respect for their own part the rights and freedoms it embodies; as is shown by Article 14 (art. 14) and the English text of Article 1 (art. 1) ("shall secure"), the Convention also has the consequence that, in order to secure the enjoyment of those rights and freedoms, those authorities must prevent or remedy any breach at subordinate levels.[14]

### 1.3.2.2 Title

The title of the Convention reads as 'Convention for the Protection of Human Rights and Fundamental Freedoms'/'Convention de Sauvegarde des Droits de l'Homme et des Libertés Fondamentales'. From this, one can discern the general nature of the Convention provisions, as well as the general purpose, namely their 'protection' ('sauvegarde').

The title of the Convention is also conveniently referred to as the 'European Convention of Human Rights' ('La Convention Européenne des Droits de l'Homme'), with fundamental freedoms being implied in these short titles. It should be noted that, unlike the French short title that remains unchanged wherever and whenever is used, the English version is also encountered as 'the European Convention *on* Human Rights'. The difference between a Convention 'of' human rights, as opposed to a Convention 'on' human rights is nothing but fundamental. The former recognises its preponderant status close to the *one and only* document, while the latter version suggests *a* Convention *on* something among other things. In addition, as Pieter Drost has explained:

A clear distinction must be made between treaties *of* human rights and treaties *on* human rights. The first category creates individual rights; the second creates merely governmental obligations. If the international legal order has the essential function to afford protection against the state, and to guarantee the individual assistance by the state, it is necessary to create individual human rights under international law.[15]

---

14 *Ireland* v. *the United Kingdom* [1978] no. 5310/71, para. 239. See also the quotation of Article 1 in the French translation of that judgment, para. 236: 'Les Hautes Parties Contractantes reconnaissent – en anglais – "shall secure" – à toute personne (...) Convention.'
15 Drost, *Human Rights*, p. 174.

### 1.3.3   The nature and structure of the Convention rights: the centrality of private life/personality as a core value

Section I of the Convention contains the substantive rights against which the state's international liability arises. The nature and structure of these rights can first be seen by a literal reading of their respective provisions, i.e. Article 2: the right to life; Article 3: prohibition of torture and inhuman or degrading treatment, etc. At a basic level, the Convention is studied on an Article-by-Article basis, as reflected in the applicants' claims and Court's decisions. There are, however, broader issues of human rights protection in the wider context to which the applicant's circumstances often relate which accordingly require a broader approach. To this aim, it is important to note that the Convention is not simply a collection of various human rights interests but constitutes an integrated whole. As the Court constantly reiterates, '[t]he Convention must also be read as a whole, and interpreted in such a way as to promote internal consistency and harmony between its various provisions.'[16]

In this respect, due attention has to be paid to the first component of Article 8 that guarantees respect for 'private life', a term whose broadness accounts by far for the most positive obligations claims.[17] The concept of private life has long been connected to the development of one's 'personality'[18] (or 'personal development'[19]), an interpretation that satisfactorily encapsulates the ultimate core of a person's existence. It has been made clear since the early jurisprudence of the former European Commission of Human Rights (hereinafter, the Commission)[20] that

---

16  *Stec and Others* v. *the United Kingdom* (dec.) [2005] nos. 65731/01, 65900/01, para. 48. See also *Kjeldsen, Busk Madsen and Pedersen* v. *Denmark* [1976] nos 5095/71, ..., 5926/72, paras 52 and 54; *Klass and Others* v. *Germany* [1978] no. 5029/71, para. 68; *Soering* v. *the United Kingdom* [1989] no. 14038/88, para. 103; *Kudla* v. *Poland* [2000] no. 30210/96, para. 152.

17  L. Wildhaber, 'The European Court of Human Rights in Action' (2004) 21 *RLR* 83–92, p. 84: 'In a dynamic instrument, Article 8 has proved to be the most elastic provision.'

18  This approach has been influenced by the German constitutional provision of Article 2 of the Basic Rights (*Grundrechte*) of 1949: 'Everybody has the right to the free development of his personality, as long as he does not violate the rights of others and does not contravene the constitutional order or moral laws.' For analysis of earlier case-law, see P. Duffy, 'The Protection of Privacy, Family Life and Other Rights Under Article 8 of the European Convention on Human Rights' (1982) 2 *YbkEL* 191–238, pp. 191, 194, 224; L. Loucaides, *Essays on the Developing Law of Human Rights* (Dordrecht: Martinus Nijhoff, 1995), chapter 4: 'Personality and Privacy under the European Convention on Human Rights', pp. 83–107.

19  *Pretty* v. *the United Kingdom* [2002] no. 2346/02, para. 61; *Van Kuck* v. *Germany* [2003] no. 35968/97, para. 69; *Campagnano* v. *Italy* [2006] no. 77955/01, para. 53; *Evans* v. *the United Kingdom* [2007] no. 6339/05, para. 71; *Farcas* v. *Romania* (dec.) [2010] no. 32596/04, para. 68 (available in French only); *Ozpinar* v. *Turkey* [2010] no. 20999/04, para. 45 (available in French only).

20  Under the provisions of Protocol 11, the European Commission and the European Court on Human Rights joined together in a single body, the European Court of Human Rights, in 1999.

For numerous anglo-saxon and French authors the right to respect "private life" is the right to privacy, the right to live, as far as one wishes, protected from publicity.... (§) In the opinion of the Commission, however, the right to respect for private life does not end here. It comprises also, to a certain degree, the right to establish and to develop relationships with other human beings, especially in the emotional field for the development and fulfilment of one's own personality.[21]

Under this clarification, the scope of Article 8 targets the necessary conditions that allow the individual to develop their personality, or, put in negative terms (perhaps more accurately), those critical conditions without which the personality of an individual cannot develop. Such conditions have been recognised in Article 8 case-law as including the 'physical and psychological integrity' of a person and the possibility to 'develop relationships with other human beings'. To the extent that these specific interests are vital to the development of one's personality, they are valued in their own right, something that is also confirmed by the fact that in some judgments direct reference to the more general and unifying core value of personality is often omitted.[22]

The generous interpretation of 'private life' as the development of one's personality (or personal development) not only succeeds in specifying an otherwise open-ended term but also, more importantly, interconnects all human rights around a central concept through which the long-professed holistic reading of the Convention provisions can be achieved. As Commissioner Loukis Loucaides (as he was then) has noted in analysing earlier Article 8 jurisprudence:

> [t]he personalised inclination of the system [of the Convention] is indicated by the particular human rights which are expressly recognised and protected and which constitute aspects of personality of the

---

21 *X. v. Iceland* (dec.) [1976] no. 6825/74, p. 87, as quoted by Loucaides, *Essays*, p. 87, who also explains that 'from the first years of application of the Convention [its organs] have felt the need to protect the right to privacy on the basis of the requirements of personality.', citing an admissibility decision of 1969, no. 2929/66, pp. 99–100, see also pp. 86–87 and footnote 11. For earlier case-law, see *Bruggeman and Scheuten* v. *Germany* (dec.) [1976] no. 6959/75, para. 57; *McFeeley and Others* v. *the United Kingdom* (dec.) [1980] no. 8317/78. See also *Taliadoroi and Stylianou* v. *Cyprus* (dec.) [2008] nos 39627/05, 39631/05, paras 52–54; *Reklos and Davourlis* v. *Greece* [2009] no. 1234/05, paras 39, 40; *Bigaeva* v. *Greece* [2009] no. 26713/05, para. 23.

22 See, e.g., *Niemietz* v. *Germany* [1992] no. 13710/88, para. 28; *Costello-Roberts* v. *the United Kingdom* [1993] no. 13134/87. In *Botta* v. *Italy* [1998] no. 21439/93, para. 32, it has been explained that '[p]rivate life, in the Court's view, includes a person's physical and psychological integrity; the guarantee afforded by Article 8 of the Convention is primarily intended to ensure the development, without outside interference, of the personality of each individual in his relations with other human beings' (cited case omitted).

individual in a democratic and pluralistic society (the right to respect for private and family life, home and correspondence, freedom of thought, of expression and of association, the right to education, the right to marry, etc.).[23]

In that connection, the holistic reading of the Convention concerns in essence a central protected interest (i.e. personality) around which various degrees of severity and contextual applications are specified in the remaining rights whose exact scope is fixed in the Court's jurisprudence.[24]

Where contextual applications are concerned, such as the right to marry, preference is given to the *lex specialis* (Article 12) due to the degree of specificity entailed in the express provision.[25] A link to the central protected interest of one's private life/personality, through a reference or a parallel examination of the *lex generalis* (Article 8), will always be useful for a better appreciation of the interconnection and holistic reading of the Convention provisions.[26]

### 1.3.4 The object and purpose of the Convention

It is important at this early stage of the study to acquire an understanding of the political significance of positive obligations that places the question of their legitimacy and far-reaching scope within the object and purpose of the Convention.

The European Convention of Human Rights is first and foremost a peace project. It was founded as a regional international institution following the setting up of the United Nations and the Universal Declaration of Human Rights in the aftermath of the Second World War (WWII), an event that is remembered as the most catastrophic war in human history for the unprecedented number of casualties and the sickness and perversity of the atrocities committed. Within the geo-

---

23 Loucaides, *Essays*, p. 85. It should also be stressed that freedom of expression and of association, as guaranteed by Articles 10–11 have a personal dimension in addition to their collective value for a democratic society. See, e.g., *Lingens* v. *Austria* [1986] no. 9815/82, para. 41: 'the Court has to recall that freedom of expression, as secured in paragraph 1 of Article 10 (art. 10–1), constitutes one of the essential foundations of a democratic society and one of the basic conditions for its progress and for each individual's self-fulfilment.' *Steel and Morris* v. *the United Kingdom* [2005] no. 68416/01, para. 101; *Dlugolecki* v. *Poland* [2009] no. 23806/03. See also *Molka* v. *Poland* (dec.) [2006] no. 56550/00, discussed in chapter 3.

24 See, e.g., *Costello-Roberts* v. *the United Kingdom* [1993] no. 13134/87; *Goodwin* v. *the United Kingdom* [2002] no. 28957/95.

25 Duffy, 'The Protection of Privacy, Family Life and Other Rights under Article 8 of the European Convention on Human Rights'.

26 See, e.g. *Abdulaziz, Cabales and Balkandali* v. *the United Kingdom* [1985] nos 9214/80; 9473/81; 9474/81; *Goodwin* v. *the United Kingdom* [2002] no. 28957/95.

political area of the Council of Europe, differences between member states on human rights issues can peacefully be adjudicated by the Convention's institution.[27] The standing of the Convention as an international adjudicator has boldly been affirmed in cases concerning the preservation and actual enjoyment of property (including physical access) of individuals who have forcedly been displaced following a military operation.[28]

However, the Convention's plan to advance the objective of peace goes beyond the international adjudication of human rights issues between the contracting states. As is clear from the preamble of the treaty, peace is the categorical and ultimate objective that has to be achieved through the intermediate objectives of democracy, human rights (and fundamental freedoms) and the rule of law. All these objectives are indispensable in guaranteeing a solid institutionalised framework at the domestic level capable of inducing a civilised and advanced political culture. In other words, the Convention aims at the foundations of peace by creating a European culture that has a sweeping effect on whole generations of people, rather than serving as a mere adjudicator of human rights complaints after peace has been broken. Every single complaint brought by an individual residing within one of the contracting states is an opportunity to advance and continuously maintain the political culture of democracy, human rights and the rule of law. Every victory won at the individual level is a victory towards an advanced civilised culture and, by extension, a victory towards peace.

The realisation of the core intermediate objectives of the Convention presupposes an additional intermediate objective, which is the Convention itself. This fundamental assertion is highlighted as follows:

27 Since it was set up in 1959, the Court has delivered judgments in three inter-state cases: *Ireland* v. *the United Kingdom* [1978] no. 5310/71; *Denmark* v. *Turkey* [2000] no. 34382/97; *Cyprus* v. *Turkey* [2001] no. 25781/94. At the time of the application of *Georgia* v. *Russia*, lodged with the Registry on 26 March 2007, a further 17 inter-state applications were dealt with by the former European Commission of Human Rights. See, further, S. Greer, *The European Convention on Human Rights: Achievements, Problems and Prospects* (Cambridge: Cambridge University Press, 2006), 'Inter-state complaints', p. 25.

28 *Loizidou* v. *Turkey* [1995] no. 15318/89; *Demades* v. *Turkey* [2003] no. 16219/90; *Xenides-Arestis* v. *Turkey* [2005] no. 46347/99; *Epiphaniou and Others* v. *Turkey* [2009] no. 19900/92; *Dokic* v. *Bosnia and Herzegovina* [2010] no. 6518/04. The dissenting opinion of the French judge Pettiti in the *Loizidou* case has to be cited if only to show different visions about the role of the Court in international affairs and peace: 'The movement of displaced persons from one zone to another, an exodus which affected both communities, was the consequence of international events for which responsibility cannot be ascribed on the basis of the facts of the Loizidou case but has to be sought in the sphere of international relations'.

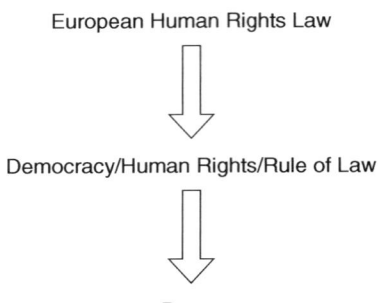

European Human Rights Law

Democracy/Human Rights/Rule of Law

Peace

The Convention has first to establish a supranational system that sets itself over and above national sovereignty. It produces European human rights law that creates and guarantees individual human rights under international law. In such a system there are three fundamental characteristics:

1    The decisions of the European Court of Human Rights are *binding*.[29] The Court is able to order an award of just satisfaction under Article 41 and ask for action on the part of the respondent state where there is a continuing effect of human rights violation in the applicant's circumstances.[30] The Committee of Ministers supervises the state's compliance and intensifies its monitoring over repetitive cases concerning similar human rights complaints against the same state.[31]

2    The state shall secure the Convention rights to '*everyone*', as expressly stated in Article 1 or implied and stated in paragraph 1 of other Articles ('*everyone* has the right to ...', or '*no one* shall be ...').[32]

3    *Individual Petition* to the European Court is secured under Article 34 (ex Art. 25), which has become obligatory since 1987.[33] This right is complemented by corresponding rights of access to a human right

---

29  Loucaides, *Essays*, p. 4: 'The provisions of the European Convention in contrast with those of the Universal Declaration, are legally binding and may be enforced through the judicial organs of the Convention.'

30  *Fadeyeva* v. *Russia* [2005] no. 55723/00.

31  Resolution *Res(2004)3* of the Committee of Ministers on a judgment revealing an underlying systemic problem (adopted on 12 May 2004). See also *Broniowski* v. *Poland* [2004] no. 31443/96; *Lukenda* v. *Slovenia* [2005] no. 23032/02; *Cocchiarella* v. *Italy* [2006] no. 64866/01; *Rumpf* v. *Germany* [2010] no. 46344/06; *Vassilios Athanasiou and Others* v. *Greece* [2010] no. 50973/08. Cf. *Wolkenberg and Others* v. *Poland* (dec.) [2007] no. 50003/99.

32  *Austria* v. *Italy* (dec.) [1961] no. 788/60.

33  Before 1987, individual petition was available to those states that had opted for it, e.g. the United Kingdom in the 1960s, France and Turkey in the 1980s.

claim under both admissibility criteria (Article 35.1) and procedural obligations for a domestic remedy (Article 13).[34]

These three fundamental characteristics are closely interdependent and have a combining effect that comes down to one reality (the current living experience) that the Convention exists as an independent and autonomous legal authority that responds to the human rights claims of the ordinary individual. Therefore, the agenda for the development of European human rights law and, by extension, any advances needed in the current human rights standards, are informed and pursued directly by the ordinary individual.[35] It is within this context that the additional objective of 'greater unity' between member states, as is also mentioned in the Convention's preamble, can best be appreciated. Unity is the result of the combining effort of European individuals who through their own initiative and persistence advance European human rights law. Any given case that is pursued at the European level can have an effect on three levels: (1) the applicant's circumstances, (2) the respondent state's legal system and (3) that of other member states falling short of the European standards (as they are exposed to similar complaints before the Court). Accordingly, the interrelation of the intermediate objectives that have to be secured in priority in order to safeguard the final objective of peace can be described as follows:

34 W. Friedmann, *The Changing Structure of International Law* (London: Stevens & Sons, 1964), p. 244: 'this Convention signifies a revolutionary advance in the legal position of the individual. The right of an individual to bring complaints, culminating in the compulsory jurisdiction by a supra-national court, against violations of his rights by the state of his own nationality, is a derogation from the principle of absolute state sovereignty with regard to nationals'. K. Boyle and H. Hannum, 'Individual Applications under the European Convention on Human Rights and the Concept of Administrative Practice: the Donnelly Case' (1974) 68 *AJIL* 440–453, p. 440: 'The most distinctive feature of the European Convention on Human Rights is the optional procedure under [ex] Article 25'. P. Drost, *The Crime of State: Penal Protection for Fundamental Freedoms of Persons and Peoples*, Book I: *Humanicide* (Leyden: A.W. Sijthoff, 1959), p. 82: 'Human rights and fundamental freedoms, whether they are ordained in national constitutions or proclaimed in international conventions, in so far as they relate to norms of action and forms of organization of the state and do not confer rights and remedies to the private person at law, belong to the province of politics and economics more than to the department of law. [§] Constitutions and treaties often are not much more than empty words and printed paper. Words are usually plentiful and paper always patient.'
35 X. Ροζάκης (Ch. Rozakis) (former vice-president of the Court), *Η Προστασία των Ανθρωπίνων Δικαιωμάτων σε μία Μεταβαλλόμενη Ευρώπη* (Athens: Αντ. Ν. Σάκκουλα, 1994). L. Wildhaber (former president of the Court), 'A Constitutional Future for the European Court of Human Rights?' (2002) 23(5–7) *HRLJ* 161–165, p. 162: 'the mechanism of individual applications is to be seen as the means by which defects in national protection of human rights are detected with a view to correcting them and thus raising the general standard of protection of human rights.'

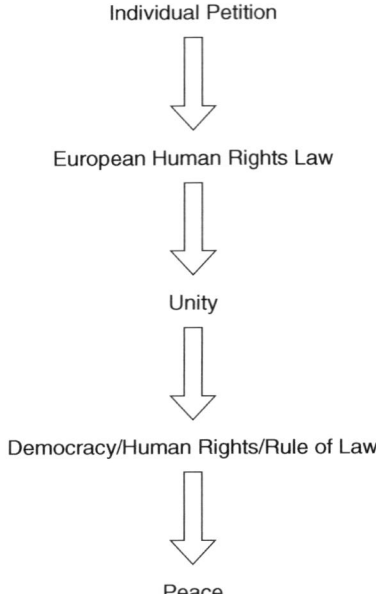

Individual Petition

European Human Rights Law

Unity

Democracy/Human Rights/Rule of Law

Peace

It should be noted that in no period in the history of humankind the ordinary individual could exercise such a direct and personal pressure through a normal institutional framework to influence important constitutional issues at both national and international levels. The emergence of the ordinary individual as an active international player in the shaping of the political culture is an overwhelming and unprecedented experience. It is this experience that explains the advanced and very advanced kind of human rights claims that are brought before the Court on the state's positive obligations. In that connection, positive obligations reflect the Court's response to social forces, as expressed in individual petitions, in redirecting the Convention as a 'living instrument' accordingly.[36]

In turn, positive obligations acquire their own significance within the Convention's interconnected aims, whose structure begins and ends with the participation of the individual and the preservation of peace, respectively. As positive obligations concern the active protection of human rights in circumstances in which the state does not directly interfere, the participatory ability of the ordinary individual now extends to all areas in

---

36 Greer, *The European Convention*, p. 170: 'by the end of the twentieth century the entire original raison d'être for the Convention had undergone subtle, yet fundamental, transformation.' citing P. Mahoney, 'Speculating on Future of the Reformed European Court of Human Rights' (1999) 20 *HRLJ* 1–4.

which human rights can be relevant, thereby signalling the most advanced review of the state's business ever attempted in international law. Therefore, when the legitimacy or the conceptual limits of positive obligations are discussed, it is important to have in mind the opportunities for the ordinary individual and, by extension, for international peace that have resulted from the development and application of positive obligations within the system of the Convention.

## 1.4 The doctrinal justification of positive obligations

### 1.4.1 Early studies

In this sub-section we give a brief account of important writings that influenced the application of positive obligations in the Court's jurisprudence in the late 1970s. The argumentation developed prior to that period exhibits the origins of the debate and help us understand that the core base of the current, more expanded scope of positive obligations has been and still remains the active protection of human rights from acts of interference of private parties. This is also an opportunity to pay homage to the scholarly debate of the 1960s and 1970s that took place at both national and international levels and which cannot possibly be exhausted here. For our purposes, we need only to present key points of justification of positive obligations from the ground already covered in previous commentary, and move on.

Some of the most important writings tackling the issue of human rights violations by private parties are contained in a book of individual articles entitled *Privacy and Human Rights*. In his contribution, ' "Twenty Years" Experience of the Convention and Future Prospects', Phedon Vegleris has pointed out:

> The only *qualitative* difference between private infringements of this kind [on human rights] and those which may be perpetrated by public authorities is that the private individual, unless he manages to establish a de facto government, can never legally remove or impair any of these rights or freedoms, either generally or individually.[37]

This explanation affirms the basic point that when human rights are violated by non-state actors, these rights have still a binding effect, and hence they are legally actionable. Therefore, it is the responsibility of the state to regulate private conduct and duly enforce the regulated

---

37 P. Vegleris, in A.H. Robertson (ed.), *Privacy and Human Rights*, p. 382.

standards. In this regard, the sovereign state becomes accountable for acts of interference of private parties.[38]

It is worth noting that some of these contributions were written by self-exiled scholars in a Europe characterised by communist regimes in the East and dictatorships in the South. In spite of that bleak political climate, the protection of human rights against private actors was dynamically campaigned for.

Beyond general justifications, it is pertinent to establish that the Convention has the necessary internal resources to channel legitimately, as well as effectively, the responsibility of the state within its supranational system. In the same book of articles, Jan De Meyer has argued that the protection of human rights from private interference should be organised by holding the state indirectly responsible. In particular, he wrote that

> without the text of the Convention having to be amended or a new protocol drafted, violation by private individuals of the rights protected by the Convention can be sanctioned indirectly, under the existing text, by the organs responsible for ensuring that the Convention is respected by the contracting States, if the responsibility of such a State is involved. Such a case could arise if a State had failed in its duty to provide due protection and, in particular, had failed to take the necessary steps to prevent or punish the offence or ensure effective redress for the victim, for where the State's responsibility is involved in this way it follows that it is the State itself which has infringed the rights protected.[39]

De Meyer based his position on the express wording of the Convention rights and the background information of the drafting history. In particular, he explained that the state's indirect responsibility for human rights violations by private parties is deduced from the express wording of the following provisions:

38 M.-A. Eissen, 'La Convention Européenne des Droits de l'Homme et les Obligations de l'Individu: une Mise à Jour', in *Amicorum Disciplorumque Liber René Cassin III: Protection des Droits de l'Homme dans les Rapports Entre Personnes Privées* (Paris: Pédone, 1971), pp. 151–162, p. 156: 'How does a private individual encroach on the rights of another if the state does not authorise the individual's acts in the name of a private interest, which is both legitimate and sufficiently important?' (translation). G. Malinverni, in W. Haller *et al.* (eds), *Im Dienst an der Gemeinschaft*, p. 559: 'the Strasbourg organs have deducted from the Convention the obligation of the member states to make sure that the rights and liberties of the Convention cannot be prejudiced in any circumstance, irrespective of whether the interference, which can be attributed to the State, originates from the State itself or a private individual or even from a state agent, which authorises or tolerates that act ... If a violation of a fundamental right is caused by an act of a private individual, it is not him who should be responsible, but the State.', (translation).

39 J. De Meyer, in A.H. Robertson (ed.), *Privacy and Human Rights*, p. 273.

- Article 1: To secure the Convention rights to everyone.
- Article 13: To guarantee an effective remedy notwithstanding that the violation has been committed by persons acting in an official capacity.[40]
- Article 17: To prohibit abuse of the Convention rights by any state, group or person engaged in any activity.[41]
- The terms 'Everyone has the right' in Articles 1, 2, 5, 6, 8, 9, 10, 11, 13 or 'no one shall' in Articles 3, 4.[42]

Any of these provisions, taken alone or in combination, suffices to establish positive obligations as inherent into the system of the Convention.

In addition, De Meyer cites the drafting history of Article 8 from the *travaux préparatoires* to remind that a proposal to include 'the right to freedom from governmental interference' in the first paragraph of Article 8 was removed by the drafting Conference.[43] Although the drafting papers do not influence the interpretation of the Convention, which has long

---

40 See also P. Mertens, *Le Droit de Recours Effectif devant les Instances Nationales en cas de Violation d'un Droit de l'Homme* (Brussels: Editions de l'Université de Bruxelles, 1973), p. 110, who pointed out that '[t]he status of the actor of the violation is indifferent.' (Ch. III, sec. III: 'L'article 13 de la Convention de sauvegarde et la responsabilité de la puissance publique'), and for analysis of earlier case-law, see pp. 111–141. Mertens quotes Henri Rolin at pp. 105–106: 'It appears that from the moment that the states are under an obligation to ensure the protection of individuals against any violation, including those emanating from a state agent, this protection means to prevent or sanction violations committed by parties other than State officials or agents, namely, by private individuals. It follows, therefore, that as far as they are concerned, there is also an obligation [for the State]. The State that ratifies the Convention links also its nationals, namely all individuals who reside in its territory' (translation), from the book of articles entitled *La Protection Internationale des Droits de l'Homme dans la Cadre Européen* (Dalloz, 1961), p. 410.

41 See also J. Rivero, 'La Protection des Droits de l'Homme dans les Rapports entre Personnes Privées', in *Amicorum Discipulorumque Liber René Cassin III: Protection des Droits de l'Homme dans les Rapports Entre Personnes Privées* (Paris: Pédone, 1971), pp. 311–322, p. 318. J. De Meyer, in A.H. Robertson (ed.), *Privacy and Human Rights*, p. 261. Declaration of the Rights of Man and of the Citizen (1789), Article 4: 'Liberty consists in the freedom to do everything which injures no one else; hence the exercise of the natural rights of each man has no limits except those which assure to the other members of the society the enjoyment of the same rights. These limits can only be determined by law'.

42 De Meyer, ibid., p. 260: 'The Council of Europe Consultative Assembly has since been moving unmistakably towards a progressive interpretation of Article 8; this is revealed especially clearly in its resolution of 23 January 1970, where it states explicitly that the "right to privacy afforded by Article 8 of the Convention ... should not only protect an individual against interference by public authorities, but also against interference by private persons or institutions, including the mass media", see also pp. 162 and 275.

43 Ibid., p. 264. For discussion of earlier case-law, see G. Malinverni, in W. Haller *et al.* (eds), *Im Dienst an der Gemeinschaft*, p. 555.

been treated by its Court as a 'living instrument',[44] they show nevertheless that even in those very early years the Convention was not meant to exclude protection of human rights from private interference.

The influence of these writings on the application of positive obligations in the Court's jurisprudence can be seen in the connection between the above-mentioned book of articles submitted for an international conference in Brussels, the first case on positive obligations against Belgium (i.e. *Marckx* v. *Belgium*) and the express reference to one of the articles from that book by the lawyer representing Paula Marckx in the homonymous case.[45] It should also be noted that learned scholars and lawyers are often nominated by the states as judges or for other influential posts in the Convention's institution (e.g. Jan De Meyer, Torkel Opsahl, Marc-André Eissen). This final note adds nothing to the internal legitimacy of positive obligations but highlights the trading and streamline of thoughts and the human factor involved in the development of institutions.[46]

### 1.4.2  The first positive obligations cases

The application of positive obligations in the Court's jurisprudence begins with the judgments in the cases of *Marckx* and *Airey* in 1979. In both these cases, the Court's ruling should be considered quite ahead of its time, even by current standards, in that the issue of protection of human rights against acts of interference from private actors was either not relevant (as in *Marckx*) or did not concern the general question of the state's indirect responsibility as such (as in *Airey*).

However, as already noted, in spite of the current expanded scope of positive obligations, their core base has been and still is the active protection of human rights from acts of interference of private parties, whose causal relation to the violation complained of requires an effective response from the state (see detailed discussion in the following chapters).

44  See case-law cited in note 12.
45  In *Marckx* v. *Belgium* (dec.) [1975] no. 6833/74, the applicant cites (at p. 130) the article of Torkel Opsahl, 'The Convention and the Right to Respect for Family Life Particularly as Regards the Unity of the Family and the Protection of the Rights of Parents and Guardians in the Education of Children', in A.H. Robertson (ed.), *Privacy and Human Rights* (Reports and Communications Presented at the Third International Colloquy about the European Convention on Human Rights, Organised by the Belgian Universities and the Council of Europe, with the support of the Belgian Government: Brussels, 30 September–3 October 1970), (Manchester: Manchester University Press, 1973), pp. 255–275.
46  With reference to the previous note, see also the argument of Commissioner Torkel Opsahl before the Court in *Airey* v. *Ireland* [1979] no. 6289/73, p. 22: 'I do not think that this Court would accept any description of the European Convention as one containing essentially "negative" rights or endorse the out-dated *laissez-faire* concept of human rights which would find anything in order so long as there was no interference by a public authority in the particular situation.', Cour/Misc.(79)19 (the Court's verbatim record).

These issues would become more apparent in subsequent case-law, such as *X and Y* of 1985 in which positive obligations were examined in relation to a violation of a human right that was caused by a private individual.[47]

For the purposes of the current study, the case *of X and Y* needs to be discussed first to preserve the order by which the understanding of positive  obligations has developed since the beginning of the scholarly debate, making more accessible in that way the core principles and justifications of the state's positive obligations. It is only then that the judgments of *Marckx* and *Airey* should be introduced to stress the expanded scope of positive obligations that we elaborate in more details in the following chapters.

### 1.4.2.1 X and Y

The case of *X and Y* concerned the rape of the second applicant (the incident occurred on the day after Miss Y's sixteenth birthday) who could not initiate criminal law proceedings against the perpetrator due to her being mentally handicapped. The applicants complained that the state did not make available a criminal law remedy against rape in the circumstances of the victim. It was admitted by the government that rape attracted generally a punishment in criminal law which could not apply in her case due to the applicable procedural requirements. However, it argued that an alternative remedy was available in civil law, although if this had been a serious argument, a preliminary objection on the non-exhaustion of domestic remedies would have already been made.

When a private party violates a human right of another individual, the liability of the state is sought over its failure to protect the victim in the given circumstances. In the cases of rape or other forms of bodily harm, the basic content of protection and, by extension, of positive obligations is to regulate the commission of offences against the person and prescribe sanctions of an appropriate deterring effect that must be backed up by law-enforcement procedures in order to ensure due compliance of law. In *X and Y*, the fact that criminal law sanctions were not enforceable or applicable in the applicant's circumstances meant in practice that no prior regulation existed in criminal law. Only civil law remedies were available, for which enforcement proceedings could be initiated. The state was found in violation of its positive obligations on the ground that the protection offered (i.e. civil law remedy) could not guarantee the appropriate deterring effect in relation to the human rights interest concerned (i.e. respect for private life under Article 8) and the higher degrees of severity therein (i.e. 'where fundamental values and essential aspects of private life are at stake').[48]

47 *X and Y* v. *the Netherlands* [1985] no. 8978/80.
48 Ibid., para. 27.

*New,*
*Nellatu!*

The case of *X and Y* constitutes what can conveniently be called the *classic* positive obligation case that arises when the state is rendered 'indirectly' responsible for its failure to actively protect an individual, either at all or adequately (as in that case) from acts of interference of another private actor.

### 1.4.2.2 Marckx

The Court applied, for the first time, positive obligations as 'inherent' in the effective protection of human rights in the case of *Marckx*.[49] The main complaint under Article 8 concerned the lack of appropriate administrative measures that would establish a legal bond between an unmarried mother and her child from the mere fact of birth. Positive obligations were justified by simply pointing to the first paragraph of the Convention right that was engaged in the applicant's circumstances. There was no need to seek additional justifications or the combined effect of various Convention Articles.

The Court's reasoning in that case closed conclusively the issue of legitimacy of positive obligations in the legal order of the Convention or, more accurately, that legitimacy was never questioned, given that positive obligations were recognised as 'inherent' in the provisions of paragraph 1 of the substantive rights of the Convention.

In order to illustrate this point further, the focus of the Court's approach has to be highlighted. The main defence in the government's submission was that the current domestic law favours the traditional family on grounds relating to morals and public order (as the legitimate aims of interference under the second paragraph of Article 8).[50] In addressing this argument, the Court did not rule on the legitimacy and justifiability of these aims but concentrated on the question that protection of the right to respect for family life applies to 'everyone', including an unmarried mother.[51] The main issue was of how an 'illegitimate family' had been protected by the state and not whether an interference could be justified. In particular, the Court reasoned:

> [the object of Article 8] does not merely compel the State to abstain from such interference: in addition to this primarily negative undertaking, there may be positive obligations inherent in an effective "respect" for family life.... As envisaged by Article 8 (art. 8), respect for family life implies in particular, in the Court's view, the existence in domestic law of legal safeguards that render possible as from the moment of birth

---

49  *Marckx* v. *Belgium* [1979] no. 6833/74, para. 31. For earlier attempts to use positive obligations terminology, see *the Belgian linguistic Case* [1968] nos 1474/62, …, 1994/63; 2126/64 (Article 2 of Protocol 1).

50  See also *Marckx* v. *Belgium* (dec.) [1975] no. 6833/74.

51  *Marckx* v. *Belgium* [1979] no. 6833/74, para. 31.

the child's integration in his family. In this connection, the State has a choice of various means, but a law that fails to satisfy this requirement violates paragraph 1 of Article 8 (art. 8–1) without there being any call to examine it under paragraph 2 (art. 8–2).[52]

It is clear from this passage that since the state has 'inherent' positive obligations to actively protect the human rights of an individual, a core content of protection has to be guaranteed by virtue of paragraph 1 of the Convention right. The judgment in *Marckx* makes clear that the state is under a positive obligation to assist the integration of a child into a family environment, including the offspring of non-marital women. If the measures taken by the state's administration do not comply with this obligation, they fall foul of the Convention without being necessary to examine any defences on a justifiable interference under the legitimate aims of paragraph 2.[53]

Having said that, it should also be noted that the state had expressly invoked paragraph 2 of Article 8 to support its position, as can be seen in the text of the Commission's admissibility decision. In principle, the legitimate aims listed in paragraph 2 can never be excluded from the judicial examination when they are relied upon in a state's defence. The state is entitled to argue its case and the Court should respond as to whether the arguments presented can or cannot be accepted. Of course, it can be argued that it was obvious that no legitimate aims of interference could be engaged in that case. In law, however, nothing is obvious until stated. If the obvious has been explained in previous jurisprudence, then express reference to these authorities should be made.[54]

The key explanation of the Court's approach in *Marckx* is not that legitimate limitations cannot be justified, but that they are not relevant. The irrelevance of paragraph 2 aims is seen from the fact that there is simply no issue of prior interference over which a limitation to a human right could be justified under one of the legitimate aims listed in that paragraph. In that respect, the main question before the Court concerned the positive obligation to actively facilitate the integration of a family. The state was found in violation of Article 8 due to the inefficient manner of

52 Ibid.
53 Duffy, 'The Case of Klass and Others: Secret Surveillance of Communications and the European Convention on Human Rights', p. 200; C. Forder, 'Legal Protection under Article 8 ECHR: *Marckx* and Beyond' (1990) 37(2) *NILR* 162–181, p. 179.
54 Previous cases arising from the same context had been rejected or had reached an opposite outcome, *Marckx* v. *Belgium* [1979] no. 6833/74, para. 58: 'As recently as 22 December 1967, the Commission rejected under Article 27 (2) (art. 27–2) – and rejected de plano (Rule 45 (3) (a) of its then Rules of Procedure) – another application (No. 2775/67) which challenged Articles 757 and 908 of the Belgian Civil Code; the Commission does not seem to have been confronted with the issue again until 1974 (application no. 6833/74 of Paula and Alexandra Marckx).'

the applicable procedure, which was so cumbersome that it was leaving the applicant's child motherless for certain days.

The Court's reasoning, as quoted in the passage above, has confirmed that the protection of human rights has a universal application that cuts across the board. The fact that the freestanding imperative of human rights (i.e. not conditioned to a prior act of interference) can be discerned  in the very first case in which positive obligations were imposed by the Court is of tremendous importance.

The universal imperative of human rights protection does not, however, mean that universal legal principles and justifications apply in all circumstances. Clearly, when positive obligations are examined in relation to acts of interference by a private party, the existence of a causal link between the act complained of and the ensuing human rights violation creates a stronger imperative to react upon a given event. In contrast, where acts of interference are absent, the protection of human rights proceeds upon different justifications and, therefore, different evaluative principles should apply. As a preliminary point, which is explored fully in the following chapters, the only possibility to restrict protection in *Marckx* under paragraph 1 of the Convention rights would be to show that a Convention right had not been engaged in the applicant's circumstances or that the cost of protection would be disproportionate, and hence impractical. Neither of these parameters applies in circumstances such as those of *Marckx* and, therefore, a core positive obligation is imposed.

### 1.4.2.3 Airey

The case of *Airey* arose from a wife's decision to separate from her abusive husband.[55] In this context of relationships between private individuals, the positive obligations of the state concern regulations that prescribe appropriate sanctions in the event of physical violence. If violence occurs within a marital relationship, then the possibility of separation should easily be accessible to the victim (see discussion above, pp. 12–14, on the right to develop one's personality under the provisions of Article 8). The general question of whether such a situation raises the indirect responsibility of the state in the form of positive obligations was not discussed as such in the Court's judgment, because it had been presupposed by both the applicant and the respondent state.

Indeed, the main issue before the Court was whether legal separation was practically available to the applicant. As discussed in *X and Y* above, the corollary of an effective regulatory framework is to guarantee enforcement and remedial procedures in order to implement in practice the regulatory standards of law. In *Airey*, legal separation had been regulated and existed as such in the domestic legal order but was not practically accessible to the

55 *Airey* v. *Ireland* [1979] no. 6289/73.

applicant due to the high financial cost of litigation. Consequently, the state was found in violation of its positive obligation under Article 8 on the grounds that the regulated measure was not effective in the applicant's circumstances. This case is further discussed in Chapter 4, which is devoted to the procedural aspect of positive obligations.

The favourable judgments of *Marckx* and *Airey* complete each other in covering both the substantive (in *Marckx*) and procedural (in *Airey*) content of positive obligations that are indispensable for the effective protection of human rights. Indeed, seizing the opportunity, as presented by the facts of these cases, the Court, in two judgments in the year of 1979, moved expeditiously to lay down the general framework and scope of positive obligations. The judgments of *Marckx* and *Airey* are not only the beginning of the application of positive obligations in the jurisprudence but reveal also their more expanded and sophisticated content that only the recent case-law has started to explore.

### 1.4.3 Subsequent studies

A major study that has exclusively been made on the state's positive obligations under the Convention is the doctoral thesis *Positive Verpflichtungen der Staaten in der Europaischen Menschenrechtskonvention* (2003) by Cordula Dröge.[56] The author presents a 'normative' categorisation of positive obligations within which the study, understanding and development of positive obligations can be undertaken through a more 'holistic' human rights theory as *liberales, soziales und multidimensionales Grundrechtsverständnis* (liberal, social and multidimensional understanding of fundamental rights).[57] The division of these categories breaks down to a 'horizontal' and 'social' dimension within which the case-law of the Court can fit. The former concerns the protection of human rights between private parties,[58] while the latter encompasses what does not fall within the former category[59] and 'comprise not only the so-called economic and social rights, but also rights to legislative action, for example to enact the laws necessary for the enjoyment of right in a given national system'.[60]

Another major study is the work of Alastair Mowbray, *The Development of Positive Obligations under the European Convention on Human Rights by the European Court of Human Rights* (2004) in which important cases are identified and categorised on an Article-by-Article basis.[61] Because of its more limited

---

56 C. Dröge, *Positive Verpflichtungen der Staaten in der Europaischen Menschenrechtskonvention* (Heidelberg: Springer, 2003).

57 Ibid., p. 196.

58 Ibid., p. 281.

59 Ibid., p. 382.

60 Ibid.

61 A. Mowbray, *The Development of Positive Obligations under the European Convention on Human Rights by the European Court of Human Right* (Oxford: Hart, 2004) covering the jurisprudence until the year of 2002.

scope, or it may have been a conscious choice by the author, it provides an unbiased account of the jurisprudence in a cases-and-materials fashion. Categorisations in horizontal, social or any other dimension play no role at all, an observation that points to the fact that positive obligations are not exactly the occasion that satisfies or links all previous literature on human rights.

It should be noted that in those studies, a critical explanation (exegesis) on the actual operation of positive obligations is largely absent, with the result that every positive measure may be classified as a positive obligation (see, for example, the case of *McCann and Others*) and/or categorised for the sake of categorisation.[62] Although the 'holistic' appreciation of human rights is a valid point that reflects also the current political climate, the term 'social' cannot be used every time a positive action is required from the state 'for lack of a better all encompassing description,…, to differentiate them from positive obligations of the horizontal dimension'.[63] Indeed, there is no basis at all in putting the cases of *Osman* and *Powell and Rayner* in the 'horizontal' basket and *Z and Others* and *Guerra and Others* in the 'social' one.[64]

In the following section, we deal with the issue of horizontality which has attracted considerable scholarly commentary, if only to show that the normal function of the state to regulate private activities has been presented as a *new* issue under a new name (i.e. 'horizontality'), which is marketed as a new normative category recycling over and again the same question of *if* the state must guarantee human rights in the relationships between private individuals.

*1.4.3.1 The horizontality issue: forced or dangerous?*

THE FORCED DEBATE

One of the most widely cited books in recent times on the issue of horizontality is *Human Rights in the Private Sphere*[65] by Andrew Clapham from his doctoral thesis, 'The Privatization of European Human Rights'.[66] The author starts from the point that 'the State should not be considered to have a

---

62 Without having to go into a review, starting from the very first case that is covered by Mowbray, *The Development*, p. 7, (i.e. *McCann and Others* v. *the United Kingdom* [1995] no. 18984/91), it is noted that the Court at no point refers to positive obligations in its judgment. An explanation is, therefore, required as to why *McCann and Others* is classified as a positive obligation case. Cf. discussion of *McCann and Others* in Chapter 2, pp. 76–78.

63 Drögue, *Positive Verpflichtungen*, p. 382.

64 Ibid., pp. 381–382.

65 A. Clapham, *Human Rights in the Private Sphere* (Oxford: Oxford/Clarendon Press, 1993), cited by, *inter alios*, Drögue, *Positive Verpflichtungen*, pp. 60, 82, and O. Cherednychenko, 'Towards the Control of Private Acts by the European Court of Human Rights?' (2006) 13 *MJ* 195–218, p. 198.

66 A. Clapham, 'The Privatization of European Human Rights' (DPhil thesis, European University Institute, 1991).

monopoly over the abuse of power'[67] and sets off to 'challenge the presumption that the fundamental rights and freedoms contained in the European Convention on Human Rights are irrelevant for cases which concern the sphere of relations between individuals'.[68] He concludes that the 'thesis presented in this study is that the European Convention on Human Rights ought to be interpreted so that it is applicable where victims face abuse from private actors'.[69] He coins a more enhanced term which is explained as 'it is the application of human rights law to the actions of private bodies which I label "human rights in the private sphere" or "the privatisation of human rights"'.[70]An even more enhanced term is also discussed which is the 'ecological' liability of the state, quoting Evrigenis, who had argued that

> [the State] is not merely answerable for violations committed by itself but also, in a more general sense, for all violations committed within its territory. One could say, indeed, that the modern State has a kind of 'ecological liability' in the human rights field.[71]

The method used in taking up the research challenge is comparative, while the first Part of the thesis is devoted to the legal system of the United Kingdom. In the record of history, however, the assertion that the rights of individuals are violated by other individuals in the relationships between themselves is as old as the first organised human society since time immemorial. That states regulate private relationships and behaviour is something that is also traced from those times.[72] With regard to the comparative study adopted, it is admitted that

---

67  Clapham, *Human Rights*, p. 9.
68  Ibid., p. 1.
69  Ibid., p. 343.
70  Ibid., p. 1.
71  Ibid., p. 183, citing D. Evrigenis, 'Recent Case-Law of the European Court of Human Rights on Article 8 and 10 of the European Convention on Human Rights' (1982) 3(1–4) *HRLJ* 121–139, p. 137.
72  P. Vegleris, in A.H. Robertson (ed.), *Privacy and Human Rights*; J. De Meyer, in A.H. Robertson (ed.), *Privacy and Human Rights*; G. Ténékidès, 'La Cité d'Athènes et les Droits de l'Homme', in F. Matscher and H. Petzold (eds), *Protecting Human Rights: The European Dimension: Studies in Honour of G.J. Wiarda* (Köln: Heymann, 1988), pp. 605–637; Decalogue; etc. See also E. Thompson, *The Making of the English Working Class* (London: Penguin, new edn, 1991): 'Not only freedom from the intrusions of the State but also belief in the equality of rich and poor before the law was a source of authentic popular congratulation. Sensational reading-matter, such as the *New Negate Calendar: or Male-factor's Bloody Register*, recorded with satisfaction ... such cases as that of Leeds' "domineering villanous lord of the manor" who was executed in 1748 for killing one of his own tenants in a fit of temper.', p. 90. 'In 1776 Wilkes went so far as to plead in the House of Commons for the political rights of the "meanest mechanic, the poorest peasant and day labourer", who, "has important rights respecting his personal liberty, that of his wife and children, his property however considerable, his wages ... which are in many trades and manufactures regulated by the Parliament."', p. 91.

[a]ll the above arguments have been taken out of context, and from various diverse traditions and disciplines, and none of them are really addressed to the question of human rights; but, the question of human rights in Europe does arise in each of the contexts referred to above – family life, work life, administrative life, sexual life.[73]

From the limited discussion on 'human rights' and the 'international obligations' of the states under the Convention, it is suggested that the European Court should follow the development of the Inter-American Court of Human Rights in the case of *Velasquez Rodriguez* in 1988,[74] as

in the Americas the Commission and the Court of Human Rights already deal with private action and the threat to human rights; therefore according to the European Court's own contextual evolutive method of interpretation the European Court should similarly offer practical and effective protection even where the link to the state cannot be easily established.[75]

However, it should be stressed that in that case the Inter-American Court examined the state's obligations in circumstances arising out of the disappearance of an individual. In scholarly commentary, the *Velasquez Rodriguez* case is also discussed in relation to procedural obligations in the form of legal safeguards (e.g. investigations) that state agents must take in *ex post facto* circumstances in order to enforce the law.[76] In Europe, the issue of human rights protection against non-state actors is not restricted to such basic issues, not to mention that private actors are not clearly involved in cases where a known disappearance phenomenon is observed.[77]

---

73  Clapham, *Human Rights*, p. 132.
74  *Velasquez Rodriguez* v. *Honduras* [1988] I.A. Ct. of Human Rights, Series C, No. 4; (1988) 9 *HRLJ* 212.
75  Clapham, *The Privatization*, pp. 165–166.
76  See, e.g., F. Ni Aolain 'The Evolving Jurisprudence of the European Convention Concerning the Right to Life' (2001) 1 *NQHR* 21–42, who makes a comparative reference to the case of *Velasquez Rodriguez* in analysing the development of *ex post* legal safeguards in justifiable lethal operations of the police, as seen in *McCann and Others* v. *the United Kingdom*, p. 33.
77  *Velasquez Rodriguez* v. *Honduras* [1988] I.A. Ct. of Human Rights, Series C, No. 4, paras 119, 147, 150. and para. 182: 'The Court is convinced, and has so found, that the disappearance of Monfredo Velasquez was carried out by agents who acted under cover of public authority. However, even had that fact not been proven, the failure of the State apparatus to act, which is clearly proven, is a failure on the part of Honduras to fulfil the duties it assumed under Article 1 (1) of the Convention, which obligated it to guarantee Monfredo Velasquez the free and full exercise of his human rights.' For similar case-law of the European Convention, see, e.g., A. Reidy, F. Hampson, K. Boyle, 'Gross Violations of Human Rights: Invoking the European Convention on Human Rights in the Case of Turkey' (1997) 15(2) *NQHR* 161–173; C. Buckley, 'The European Convention on Human Rights and the Right to Life in Turkey' (2001) 1 *HRLR* 35–65; Greer, *The European Convention*, pp. 27–28. See further discussion in Chapter 4, pp. 200–201.

Clapham closes the theory part of his study in French quoting a passage from a 1971 article of Marc-André Eissen.[78] However, the French article, which had been cited by Andrew Drzemczewski[79] in 1979, and later, once again, by Dean Spielmann in 1995 and 1998,[80] does not deal with the general issue of *if* the Convention rights are relevant for cases which concern the sphere of relations between individuals (the *if* question), as Clapham argues, but with the pertinent question of *how* human rights protection in private relationships can be organised within the supranational system of the Convention. All authors mentioned above had put forward a specific proposal (discussed below in 'the *drittwirkung proposal*' sub-section, pp. 42–43), taking the *if* question as their working base.

In addition, the discussion of the Commission's inadmissibility decision in 1985 in *Van der Heijden*, in which it was stated that '[the Commission] may not receive applications directed against individuals – in this case, Foundation, which is a private law corporation' due to the operation of the former Article 25, para. 1 (current Article 34),[81] does not prove that human rights protection against private parties had not been recognised by the Convention so as to justify a comparative analysis that suggests the paradigm of *Velasquez Rodriguez*.[82] It comes as a surprise that the author himself is aware that positive obligations have already been part of the jurisprudence, as he gives a brief discussion of the relevant cases, such as *Airey* (1979); *X and Y* (1984); *Hughes* (1986); *Plattform 'Ärzte für das Leben'* (1988); *Powell and Rayner* (1990), which prove that the Court has answered

---

78 Clapham, *Human Rights*, p. 133, quoting a passage from M.-A. Eissen, in *Amicorum Disciputorumque Liber René Cassin III: Protection des Droits de l'Homme dans les Rapports Entre Personnes Privées*, p. 162. For a translation of that passage in English, see J. Velu, 'The European Convention on Human Rights and the Right to Respect for Private Life, the Home and Communications', in A.H. Robertson (ed.), *Privacy and Human Rights* (Manchester: Manchester University Press, 1973), pp. 12–95.

79 A. Drzemczewski, 'The European Human Rights Convention and Relations between Private Parties' (1979) 26(2) *NILR* 163–181.

80 D. Spielmann, 'L'Effet Potentiel de la Convention Européenne des Droits de l'Homme entre Personnes Privées' (Brussels: Nemesis/Bruylant, 1995), revised as 'Obligations Positives et Effet Horizontal des Dispositions de la Convention', in F. Sudre (ed.) *L'Interprétation de la Convention Européenne des Droits de l'Homme* (Brussels: Nemesis/Bruylant, 1998), pp. 133–174.

81 *Van der Heijden* v. *the Netherlands* (dec.) [1985] no. 11002/84, 41 D. & R. 264, p. 270, cited by Clapham, *Human Rights*, p. 128. Cf. for analysis of earlier case-law, see J. De Meyer, in A.H. Robertson (ed.), *Privacy and Human Rights*; G. Malinverni, in W. Haller *et al.* (eds), *Im Dienst an der Gemeinschaft*, pp. 560–561; Loucaides, *Essays*, p. 144.

82 Cf. Mertens, *Le Droit de Recours*, p. 109: 'In fact, when private parties appear to be burdened with duties by virtue of Art. 13, then, as noted by Professor Rolin, there is no international sanction, strictly speaking, but rather a domestic "sanction that is internationally imposed"' (translation), citing Henri Rolin in the book of articles, *La Protection Internationale des Droits de l'Homme dans la Cadre Européen* (Dalloz, 1961), p. 214. G. Malinverni, ibid., pp. 560–561.

the *if* question by rendering the state indirectly responsible for violations of human rights by non-state actors.[83]

Moreover, the *if* question (i.e. if human rights are relevant in private interactions) is not conditioned on the 'publicness' of private activities. From the limited discussion of the technical issue of how the protection of human rights in the private sphere can be organised under the capabilities of the system of the Convention (the *how* question), special attention is given to the admissibility case of *Hughes*.[84] The case concerned a part-time cleaner at a private high school who had taken time off due to his suffering from chest pains but returned to the school to collect his wages and on that day he was discovered collapsed in the school's premises. The complaint before the Commission was about the failure of the domestic law to sanction in negligence any delays in taking prompt emergency steps to help an individual in such circumstances (i.e. to call an ambulance immediately). However, it cannot be said that the positive obligation of the state only arises because 'education is usually considered a function of the state and all private schools are to some extent subsidised by the state whether through grants, scholarships and tax relief'.[85] At no point in the Commission's reasoning did the question of whether the school is public or private play any role in deciding the admissibility issue.[86] Not to mention that when a part-time cleaner collapses in a school or a cinema theatre, this fact alone does not bring the case within the context of education or culture. If the applicant's husband went to his workplace for purposes relating to the employment contract, then the corresponding context is that of health and safety in the workplace. Alternatively, if his contract had been suspended or not applicable in the circumstances concerned, then the case should be looked at in the context of occupiers' liability for accidents occurring in their premises.

As regards the only pertinent question of how to determine the content of positive obligations, there is one single proposal that 'a "but for" test could be utilized to fix [the state's] responsibility where there was a high probability that the private violation could have been prevented by state action'.[87] With reference to the case of *Hughes*,[88] it should be said that the domestic judge relied on medical evidence to find that 'even if an ambulance had been summoned immediately, it would have been too late'. As a

---

83  *Airey* v. *Ireland* [1979] no. 6289/73; *X and Y* v. *the Netherlands* [1985] no. 8978/80; *Hughes* v. *the United Kingdom* (dec.) [1986] no. 11590/85; *Plattform 'Ärzte für das Leben'* v. *Austria* [1988] no. 10126/82; *Powell and Rayner* v. *the United Kingdom* [1990] no. 9310/81.

84  *Hughes* v. *the United Kingdom,* ibid.

85  Clapham, *Human Rights,* p. 206.

86  See also *Powell and Rayner* v. *the United Kingdom* [1990] no. 9310/81 from the same period.

87  Clapham, *Human Rights,* p. 214, referring to the case of *X and Y* v. *the Netherlands* [1985] no. 8978/80.

88  For the application of this proposal to other cases, see Clapham, *Human Rights,* pp. 196–197, 199, 201, 206, 214, 240.

result, the civil law action for compensation failed to establish an element of causation between the harm suffered by the individual and the employer's negligence. The Commission agreed with the domestic decision and stated that 'the existence of any express obligation to take prompt emergency action would not have been of any avail to the applicant's husband'. In analysing this point, Clapham explains that

> This phrase [Everyone's right to life shall be protected by law, under Article 2] would not seem to impose positive obligations or responsibility for omissions on private individuals. However, even if we grant that Article 2 implies that everyone is bound to take positive measures to guarantee other people's right to life, and that in these circumstances the teachers owed the deceased such a duty, we still have to show that *but for* the government's lack of legislation this particular duty probably would have been avoided. It is unlikely, with regard to the facts as they emerge from that decision, that legislation or other administrative measures would have had the effect of preventing the loss of life.[89]

To check the seriousness of this approach, we have to contradict it with the following factual hypothesis: on the following day of the Commission's decision, another employee at the same private school is found on the floor. The staff again stay aloof of the incident and with a two-hour delay they call the police first (as in *Hughes*), although no criminal act is suspected. Once at the scene the police call the ambulance service (as in *Hughes*) and in hospital, the employee dies after some minutes. Medical evidence could well suggest this time that a prompt transfer to the hospital would have saved the employee's life. Therefore, can it ever be suggested that positive obligations in the form of a prior 'legislation or other administrative measures' arise for the state upon circumstantial chances of *ex post* results?

The *ex post* assessment, which is perfectly suitable for examining negligence in the duty of care in a civil law action for compensation, sits uneasily with the constitutional complaint before the Court which exclusively concerns the determination of the minimum structure of a system of protection that is presupposed to exist in known contextual circumstances. Indeed, when the Court considers the state's positive obligations, the examination focuses not on the individual responsibility of private parties, but rather on the state's prior regulations of health and safety standards and the relevant administrative practices that guarantee their implementation. In that connection, a given *ex post* result cannot be relied upon to negate the positive obligation that the Convention imposes on the state's legal system as a whole. Unlike tortious (civil law) principles assessing the level of compensation, at the European level, we are concerned with the preliminary issue of setting the very minimum standards against which any

89 Ibid., p. 206.

negligence will come to be assessed *ex post*. In this account, the only pertinent question in *Hughes* is whether the state had regulated in advance
health and safety standards in the workplace or occupiers' premises that are
open to the public. The text of the Commission's decision does not inform
of the applicable regulatory framework at the domestic level. Under current
law, health and safety measures are duly regulated in the respondent state's
legal system and, therefore, the 'but for' causation test to examine a
remedial action in *ex post* circumstances remains unchallenged.[90]

The 'but for test' has also been argued, probably for the first time in
history, in the context of violence against the person. With reference to the
case of *X and Y*, it has been proposed that 'States will be liable under
the Convention, where, "but for" the absence of legislation prohibiting the
behaviour complained of, the violation of human rights would probably not
have occurred.'[91]

From the foregoing analysis, it can be said that the issue that 'the Convention rights are relevant for cases which concern the sphere of relations
between individuals' concerns a message that was sufficiently communicated in informed scholarly commentary in the 1960s and 1970s. The
debate closed after that message was officially announced in the judgments of *Marckx* and *Airey* in 1979 which made it unequivocally clear that
the protection of human rights against private actors raises the state's indirect responsibility in the doctrinal form of positive obligations.

The reason why the study of positive obligations is not moving fast
enough is because it is still trapped in the circular general debate over the
very relevance of the Convention rights in the private sphere in which the
same things are stated over and over again, setting the perspective from
which human rights protection within the system of the Convention has to
be approached. In addition, as the subject matter of study is ultimately
destined to lay people (as represented by legal practitioners), scholarly
debate should be reasonably accessible to them. In this respect, the jargon
of 'horizontality', 'privatization of human rights' and 'ecological liability
of the state' for non-ecological issues, is far from helpful.

Closing this sub-section, we adopt a rather fashionable technique by
quoting a passage from an article by Murray Hunt, who points out:

> The vocabulary of "horizontality" commits participants in the discourse
> to a prior assumption about the separateness of the public and private
> spheres which is highly controversial. It concedes the starting point in
> the debate to those who believe there to be a firm distinction between
> the public and the private spheres.... The [geometric] metaphor

---

90 K. Williams, 'Medical Samaritans: Is There a Duty to Treat?' (2001) 21 *OJLS* 393–413,
    'The existence of duty does not necessarily lead to a finding of liability, of course, since a
    claimant must go on to show breach and causation', page corresponding to footnote 104.
91 Clapham, *Human Rights*, p. 196.

presupposes that there is a fundamental distinction between public and private spheres of law's operation, and by framing the debate in this way it "assumes the very thing that needs to be debated".[92]

Subsequently, and in growing realisation (at last) that positive obligations are being imposed on the states to actively protect human rights in the private sphere, the 'horizontality' debate has turned to the alleged 'dangerous' or 'disastrous consequences' for the national private law. Some key arguments supporting this position have to be addressed here, as they re-open the question of legitimacy of positive obligations in the system of the Convention.

In this section, we respond to the points raised by Olha Cherednychenko in the article 'Towards the Control of Private Acts by the European Court of Human Rights?'[93] in relation to the case of *Pla and Puncernau*. In that case, the Court dealt with a domestic courts' interpretation of a clause in a will that it found to be discriminatory in violation of Article 14 taken in conjunction with Article 8. The applicants complained that in determining inheritance rights, the High Court of Justice and the Constitutional Court had breached their right to respect for private and family life by unjustifiably discriminating against the first applicant on the ground of his filiation (a distinction was made between adopted and biological children).

We quote the passage from the judgment that was made the subject of particular discussion:

> Admittedly, the Court is not in theory required to settle disputes of a purely private nature. That being said, in exercising the European supervision incumbent on it, it cannot remain passive where a national court's interpretation of a legal act, be it a testamentary disposition, a private contract, a public document, a statutory provision or an administrative practice appears unreasonable, arbitrary or, as in the present case, blatantly inconsistent with the prohibition of discrimination established by Article 14 and more broadly with the principles underlying the Convention.[94]

---

92 M. Hunt, ' "The Horizontal Effect" of the Human Rights Act: Moving Beyond the Public–Private Distinction', in J. Jowell and J. Cooper (eds), *Understanding Human Rights Principles* (Oxford: Hart, 2001), pp. 161–178, p. 173, citing S. Sedley, *Freedom, Law and Justice* (London: Sweet & Maxwell, 1999), p. 23. See also D. Oliver, *Common Values and the Public–Private Divide* (London: Butterworths, 1999). For a comparative study, see S. Fredman, *Human Rights Transformed: Positive Rights and Positive Duties* (Oxford: Oxford University Press, 2008).

93 Cherednychenko, 'Towards the Control of Private Acts by the European Court of Human Rights?'

94 *Pla and Puncernau* v. *Andorra* [2004] no. 69498/01, para. 59 (cited case omitted).

Cherednychenko expressed strong concerns about 'disastrous consequences' from such an approach for the private autonomy and freedom of contract, as guaranteed by the state's private law, citing in support a US academic arguing about 'the unsettling effect on private transactions' by 'the ubiquitous Convention rights'.[95]

With regard to these legitimate concerns, it should be said, first, that there is no such thing as absolute private autonomy. Private autonomy is cherished but is regulated by private law in accordance with the values of the society, as expressed by its constitution and the social pressure to which the legislator responds.[96] Not only do human rights help inform the content of private law, but social rights as well (see minimum national wage implied in freely negotiated employment contracts).[97]

The other argument about 'the unsettling effect on private transactions' by 'the ubiquitous Convention rights' has to be addressed by analysing the word 'ubiquitous' with reference to the judges' own reasoning.

The first point to note is that the Court did not review the clauses of the will, which is by its very nature selective and 'discriminatory', and as judge Garlicki said in his dissenting opinion, '[t]he whole idea of a will is to depart from the general system of inheritance, that is, to discriminate

95  Cherednychenko, 'Towards the Control of Private Acts by the European Court of Human Rights?', p. 207, citing R. Kay, 'The European Convention on Human Rights and the Control of Private Law' (2005) 5 *EHRLR* 466, p. 479.

96  J. Rivero, in *Amicorum Disciplorumque Liber René Cassin III: Protection des Droits de l'Homme dans les Rapports Entre Personnes Privées*, p. 322: 'those who would escape the state's arbitrariness, if only to fall under the domination of private powers, will only manage to change master.... To recognise but liberties that remain a dead letter in private relationships, would constitute an aberration or a hypocrisy from the part of the State, this hypocrisy that is precisely denounced by the Marxist critique of the bourgeois state.', (translation). See, comparatively, P. Benson, 'Equality of Opportunity and Private Law', in D. Friedmann and D. Barak-Erez (eds), *Human Rights in Private Law* (Oxford: Hart, 2001), pp. 201–243, p. 229, who points to 'an early instance of the State's exercise of its police power to regulate private transactions and property in furtherance of the common good and therefore as the exercise of a legislative function', referring also to early writings of B. Wyman, 'The Law of Public Callings as a Solution of the Trust Problem' (1904) 17 *Harv. L. Rev.* 156 and N. Arterburn, 'The Origin and First Test of Public Callings' (1927) 75 *U Pa. L. Rev.* 411, and courts decisions, *Munn* v. *Illinois* 94 US 113 (1876) (US Sup. Ct.) (per Waite, C.J.) and *People* v. *Budd* (1889) 117 NY (NY CA) (per Andrews, J.).

97  J. Rivero, in *Amicorum Disciplorumque Liber René Cassin III: Protection des Droits de l'Homme dans les Rapports Entre Personnes Privées*, p. 312. See also S. Simitis, 'The Rediscovery of the Individual in Labour Law', in R. Rogowski and T. Wilthagen (eds), *Reflexive Labour Law* (Deventer: Kluwer, 1994), pp. 183–205, who starts from the point that '"Constitutionalization" emerges as the highest degree of juridification of labour relations', p. 183, to explain that '[t]he legislator was thus forced to override the otherwise infallible maxim "qui dit contractual dit juste" and in the name of social stability to impose the basic security which supposedly would have been provided to the employee through the individual agreement of his or her working conditions.', p. 185.

between potential heirs.'[98] In that case the clauses of the will in question did not provide for any distinction between biological and adopted children. It was the interpretation of the domestic court that made this distinction discriminatory within the scope of Article 14. In that respect, the European judges have treated the complaint as an interference of the state, rather than as a positive obligation and reasoned that '[i]n the present case, the Court does not discern any legitimate aim pursued by the decision in question or any objective and reasonable justification on which the distinction made by the domestic court might be based.'[99]

Moving beyond the observation that the Court has reviewed the domestic courts' approach rather than the private dealings, it can still reasonably be argued that by intervening in a case arising from a will dispute, the European judges may have gone too far. There is, however, a fundamental difference between criticising one isolated judgment and proclaiming 'disastrous consequences' and 'the unsettling effect on private transactions' by 'the ubiquitous Convention rights'.

It should be recalled that positive obligations have emerged in the 1970s jurisprudence as a response to human rights violations by private parties. Therefore, as a matter of accuracy, there is no general 'Control of Private Acts by the European Court of Human Rights', but a 'Control of Private Acts that Interfere with Human Rights'. Even in *Pla and Puncernau*, it is clear that private law is subjected to the Court's scrutiny if its effect allows for a behaviour that is 'unreasonable, arbitrary or blatantly inconsistent with the prohibition of discrimination established by Article 14 and more broadly with the principles underlying the Convention'.[100]

But let us set aside isolated cases with wills and say that we deal with an express violation of a human right, actual or potential, arising out of the terms of a contract between private individuals. In such private dealings, the criticism about 'the ubiquitous Convention rights', as quoted above, is misplaced, because the Convention rights are not ubiquitous, but come into play in so far as the relevant thresholds of applicability are met. These thresholds correspond to pan-European minima and concern basic human rights standards.[101] Admissibility issues and actionable

---

98 Cf. P. Benson, in D. Friedmann and D. Barak-Erez (eds), *Human Rights in Private Law*, p. 227, citing G.W.F. Hegel, 'The Administration of Justice', in *The Philosophy of Right* (Oxford: Oxford University Press, T.M. Knox, trans., 1952).

99 *Pla and Puncernau* v. *Andorra* [2004] no. 69498/01, para. 61, see also para. 46.

100 Ibid., para. 59 (cited case omitted).

101 For earlier studies, see A. Cançado Trincade, *The Application of the Rule of Exhaustion of Local Remedies in International Law: Its Rationale in the International Protection of Individual Rights* (Cambridge: Cambridge University Press, 1983); T. Zwart, *The Admissibility of Human Rights Petitions: The Case Law of the European Commission of Human Rights and the Human Rights Committee* (Dordrecht: Martinus Nijhoff, 1994), especially chapter 3: 'Competence Ratione Personae' and chapter 5: 'Inadmissibility Related to the Merits'.

thresholds determining the scope of the Convention rights are preliminary questions in the Court's examination that have already been introduced above and are further discussed in the following chapters, as a part of the technical proposal for the management of the wide scope of positive obligations.

The conclusion for the horizontality section concerns a critical starting point, as confirmed by Peter Benson, that

> the question is not whether private law in general or contract law in particular can be constrained by public policy or whether legislation may authorise and indeed bind courts to do so. It is uncontroversial that private law is and should be regulated by, and indeed be subordinated to, requirements of public policy.[102]

In the system of the Convention, the European Court reviews the standards of the states' public policy on human rights and fundamental freedoms in relation to the activities and relationships between private individuals (including activities funded or run by the state, such as schools, hospitals, industry, etc.).[103] It follows, therefore, that European human rights law does not target the intrinsic normative resources of private law but only sets pan-European minimum standards of human rights protection,[104] as the states themselves have jointly required by setting up the Convention system. Thereafter, it is for the states, as the Commission pointed out, 'to ensure that their domestic body of law is compatible with the Convention'.[105]

---

102 P. Benson, in D. Friedmann and D. Barak-Erez (eds), *Human Rights in Private Law*, p. 224. From the same book, see also A. Reichman, 'Property Rights, Public Policy and the Limits of the Legal Power to Discriminate', pp. 245–280. See also *Van Kuck* v. *Germany* [2003] no. 35968/97.

103 See, e.g., *Hughes* v. *the United Kingdom* (dec.) [1986] no. 11590/85; *Fuentes Bobo* v. *Spain* [2000] no. 39293/98; *McGinley and Egan* v. *the United Kingdom* [1998] no. 21825/93; 23414/94; *Oneryildiz* v. *Turkey* [2004] no. 48939/99; *Murillo Saldias and Others* v. *Spain* (dec.) [2006] no. 76973/01 (available in French only); *Danilenkov and Others* v. *Russia* [2009] no. 67336/01.

104 A.M. Donner, 'Transition', in F. Matscher and H. Petzold (eds), *Protecting Human Rights: The European Dimension, Studies in Honour of G.J. Wiarda* (Köln: Heymann, 1988), pp. 145–148, p. 147: '[the Convention] presents minimal requirements, not as limits but as minima. Every State is perfectly free to go beyond and create additional or broader guaranties than those provided for by the Convention.', (translation).

105 *De Becker* v. *Belgium* (dec.) [1958] no. 214/56. C. Tomuschat, 'What is a "Breach" of the European Convention on Human Rights?', in R. Lawson and M. de Blois (eds), *The Dynamics of the Protection of Human Rights in Europe: Essays in Honour of H.G. Schermers* (Dordrecht: Martinus Nijhoff, 1994), pp. 315–337: '[Every state] has to adjust its domestic system to the consequences flowing therefrom and is precluded from arguing *ex post* that it is unable to establish the judicial machinery required', p. 328.

### 1.4.4 The substantive debate: the co(i)nstitutional guarantees

It is the normal function of the state to regulate the activities of private individuals, whether the political regime is tribal theocracy, oligarchy or democracy. The novelty of human rights and fundamental freedoms, as appeared few centuries ago, was to set constitutional guarantees in order to secure the emergence of citizens (*demos/polites*) in the control of power (*cratos*), and hence, the establishment of the natural political environment of democracy, with the principle of equality and the rule of law as the absolute corollaries. Within this reality, the next phase of political science concerns the question of how the various constitutional balances are to be arranged, first, between the state (the collective entity) and the citizen as the atomic unit of that collective, and second, and at the same time, between the citizens themselves.

This question relates, in essence, to the institutional framework that offers the public authoritative forum in which various human rights issues are brought to the attention of the state so as to be debated (the absolute prerequisite), assessed and finally addressed. Human rights and fundamental freedoms are fundamental guarantees forming part of the state's constitution which can only be implemented by an institutional framework (i.e. constitution as co(i)nstitution(s)`.[106]

At the European supranational level, the institutional forum and the constitutional guarantees are provided for by the Convention itself. All balances and technical details that the Court's judgments contain form the substantive law of the Convention that gives rise to negative or positive obligations for the contracting states. The content of positive obligations is not simply exhausted with the regulation of human rights standards for the operation of the activities of private parties. It encompasses indispensably the institutional forum that has to exist at the domestic level to enable a human right claim to be raised in the first place. Specific Convention provisions under Articles 35.1 (exhaustion of domestic remedies) and 13 (domestic remedies) combined with Article 34 (individual petition) require that a basic institutional framework exist domestically. The institutional framework breaks down to public administrative structures and further procedural safeguards therein.

In order to appreciate the advanced level at which positive obligations are examined and covered in subsequent chapters, it is necessary to discuss the Court's internal debate on the improvement of quality and effectiveness of its judicial supervision. Before that, two stops have to be made to include discussion from the parallel debates at the national and international levels that are constantly informed by, and constantly inform, the system of the Convention.

---

106 From Latin: con*sti*tutio, i-*sti*-tutio; Greek: sys*ta*na, i-*ste*-mi (to make to stand); German: *ste*hen; English: to *sta*nd.

### 1.4.4.1  The national constitutional debate

The establishment of an international community of states through the setting up of international institutions in the aftermath of WWII has provided the opportunity to reinforce the constitutional guarantees and the attached institutional framework in many countries (e.g. universal voting,[107] Constitutional courts).[108]

However, the constitutional debate was seriously impaired because various intellectual schools, which had originally emerged from genuine internal social dynamics, were subsequently hijacked to serve as intellectual flags for the marketing of Cold War politics and its manicheistic propaganda that set artificial antagonistic fronts to benefit those maintaining power at both international and domestic levels.[109] Whether the justifications had been exaggerated or not, the fact is that, until very recently, in many European countries the concept of liberalism would be explored after the liberty (independence), actual or real, of the state.

The end of the Cold War era has marked a period of international stability within which European politics live a phase of normalisation, as affirmed by the considerable expansion of the European Union and the Council of Europe eastwards. The peaceful climate that has been created and the foundation of institutional justice in the form of European international law has reduced the historic role of the external enemy that has served, deservedly or not, as the ever-available excuse or purpose of the state's affairs.[110] International stability has allowed the domestic constitu-

---

107 In most European states, universal voting for all men and women of an adult age was recognised for the first time after WWII. See also Martin Luther King's campaign for electoral rights of black Americans in the USA in the 1960s. The emancipation of women through electoral rights and their active involvement in the constitutional debate that effectively ended the masculine monopoly of world politics has yet to be evaluated, given that it is only a phenomenon of modern history. See, generally, L. Snellgrove, *Suffragettes and Votes for Women* (London: Longmans, 1964). It is no accident that the applicants in the first positive obligations cases (i.e. *Marckx* and *Airey*) were women. See also K. Engle, 'After the Collapse of the Public/Private Distinction: Strategizing Women's Rights', in D. Dollmeyer (ed.), *Reconceiving Reality: Women and International Law* (Washington, DC: American Society of International Law, 1993), pp. 143–155.

108 The appetite for unilateralism of some European states has not faded away immediately or completely. See, e.g., the Suez crisis, the war against Algeria, the occupation of Northern Cyprus. Friedmann, *The Changing Structure*, pp. 22–27.

109 Cold War: from the 'December events' (aka *Dekemvriana*) of 1944 in Athens to the fall of the Berlin wall in November/December 1989. W. Keylor, *The Twentieth-Century World: An International History* (Oxford: Oxford University Press, 3rd edn, 1996), pp. 195, 259, 456.

110 Heraclitus, *On Nature*. 'War is the father of all', cited by Plutarch, *De Iside et Osiride* 48, p. 370, frag. 43; J. Locke, *Two Treatises of Government*, P. Laslett (ed.) (Cambridge: Cambridge University Press, 1988), 'The Second Treatise of Government: Concerning the True Original Extent and End of Civil Government, Ch. III: Of the State of War', p. 278. See also online publication socserv.mcmaster.ca/~econ/ugcm/3ll3/locke/government. pdf (accessed January 2011).

tional debate to concentrate more on an introspective and in-depth evaluation of the state's system that is constantly influenced by comparative examples (including the Convention's).[111] As the external enemy is no longer omnipresent, the constitutional debate is moving beyond biased language[112] to arrange objectively human rights guarantees in the great range of circumstances in which they are relevant.[113] The current advanced level and trends of constitutional debate can easily be seen in the proliferation of specialised publication fora and academic conferences.

In the following, we bullet point a non-exhaustive list of the institutional guarantees through which various balances and arrangements of human rights are organised, and move on to discuss in more detail one of these guarantees that has influenced the discourse on positive obligations at the European level.[114]

- National Parliament shapes private law in accordance with constitutional human rights provisions. Supreme Constitutional Courts are able to strike down unconstitutional legislation, or to issue declarations of incompatibility.[115]

---

111 Mertens, *Le Droit de Recours*, p. 7, quoting Elihu Lauterpacht, 'Some Concepts of Human Rights' (1965) 11 *Howard Law Journal* 265 'One of the most interesting phenomena in the history of the protection of Human Rights is the interconnection between national and international activity in the field. International consciousness of Human Rights has grown out of national consciousness of the problem; and, in turn, contemporary national concern with the situation in many parts of the world itself stems from the extent of such international awareness'.

112 C. Bird, *The Myth of Liberal Individualism* (Cambridge: Cambridge University Press, 1999), p. 3: 'A fundamental prejudice of our time, perhaps attributable to the infiltration of a party political model of deliberation into intellectual consciousness, is the expectation that political programmes and ideals coalesce into distinct ideological traditions.'

113 W. Lippmann, 'The Reconstruction of Liberalism', in C.H. McIlwain (ed.), *Constitutionalism & The Changing World* (Cambridge: Cambridge University Press, 1939), pp. 283–293, p. 286: 'In a word liberalism means a common welfare with a constitutional guarantee.' G. Malinverni, in W. Haller *et al.* (eds), *Im Dienst an der Gemeinschaft*, p. 539: 'Departing from the idea that the Convention contains fundamental rules that make up the State, several authors perceive fundamental rights as directions destined to shape the whole set of the State's legal order and to affect all aspects of individuals lives.', (translation); E.-U. Petersmann, 'State Sovereignty, Popular Sovereignty and Individual Sovereignty: From Constitutional Nationalism to Multilevel Constitutionalism in International Economic Law?' (Florence: European Union Institute Working Paper Law No. 45, 2006), available at http://cadmus.iue.it/dspace/bitstream/1814/6446/3/LAW%20 2006–45.pdf (accessed January 2011).

114 For the ongoing co(i)nstitutional debate at the domestic level, see, e.g., R. Masterman, 'Determinative in the Abstract? Article 6(1) and the Separation of Powers' (2005) 6 *EHRLR* 628–648.

115 K.-G. Zierlein, 'Functions and Tasks of Constitutional Courts', in P. Mahoney *et al.* (eds), *Protecting Human Rights: The European Perspective: Studies in Memory of Rolv Ryssdal* (Köln: Carl Heymanns Verlag, 2000), pp. 1553–1562.

- Human Rights Ombudsmen or specialised committees (e.g. independent or parliamentary) i) receive complaints, ii) undertake their own case-studies, as informed by international developments, iii) evaluate the Convention's jurisprudence, etc., iv) make specific proposals to the Parliament and other competent administrative bodies for new laws or amendments.
- Judges are empowered with broad and flexible interpretative tools to balance competing interests in accordance with the provisions of constitutional human rights.
- Rights of access are accorded to individuals i) by way of judicial review (presupposing that the state's authorities have assumed supervising control of the activities in which human rights issues are involved) or ii) through the possibility of invoking the human rights provisions of the constitution in legal disputes between private individuals (*Drittwirkung der Grundrechte*).

From the various institutional approaches listed above, it is *drittwirkung* that has mostly been associated with the discourse on positive obligations in scholarly literature. A brief account of the old discussion and a re-evaluation of its current relevance are presented in a separate section.

### 1.4.4.2 *The drittwirkung proposal*

An alternative solution for the protection of human rights from the acts of private individuals in the system of the Convention has been proposed in the form of *drittwirkung* (i.e. the third-party effect of Basic Rights). Originating in the German legal order, *drittwirkung* is a judge-made constitutional guarantee that allows private individuals to invoke the human rights provisions of the national constitution to challenge in domestic courts the acts of other private individuals, whether or not the state's private law applies under the circumstances. *Drittwirkung* has been proposed for the system of the Convention in various influential writings of the 1960s and 1970s, such as that of Eissen (1971), mentioned above, whose proposal was repeated by Drzemczewski (1979), and even post-*Marckx* by Spielmann (1995, 1998).[116] The possibility of *drittwirkung* could

---

116 M.-A. Eissen, in *Amicorum Discipulorumque Liber René Cassin III: Protection des Droits de l'Homme dans les Rapports Entre Personnes Privées*; Drzemczewski, 'The European Human Rights Convention and Relations Between Private Parties'; Spielmann, 'L'Effet Potentiel de la Convention Européenne des Droits de l'Homme entre Personnes Privées', p. 87, who has pointed out: '[i]n future, therefore, it could be contemplated that the Court sanctions indirectly domestic courts' decisions for refusing to attribute the direct horizontal effect of the Convention in the circumstances concerned. This gives us the indirect horizontal effect of the direct horizontal effect.', (translation). See also P. de Fontbressin, 'L'Effet Horizontal de Convention Européenne des Droits de l'Homme et l'Avenir du Droit des Obligations', in G. Cohen-Jonathan *et al.* (eds), *Liber Amicorum Marc-André Eissen* (Brussels: Bruylant, 1995), pp. 157–164.

only be realised under two options: first, in direct application, by allowing private individuals to be challenged before the Court through a modification of Article 25 (current Article 34) that restricts petitions against the contracting states only; and second, in indirect application, by imposing the third-party effect of *drittwirkung* as a structural/institutional obligation on the state's legal order.

Before analysing the merits of the *drittwirkung* proposal, it is first noted that such a drastic institutional change was advanced by merely counting the countries in which *drittwirkung* had been adopted, while, at the same time, it was admitted that there was a 'complex problem' surrounding *drittwirkung*.[117] But a comparative approach in the absence of a prior technical analysis in the actual merits, the operating legal principles, and the difficulties involved, including the additional ones regarding the transposition of external principles to the structures of the Convention system, cannot be justified.

If *drittwirkung* was imposed at the domestic level as an institutional guarantee, then it would not be difficult to distinguish domestic cases on their particular facts, producing a mammoth case-law system in  which it would be impossible to find the pan-European standard. As any judicial reasoning would be connected to the specific legal principles of the domestic legal order, there would be more points for distinction that would leave us with a collection of unconnected ad hoc decisions. With no European standards emerging, the Convention would lose its relevance.

By contrast, if *drittwirkung* were given direct application within the system of the Convention, justice would mainly be done at European level, with the Court acting as a federal court, which cannot be under current structures. For the history record, the Court decided that the best way forward was to question the responsibility of the state due to its indirect involvement in human rights violations by non-state actors, as had been proposed by, *inter alios*, De Meyer in the early 1970s.[118]

There are, however, further problems with the practical realisation of *drittwirkung* at the domestic level that need to be addressed, because the domestic system is the main depository through which positive obligations are implemented by the state. First, it is worth noting that the above-mentioned influential writings for the *drittwirkung* proposal have come from non-German authors. This is probably because *drittwirkung* in Germany has a *real* application and it has been made clear since the *Lüth* case[119]

---

117 Drzemczewski, ibid., p. 163.
118 For earlier bibliography for and against *drittwirkung*, see M.-A. Eissen, in *Amicorum Disciplorumque Liber René Cassin III: Protection des Droits de l'Homme dans les Rapports Entre Personnes Privées*, pp. 154–155 and footnote 8.
119 BVerfG, 15 January 1958, BVerfGE 7, 198, p. 205. BVerfG is an abbreviation of the Federal Constitutional Court of Germany (*Bundesverfassungsgericht*) and BVerfGE that of a series of its decisions (*Entscheidungen*).

– introducing the constitutional principle that the German private law may not be in conflict with constitutional values – that the dispute between private parties 'remains substantively and procedurally a civil law dispute'.[120] Indeed, a clear distinction between private and public law is still widely observed in the German legal order.[121]

In addition, there are some critical parameters that prevent or facilitate the application of *drittwirkung* domestically. By way of example, if *drittwirkung* is proposed in the French legal system, then we need to see that in the German Basic Rights the right to develop one's personality stands as a cornerstone value capable of inducing the development of more narrow human rights interests.[122] If this is absent, then it is difficult to see against which value a constitutional balance will be assessed and how it will be explained in detail so as not to undeservedly interrupt the normal functioning of private law. And are such constitutional human rights balances sufficiently explained or simply pronounced by the Conseil Constitutionnel?[123] Accordingly, it is not the *drittwirkung* that has been proposed but a profound change of the national legal structure.

The judicial action between individuals over constitutional rights, as permitted by *drittwirkung*, has further implications that relate to the normal functioning of private law and the retroactivity of legal liability of private parties. One of the main functions of law is to educate people's behaviour and ensure a climate of stability and economic development.[124] The private individual reasonably expects to know where their rights extend and where they are limited. An individual does not exactly violate a legal standard when that standard is discovered for the first time in the very judicial case against that individual. This is the logic behind the entrenched principle of *nulla poena sine lege* that has been codified under Article 7 of the Convention in respect of criminal liability, as follows: '[n]o one shall be held guilty of any criminal offense on account of any act or omission which did not constitute a criminal offense under national or international law at the time when it was committed.'

---

120 See, e.g., Cherednychenko, 'Towards the Control of Private Acts by the European Court of Human Rights?', footnote 36.
121 M. Kumm, 'Who is Afraid of the Total Constitution? Constitutional Rights as Principles and the Constitutionalization of Private Law' (2006) 7 *GLJ* 341–370.
122 German Basic Law: Article 2 (1): 'Everyone has the right to free development of his personality in so far as he does not violate the rights of others or offend against the constitutional order or against morality.'
123 Kumm, 'Who is Afraid of the Total Constitution? Constitutional Rights as Principles and the Constitutionalization of Private Law', p. 367.
124 P. Benson, in D. Friedmann and D. Barak-Erez (eds), *Human Rights in Private Law*, p. 221: 'protected interests must be determinable as such *independently of and prior to* the defendant's wrongful action, intentional or not. This requirement reflects the logic of the fundamental idea at common law that there can be no liability for non-feasance.'

Moreover, as a matter of general policy, the constitutional debate is not only made by putting private parties to fight in adversarial positions, because the direct adversarial contact contributes towards and exasperates old complexes of class divisions. The constitutional debate can be made in other ways (see some institutional options above) or in other fora – mainly, the Parliament that can regulate in advance the contextual application of human rights in private law and in a more informed and detailed manner.[125]

Despite the above criticism on the *drittwirkung* constitutional principle, we are not entitled to conclude that the whole *drittwirkung* proposal has been overrated. This is because *drittwirkung* offers the unique possibility of institutionalising access to enforce the constitutional contract in the absence of institutional access (e.g. judicial review of the decisions of the competent public administration supervising the given activity of private parties). It is this uniqueness that captivated the minds of all those scholars who readily proposed its application in the system of the Convention.[126] *Drittwirkung* does not wait for the Parliament to decide if and when it would be a good idea to address a human right issue in a given context of private relationships nor is influenced by external considerations, such as the voting power of various social factions.

The *drittwirkung* debate has always been an enlightened one, since it was officially launched in the freedom of expression case of *Lüth*. It should be noted that in cases that arise from special contexts in which conflicting constitutional rights (e.g. reputation versus freedom of expression) are

125 J. Rivero, in *Amicorum Discipulorumque Liber René Cassin III: Protection des Droits de l'Homme dans les Rapports Entre Personnes Privées*, p. 316: 'But it is the law, and the law only that can fix these borders. Thus, the liberal thought, in its most orthodox form, underlines the need to guarantee the peaceful co-existence of liberties in the relationships between private individuals, while the state is conferred with an exclusive competence.', (translation). In *Plattform 'Ärzte für das Leben'* v. *Austria*, the Court dealt with a complaint that the state did not guarantee the applicants' right to demonstrate (Article 11), as they were obstructed by a counter-demonstration. The government argued that unlike other provisions of the state's constitution that apply to relations between individuals, the corresponding provision to Article 11 of the Convention did not have this effect (para. 29). However, although no *drittwirkung* effect could apply in such circumstances at the domestic level, both the Commission and the Court found that the state through the legislator had already regulated the private relationship concerned in criminal law and provided for enforcement duties of public officials empowering them to disperse an unlawful demonstration (para. 33). For a detailed account of the domestic legal framework, see the Commission's admissibility decision of 17 October 1985.

126 K. Partsch, 'Written Communication', in A.H. Robertson (ed.), *Privacy and Human Rights* (Manchester: Manchester University Press, 1973), pp. 275–282, p. 281.

involved,[127] the intervention of the judiciary to determine legal balances is rather common ground[128] and pragmatic, and has been the practice in many states.[129] But to develop a fully fledged theory that has persisted and expanded for some decades and is celebrated in every occasion, must, first, be approached seriously as a declaration of the independence of the judiciary and the demos (within the meaning of the separation of powers) to develop and enforce the constitutional guarantees.[130]

127  For detailed discussion of *drittwirkung* in the German legal order, see, e.g., B. Markesinis and S. Enchelmaier, 'The Applicability of Human Rights as Between Individuals under German Constitutional Law', in B. Markesinis (ed.), *Protecting Privacy* (Oxford: Oxford University Press, 1999), pp. 191–243. Most of the cases discussed in that contribution concern freedom of expression issues (expression versus reputation). From the very limited discussion of cases not arising from such a context, we note the action of a farmer against the granting of permission to a private power-generating company to build a nuclear power station near a village. In such circumstances not involving competing constitutional rights, a constitutional review was not allowed, as the 'court came to the conclusion that Parliament had done its utmost [through regulation] to prevent all reasonably foreseeable danger', p. 220, citing BVerfGE 49/89 (Kalkar), pp. 141, 142 (August 1978). In general, *drittwirkung* has been and is still dominant when competing constitutional interests are involved, as in freedom of expression cases. As expression is infinite, any disputes between private parties call for judicial intervention to determine the exact borders, while the ad hoc assessment of facts is pertinent. Commenting on the case of BVerfGE 93, 266 ('Soldiers are Murderers' II), 292, 3 (October 1995), arising, once again, from the freedom of expression context, the authors admit that '[s]ince all circumstances of the case have to be taken into consideration, the result of such weighing is not predictable in advance.', p. 233.
128  Most of the constitutional human rights are not absolute, e.g., Article 5 of the 1949 German Constitution (*Grundgesetz*) protects free speech, but Article 5 (2) makes protection subject to qualifications and provisions of law. See also Article 118 of the 1919 Weimar Constitution. See, much earlier, Declaration of the Rights of Man and of the Citizen (1789), Article 4 (quoted in note 41 above) and Article 11: 'The free communication of ideas and opinions is one of the most precious of the rights of man. Every citizen may, accordingly, speak, write, and print with freedom, but shall be responsible for such abuses of this freedom as shall be defined by law.'
129  J. Rivero, in *Amicorum Discipulorumque Liber René Cassin III: Protection des Droits de l'Homme dans les Rapports Entre Personnes Privées*, discussing an anti-demonstration case (that is, from the enlarged freedom of expression context) in a French administrative court in 1933, p. 314. In the system of the Convention, positive obligations were not developed from cases involving competing human rights interests, see, e.g., the freedom of expression case of *Sunday Times* v. *the United Kingdom* [1979] no. 6538/74, from the same period in which positive obligations were applied for the first time in the cases of *Marckx* and *Airey*. See also early parallel developments in the jurisprudence of the US Supreme Court in balancing competing interests in freedom of expression cases: *Dennis* v. *United States*, 341 U.S. 494 (1951), concurring opinion by Frankfurter, J.; *Barenblatt* v. *United States*, 360 U.S. 109 (1959); *Konigsberg* v. *State Bar*, 366 U.S. 36 (1961). L. Frantz, 'The First Amendment in the Balance' (1962) 71 *YLJ* 1424.
130  J. Bomhoff, 'Lüth's 50th Anniversary: Some Comparative Observations on the German Foundations of Judicial Balancing' (2008) 9 *GLJ* 121–124, p. 124: '*Lüth*, in this view, becomes the embodiment of the European legal culture's will to believe that a formal, legal conception of the judicial weighing of interests or values is possible. Balancing, in this German or Continental view, does not have to be about policy choices, compromises

In short, *drittwirkung* can work well in a rigorous legal system where private relationships are regulated in advance by the legislator so as not to put the judiciary in a difficult position to hear a constitutional complaint due to the wide implications explained above. Accordingly, the open possibility of a constitutional claim motivates the state's legal mechanism to act in advance and realise the constitutional guarantees of which human rights are seen as basic. In that connection, the intellectual influence of *drittwirkung* for the development of positive obligations of the state within the system of the Convention is undeniable and continuous.

### 1.4.4.3 The international debate: international responses to international phenomena

The protection of human rights of individuals from acts of other private parties should not be questioned as such, because this is one of the basic and natural functions of the modern state of citizens. It is argued, however, that these are matters for the national state to solve, meaning practically that positive obligations should not be imposed by the Convention.[131] It is generally admitted that by engaging the state's liability for the acts of private parties, a great range of socio-economic issues have passed under European supervision, whose standards may conflict with the public policies of the elected legislators. It suffices, however, to point that the Convention is an independent source of power to which the states have voluntarily consented and, therefore, wherever and whenever a human right violation occurs, the state is answerable to the Convention's system. However, additional justifications exist and should be stated, if only to appreciate the potential of positive obligations and their advanced application and development that we cover in the following chapters.

First, it should be stressed that human rights and fundamental freedoms are constitutional guarantees that cannot easily be swept away by majoritarian policies of the government of the day. Although the social revolutions of liberalism, socialism and feminism have essentially

---

or *ad hocery*, but can be about interpreting constitutional rights within a pyramidal, "objective" system of values. Balancing is not a discretion or an option; it can be a necessity, a constitutional obligation.'

131 *Powell and Rayner* v. *the United Kingdom* (dec.) [1986] no. 9310/81 (Report of 19 January 1989): 'In the submission of the Government, while the scope of Article 8 is wide, the Article could not on its proper construction be extended to provide guarantees against any act which directly or indirectly affects a person's comfort or enjoyment of his private or home life. Still less could the Article be interpreted as requiring a State to take positive steps to prevent or control the activities of non-Governmental bodies or private individuals which incidentally have, or may have, this effect.'

achieved one thing in common, namely universal voting, there are groups of individuals such as children, the disabled, the elderly, prisoners and immigrants whose ability to exercise social and political pressure is limited.

The case of immigrants needs particular attention, as this concerns individuals in the normal condition of active adulthood. It should be mentioned that, although immigrants are not given full or any electoral rights, this does not prevent host states from adding their *gastarbeiters* (guestworkers) to their overall population (numbers in millions) in order to acquire greater voting power at the European Union level. Because the mobility of individuals in Europe, and in the world in general, is an international phenomenon of massive proportions, basic human rights issues cannot simply be left to majoritarian domestic policies. In addition, the social classes, from which the domestic bargaining had originally emerged and some human rights had been won, are now verging on extinction in some developed countries, leaving the heavy-duty immigrant worker to influence majoritarian policies in the current social bargaining process, while having no electoral rights. In other cases, the economic potential of some countries, as reflected by the private sector being taxed in their jurisdiction, is often expressed through selling services around the world and/or moving manufacturing in non-EU or non-Convention countries where human rights standards are *very* relaxed.[132]

But even if we set aside for a moment the millions of immigrants that exist in member states, domestic bargaining policies belong to the era before the internationalisation of capital, trade and labour. For more than a generation, a significant amount of important legislation that affects the lives of individuals within a given state is taken and, more seriously, is negotiated beyond national frontiers.[133] At the supranational level of the European Union, whose member states have all contracted to the Convention, a substantial number of economic and commercial issues are decided by European institutions. Therefore, it is expected that international phenomena should be tackled by international responses. The Convention is this international institution/forum with the requisite leverage to

---

132 A. Yee, 'Wreckers in Deep Water: The Largest Ship Breaking Site in the World is Fuelled by Lax Standards: But Times are Changing', *Financial Times* (Special Report – Waste & the Environment) (18 April 2007).

133 As commented by Drost in *Human Rights,* p. 196: 'Integration and co-ordination of the means of production is nowadays envisaged on the international level. The organization of labour is not limited within political boundaries, but extends over many countries of the world.' G. Mundlak, 'Human Rights and the Employment Relationship', in D. Friedmann and D. Barak-Erez (eds), *Human Rights in Private Law* (Oxford: Hart, 2001), pp. 297–328, p. 303: 'In the absence of collective backing, employees turn to courts, seeking public assistance to compensate for their alleged weakness in individual bargaining', section 2, pp. 301–305: 'Juridification and the Breakdown of the Post-Second World War Paradigm of Labour Law'.

influence international human rights standards for the activities of private individuals.[134] A good example of the Convention's indirect influence on the European Union's economic policies, or simply the self-instinct to restore the participatory ability of the individual, who is regularly faced with international decisions involving human rights issues, can be seen in the safeguards of Directive 95/46/EC on the protection of individuals with regard to the processing of personal data. Although the exact merits of this most sophisticated document are beyond the confines of this study, it suffices for our purposes to note the same aim for which the extended scope of the Convention seeks justification, namely to secure the constitutionality of human rights in order to restore the participatory ability of the individual in the bargaining process which is no longer taking place at the domestic level.[135]

It is easy, therefore, to note that it is the legal forum that has to be secured first in order to influence pan-European human rights standards in private sector activities. It pays, at this junction, to revisit the argument of the government in the case of *Hatton and Others*, in which the Court was called to adjudicate whether the granting of permission for increased night flights to a private corporation, which controls and manages an airport in central London, violated the right to private life of some individuals who suffered sleep prevention as a result. The government's main argument was as follows:

> all other principal European hub airports had less severe restrictions on night flights than those imposed at the three London airports. Paris Charles de Gaulle and Amsterdam Schiphol had no restrictions at all on the total number of Chapter 3 aircraft which could operate at night, while Frankfurt had restrictions on landings by Chapter 3 aircraft between 1 and 4 a.m. If restrictions on night flights at Heathrow

134  R. Lawson, 'Human Rights: The Best is Yet to Come' (2005) 1 *ECLR* 27–37; Petersmann, 'State Sovereignty, Popular Sovereignty and Individual Sovereignty: From Constitutional Nationalism to Multilevel Constitutionalism in International Economic Law?', arguing that '[h]uman rights require the "constitutionalization" of international law', p. 3.

135  As explained by Spiros Simitis, one of the architects of the European Data Protection project, with reference to the reinforced position of the individual employee: 'With its 1995 Directive on Data Protection, the European Union highlighted its commitment to the constitutionalisation of European law and, in particular, underlined its vision of the individual European as a rights-bearing individual; empowered through "knowledge" and thus advantaged in communicative processes of political/social/legal bargaining. As such, the move to a data protection regime founded upon notions of individual empowerment, also mirrors a recent and fundamental re-alignment in the guiding principles of regulative labour law, which has seen the paradigm of "collective laissez-faire" challenged, if not superseded, by a redirected emphasis upon the communicative empowerment of the individual employee rather than the representative function of employees' representatives.', 'Reconsidering the Premises of Labour Law: Prolegomena to an EU Regulation on the Protection of the Employees' Personal Data' (1999) 5 *ELJ* 45–62, p. 45. See also S. Simitis, in R. Rogowski and T. Wilthagen (eds), *Reflexive Labour Law*.

were made more stringent, UK airlines would be placed at a significant competitive disadvantage.... If they were forced to operate during the day they could provide fewer viable connections with regional services at both ends, making London a less attractive place in which to do business.[136]

It is clear from this passage that the government favours economic policies that are influenced by international competition. It should be reassuring for a government, even if it is found in violation of the Convention, that European uniform standards can be set with the adjudication of the given complaint. Within the geopolitical area of the Council of Europe, the European Court stands as a neutral player that can lay down minimum pan-European human rights standards to prevent the domino effect of human rights compromises, which are driven by competition responses.[137] The Court's ruling in an isolated case sets a uniform standard when individuals in other member states are able to bring their own complaint against similar compromising practices, thereby ensuring due compliance of European human rights law.

If we have to choose one case from the jurisprudence that summarises all points made above and further proves the potential of the Convention in fostering uniform human rights standards vis-à-vis the activities of private individuals, it is, perhaps, the case of *Guerra and Others* that does us this favour.[138] The applicants were forty inhabitants who lived in vicinity of a private chemical factory, which was classified as of high risk, according to the criteria of Presidential Decree no. 175 of 18 May 1988 ('*DPR* 175/88') transposing Directive 82/501/EEC of the Council of the European Communities (the 'Seveso' directive) on the major-accident hazards of certain industrial activities dangerous to the environment and the well-being of the local population. A committee of technical experts established that, due to the factory's geographical position, emissions from it to the atmosphere were often channelled towards the populated areas. The applicants complained that the state failed to provide information about the risks posed by the industrial activity and on how to proceed in the event of a major accident. Such measures were required also by Articles 11 § 3 and 17 § 2 of Presidential Decree no. 175/88 ('*DPR* 175/88').[139]

---

136 *Hatton and Others* v. *the United Kingdom* [2003] no. 36022/97, para. 107.
137 S. Goulbourne, 'Airport Noise and the Right to Family Life: A Legitimate Application of Article 8 of the European Convention?' (2002) 24 *LLR* 227–236, p. 228: 'In view of the genuinely conflicting rights and duties, arguably the European Court of Human Rights (ECHR) is ideally placed to adjudicate on the competing claims, which may be at the centre of political or economic controversies within member states.'
138 *Guerra and Others* v. *Italy* [1998] no. 14967/89.
139 Ibid., para. 39.

The Court found the state in violation of its positive obligation under Article 8 to guarantee precautionary measures in the form of pre-emptive information about potential dangers emanating from the industrial activity. Although such precautionary measures had already been regulated at the binding level of EU law, but had not been implemented by the respondent state, the applicants did not pursue their complaints in the EU institutions.[140] At the Convention's level, the fact that some measures had already been regulated was of no relevance, as positive obligations to actively protect individuals against the activities of private actors are inherent, and, therefore, they do not exist simply because of some prior national or international provisions.

The action of the applicants in *Guerra and Others* manifests in the clearest way the increasing realisation by the ordinary individual of the unique opportunity of positive obligations that empower her/him, for the first time, to directly assert the protection of human rights in the activities of private parties that the state, as the collective political entity, must regulate and continuously guarantee.

## 1.5 The on-going debate: re-evaluating the subsidiary function of the court

The culmination and concretisation of all points made above should be reflected in the technical legal framework that determines positive obligations on the ground (the *how* question). While technical details will be covered in the remaining chapters, in the introductory chapter the basics of the Court's approach have to be discerned and secured as a point of reference.

It is first noted that the European judges are continuously deliberating on the constitutional role of the Court in building a European public order of minimum pan-European standards[141] in the area of human rights and fundamental freedoms in order to achieve and continuously maintain

---

140 M. Demerieux, 'Deriving Environmental Rights from the European Convention for the Protection of Human Rights and Fundamental Freedoms' (2001) 21 *OJLS* 521–561, page corresponding to footnotes 125–128.
141 Wildhaber, 'A Constitutional Future for the European Court of Human Rights?', pp. 162–163, uses the term: 'common minimum standards' on p. 164 and points out: '[t]he Charter of Fundamental Rights, proclaimed in Nice on 7 December 2000, takes the Convention as setting out the minimum level of protection to be secured, while making clear that the minimum level did not prevent a higher level of protection.', p. 165.

the object and purpose of the Convention.[142] As Steven Greer has pointed out, '[n]o longer does [the Convention] express the identity of western European liberal democracy in contrast with the rival communist model of central and eastern Europe; it now provides an "abstract constitutional identity" for the entire continent.'[143]

It is also possible to exact the technical framework by reference to the job that needs to be done by the European judges without adopting the term 'constitutional' to describe the role of the Court.[144] Adjectives, however, are used as convenient points of reference to short-cut details that would otherwise have to be repeated at every occasion. The Court has long been seen as a constitutional court simply because 'the issues which it is called upon to decide are constitutional issues in so far as they concern fundamental rights within Europe.'[145] As the subject matter is itself constitutional, the Convention is in essence a constitutional document and therefore its institutional organ is described accordingly.[146] That there may be some functions which national constitutional courts do not perform, or perform in addition, does not affect the constitutionality of the Court's function.[147] It should also be stressed that the concept of constitution is not static so as to impose qualifying criteria of past traditions that no longer reflect current social and political realities and evolving practices and perceptions. What is currently observed, as Giorgos Pinakides has recently reaffirmed, is that 'international

142 See e.g. *Loizidou* v. *Turkey* [1995] no. 15318/89, para. 75; *Kakoulli and Others* v. *Turkey* (dec.) [2001] no. 38595/97; *Bosphorus Hava Yollari Turizm ve Ticaret Anonim Sirketi* v. *Ireland* [2005] no. 45036/98, para. 156. See also Council of Europe's Recommendation *Rec1606(2003)* of the Parliamentary Assembly of the Council of Europe on areas where the European Convention on Human Rights cannot be implemented (23 June 2003): 'All Member States of the Council of Europe have ratified the Convention which has gradually acquired, in the words of the Court, the status of a "constitutional instrument of European public order (*ordre public*) for the protection of individual human beings"'; Memorandum by the European Court of Human Rights from the Third Summit of the Council of Europe 'The Court would emphasise "the central role that the European Convention on Human Rights (ECHR) must continue to play as a constitutional instrument of European public order, on which the democratic stability of the Continent depends". Because of its pan-European dimension, moreover, the Strasbourg system provides the only framework within which it will be possible to develop a common European conception of human rights.', para. 1, (footnote omitted), available at www.echr.coe.int/eng/Press/2005/April/SummitCourtMemo.htm (accessed June 2010). See also Explanatory Report of Protocol No. 14 (CETS No. 194): Article 12 to the Amending Protocol, para. 77.

143 Greer, *The European Convention*, pp. 170–171.

144 Wildhaber, 'A Constitutional Future for the European Court of Human Rights?', section 1: A European Constitutional Court, p. 161: 'Whether the European Court of Human Rights is itself a "Constitutional Court" is largely a question of semantics.'

145 Ibid.

146 Φ. Βεγλέρης (F. Vegleris), 'Η Σύμβαση των Δικαιωμάτων του Ανθρώπου και το Σύνταγμα' [1976] *ToΣ* 385, p. 394.

147 Γ. Πινακίδης (G. Pinakides), 'Η Συνταγματική Υφή της Ευρωπαϊκής Σύμβασης Δικαιωμάτων του Ανθρώπου' (2007) 33 *ΔτΑ* 71–95.

law is being "constitutionalised" and constitutional law is being "internationalised". Within this framework, established and accepted concepts that concern the organisation of the state re-open for discussion.'[148]

Either *de jure* or de facto, the system of the Convention has managed to establish itself through the binding judgments of its Court which have all been complied with, at least at the ad hoc level (i.e. the applicant's claims), and very often at the structural level and over issues that involve positive obligations in a wide range of circumstances in which no national Constitutional court has competence or ever dared to reach (i.e. where mega-theories and principles have to meet practice).[149] The Convention is a supranational system that has set an independent and sovereign centre of power whose advent in the European legal order has not set antagonist fronts, but channels of co-operation with national systems and between them with the Convention as the common communication forum. Notable is the paradigm of English law in which the Convention's jurisprudence is directly invoked, examined and analysed in litigation proceedings and judgments.[150] Of course, such a national practice is the quintessence of a common European public order, as confirmed in the words of the former president of the Court, judge Luzius Wildhaber, that '[if] the national authorities are in position to apply Convention case-law to the questions before it, then much, if not all, of the Strasbourg Court's work is done.'[151] Although the practice of the English courts may be seen as advanced, especially from the point of view of newer member states,[152] it helps highlight the maximum practical result of the Convention's object and purpose that guides not merely the debate of whether the role of the Court is constitutional, but the more pertinent issues of the general and practical description of the constitutional job that needs to be carried out at the European level. And this job is about building a European public order that is needed as a qualitative standard-setting framework of human rights protection to guide and force changes at the domestic level, which is the only level at which human rights are a living experience.

It may not be possible or desirable to engage in a debate on whether the Convention results in 'constitutional or individual justice'.[153] It is the constitutional framework that has to be targeted in order to secure justice to an individual at the domestic level and, conversely, it is through the

---

148 Ibid., p. 76 (translation), citing Ευ. Βενιζέλος, 'Η Αντοχή του Συνταγματικού Φαινομένου στη Μετανεώτερη Εποχή' [2002] *ΤοΣ* 845, p. 855.
149 See discussion on the *drittwirkung* proposal section (pp. 46–48).
150 Human Rights Act 1998, sections 2.1, 3.1. See, e.g., *R. v. British Broadcasting Corporation ex parte Prolife Alliance* [2003] UKHL 23, citing *inter alia Haider* v. *Austria* (1995) 83 DR 66, *Huggett* v. *United Kingdom* (1995) 82A DR 98, *VgT Verein Gegen Tierfabriken* v. *Switzerland* (2002), *Sporrong and Lonnroth* v. *Sweden* (1982) 5 EHRR 35.
151 Wildhaber, 'A Constitutional Future for the European Court of Human Rights?', p. 162.
152 See, Greer, *The European Convention*, chapter 2: 'Convention compliance', p. 60.
153 For detailed discussion see, Greer, ibid., pp. 165–174.

micro-level of individual justice that any defects in the constitutional framework can be detected and addressed.[154]

It should be seen as very basic that a supranational Court should look beyond the particular facts of an isolated complaint and deliver judgments that set standards and principles of broad reach in order to target structures and legal practices at the domestic level.[155] Such standards should be able to apply in all member states, otherwise neither their legitimacy is secured nor does any European standard emerge to define a European public order. A more conscious approach is now forced by the ever-increasing number of applications pending before a judicial formation that rose in 2010 by 17 per cent to 139,650.[156]

The Court develops its approach in conformity with the subsidiary nature of the Convention. For this purpose, it has long relied on the judge-made principle of the state's margin of appreciation, whose application has not always been clear.[157] What changes in the current technical approach, as observed in recent judgments and published commentary of

154 *Karner* v. *Austria* [2003] no. 40016/98 para. 26: '[its] judgments in fact serve not only to decide those cases brought before the Court but, more generally, to elucidate, safeguard and develop the rules instituted by the Convention,..., thereby raising the general standards of protection of human rights and extending human rights jurisprudence throughout the community of Convention States.' See also *Capital Bank AD* v. *Bulgaria* [2005] no 49429/99, para. 79; *H.G. and W.G.* v. *Germany* (dec.) [1964] no. 2294/64, *Yearbook of the European Convention on Human Rights* Vol. 8, 1965, p. 320; *Ireland* v. *the United Kingdom* [1978] no. 5310/71, para. 154. M. De Salvia, 'Illustration et Défense du Système Européen de Protection Judicaire des Droits de l'Homme: Des Règles Précises pour des Obligations Claires et Partagées par les Etats' (2007) 69 *RTDH* 135–151, p. 138: 'the Court's business subscribes to the so-called framework of European public order, that is defined by its autonomy in relation to the national legal order. In this respect, the role of the Court can be of a constitutional nature. In fact, in interpreting the essential norms of the European Convention of Human Rights, the Court becomes implicitly involved in laying down principles, whose application goes beyond the given case that is brought for evaluation.', (translation).

155 F. Tulkens (a judge of the Court), 'Human Rights, Rhetoric or Reality?' (2001) 9(2) *ER* 125–134, pp. 129: 'At the outset, it should be recalled that: "notwithstanding the vital role played by international mechanisms, the effective protection of human rights begins and ends at the national level"... Human rights are not just *logos*, they are also *praxis*. That constraint means that the recognition of human rights is inseparable from the machinery used to ensure the rights' respect and protection.', citing the document of Council of Europe, 'The Effectiveness of Human-Rights Protection 50 Years After the Universal Declaration' (1998).

156 ECtHR Report: 'Analysis of Statistics 2010', p. 4, available at www.echr.coe.int (Reports section). R. Harmsen, 'The European Convention on Human Rights after Enlargement (2001) 5(4) *IJHR* 18–43, p. 38, 'Enlargement may see the Court escape these (largely self-imposed) constraints, allowing it to (re)assume its rightful place as the constitutional court of a European public order.'

157 See, e.g., C. Feingold, 'The Little Red Schoolbook and the European Convention on Human Rights' (1978) 3(1) *HRR* 21–47; Lord Lester of Herne Hill, 'Universality Versus Subsidiarity: A Reply' (1998) *EHRLR* 73–81; R. Singh, M. Hunt, and M. Demetriou, 'Is There a Role for the "Margin of Appreciation" in National Law after the Human Rights Act?' (1999) 1 *EHRLR* 15–22; I. de la Rasilla del Moral, 'The Increasing Marginal

judges writing in personal capacity, is a re-justification and re-orientation of the 'logic of subsidiarity', especially when reference is made to the case-law on positive obligations, which pose much bigger challenges due to the wide range of their application.[158] It should be noted that it is the 'logic' rather than the 'principle' that is stressed, reminding us that principles require a constant re-justification and re-interpretation to accommodate current needs. In essence, the re-alignment of subsidiarity marks the Court's abandonment of general margins allowed to the states in an effort to achieve the long-awaited *quality* of its reasoning and describe European human rights standards that educate the state and guarantee legal protection at the domestic level.[159] In this account, subsidiarity is an end aim and not the starting point, as may have appeared in the past.[160] What comes first are the domestic structures and legal principles that the Court needs to define in order for the Convention to become subsidiary to the state's legal system.

The general premises of the technical approach of the Court that affect the planning and application of positive obligations within the

---

Appreciation of the Margin-of-Appreciation Doctrine' (2006) 7 *GLJ* 611–624; Y. Arai-Takarashi, *The Margin of Appreciation Doctrine and the Principle of Proportionality in the Jurisprudence of the ECHR* (Antwerp: Intersentia, 2002); Greer, *The European Convention*, pp. 222–228.

158 Wildhaber, 'A Constitutional Future for the European Court of Human Rights?', p. 161, citing *Z and Others* v. *the United Kingdom* [2001] no. 29392/95.

159 For insightful separate opinions in earlier case-law, see *Fischer* v. *Austria* [1995] no. 16922/90, per judge Jambrek: 'It seems to me that reasoning not solely restricted to the scope and the circumstances of the case would contribute better to the quality of the Court's case-law in the service of the Convention as a living constitutional instrument on European public order.' And per judge Martens: 'This refusal to decide the question once and for all is (merely) based on the Court's doctrine that the Court "should confine itself as far as possible to examining the question raised by the case before it". This doctrine is in my opinion no more than a regrettable petitio principii. No provision of the Convention compels the Court to decide in this way on a strict case-by-case basis. This self-imposed restriction may have been a wise policy when the Court began its career, but it is no longer appropriate. A case-law that is developed on a strict case-by-case basis necessarily leads to uncertainty as to both the exact purport of each judgment and the precise contents of the Court's doctrine.... The Court rightly is wont to stress that the protection of the rights and freedoms under the Convention falls primarily to national authorities. It should, however, not overlook that the reverse side of this coin is that national authorities are obliged to seek guidance in its case-law.', para. 16 (footnote omitted). See also *Marckx* v. *Belgium* [1979] no. 6833/74, para. 58. F. Sudre, 'Les "Obligations Positives" dans la Jurisprudence Européenne des Droits de l'Homme', in P. Mahoney *et al.* (eds), *Protecting Human Rights: The European Perspective: Studies in Memory of Rolv Ryssdal* (Köln: Carl Heymanns Verlag, 2000), pp. 1359–1376, p. 1375: 'The affirmation that is regularly repeated by the Court that "it is not for the Court to determine the measures that have to be taken" by the convicted State, is a pretence [pseudo-appearance]' (translation). Greer, *The European Convention*, p. 228: 'how can the Court deliver constitutional justice effectively without addressing the unresolved constitutional issues at the core of its adjudicative method more coherently?'

160 Cf. *Eckle* v. *Germany* [1982] no. 8130/78, para. 66.

Convention system should be discussed here to support the choice in the structure of chapters and, also, to introduce the reader to some key technical issues that are fully elaborated in the following chapters.

The Court determines first the substantive law of the Convention. It explains the scope of the Convention rights and the entitlement to human rights protection taking into account the principle of equality that reminds the European judges of the potential of their decision to set a pan-European precedent. In appropriate circumstances, the capabilities and natural limits of the Convention, as well as those of the states and the economic disparities between them, are pertinent considerations in determining positive obligations in the wide range of circumstances in which the state does not directly interfere.

As long as the substantive law of positive obligations has been defined, the focus shifts on the procedural aspect of the state's obligations, that is the means by which domestic law can implement the substantive content of human rights protection. In addition, the substantive law is also defined through procedural safeguards, which are seen as inherent in the objective determination of the content of protection. As a result, the Court's review increasingly expands to the procedural framework through which interested individuals are able to participate in the enforcement and implementation of positive obligations at the domestic level. This trend coincides with the process of the Court's continuous self-evaluation, which seeks to adjust its supranational supervision to the challenges of its ever-expanding business and the long-term effectiveness of the Convention.[161]

Appropriate procedures and structures induce the dialectics of justice at the domestic level, something that is particularly encouraged by the European institution. A modern democracy should provide for, or a democracy is modern when there are institutional structures of a procedural nature that allow the individual to initiate the social debate on the active protection of human rights and participate in the implementation of protection. It is the institutional level of access that determines and updates the content of positive obligations and it is the same level that guarantees their implementation in the domestic system.

---

161  See Protocol 14, amending the control system of the Convention (adopted 13 May 2004, entered into force 1 June 2010) E.T.S. 194. E. Savarese, 'Il Protocollo N. 14 alla Convenzione Europea dei Diritti dell'Unomo' (2004) *RDI* 714–729; L. Caflisch (a judge of the Court), 'The Reform of the European Court of Human Rights: Protocol No. 14 and Beyond' (2006) 6 *HRLR* 403–415; Greer, *The European Convention*; De Salvia, 'Illustration et Défense du Système Européen de Protection Judicaire des Droits de l'Homme: Des Règles Précises pour des Obligations Claires et Partagées par les Etats'.

# 2 The application and development of positive obligations

In this chapter we study the application and development of positive obligations in extending the scope of human rights protection in the wide range of circumstances in which private individuals interact. A coherent methodological framework is proposed to determine the content of positive obligations in a realistic, consistent and predictable manner.

The general approach is to move beyond the basic and introductory Article-by-Article study of the Convention in recognition that its provisions are mostly broadly framed and the content of protection is naturally linked to other issues within the wide context of activities to which an applicant's circumstances often relate. Accordingly, the current study gives due weight to the well-known maxim that 'in law context is everything'[1] in order to assert the content of positive obligations as a system of protection that is organised and implemented in various levels.

First, the distinctive character of positive obligations in imposing the active protection of human rights has to be established. Positive obligations co-exist with other obligations requiring the state not to interfere with human rights (i.e. negative obligations) but are not an extended interpretation of the latter, as has appeared in some case-law. For this reason, a specific content of positive obligations has to be identified and be required in its own right (section 2.1).

The current study advocates a manageable scope of positive obligations which has to be defined before going into the discussion of the specific content of protection. To this aim, pertinent principles of international law are revisited in order to establish the critical condition under which the state's liability can be engaged in the circumstances in which state actors do not directly interfere. In that respect, objective elements are inserted in judicial examination to narrow considerably the apparently open-ended scope of positive obligations (section 2.2).

---

1 Taking this opportunity to pay homage to a learned judge, we only cite Lord Steyn in his opinion in *R. v. Secretary for Home Department ex parte Daly* [2001] UKHJ 26, paras 27–28.

With reference to the discussion in the introductory chapter that the Court does not recognise conceptual limits to the responsibility of the states for the acts of interference of private individuals, positive obligations are primarily managed vis-à-vis the scope of the Convention rights against which these obligations arise. In that connection, technical rather than conceptual limits are identified which can strategically be adjusted to the capabilities of the system of the Convention, as well as those of the member states. Limits of practicality are additionally recognised in their own right. Their study is divided in accordance with critical points of distinction, as observed in various contexts in which the active protection of human rights is required. Having defined a manageable scope of positive obligations, the study moves on to the specific level of protection. Aiming at a system of human rights, the content of positive obligations is organised in relation to the complete range of protection, whose effectiveness depends on core aspects of the domestic procedural infrastructure through which a more specific and ad hoc response can be determined (section 2.3).

Further divisions are included to determine the content of protection in circumstances in which legitimate aims of interference with human rights are pursued by the state through the activities of private parties, or where there are conflicts of rights in some contexts of private interactions (section 2.4).

The long division of sections and sub-sections accounts for points of distinction that correspond to critical parameters and contextual differences, which affect considerably the planning of the application and development of positive obligations in the system of the Convention. In short, the chapter's proposal is embodied in a long prioritized, and yet interconnected, breakdown of critical parameters that are considered beyond ad hoc balances to assert a manageable content of positive obligations in accordance with their potential.

Before going into the main text, it should be clarified that the discussion of the jurisprudence in this chapter does not intend to make an exhaustive presentation or collection of various approaches. Of course, other case-law can well be identified and interpreted in a different way so as to reach different conclusions. The main aim of this study is to reason a choice of principles and structures upon which to base a proposal for a coherent and workable legal framework and, therefore, our task is confined to locating 'existing',[2] as opposed to exhaustive, norms. Guidance is also drawn from the wider objectives of the Convention, the on-going internal debate on the Court's function (as discussed in Chapter 1), and

---

2   J. De Meyer, 'The Right to Respect for Private and Family Life, Home and Communications in Relations Between Individuals, and the Resulting Obligations for States Parties to the Convention', in A.H. Robertson (ed.), *Privacy and Human Rights* (Manchester: Manchester University Press, 1973), pp. 255–275, p. 273.

the Court's jurisprudence as *nomologia* whose authority is conditioned on a sufficient scientific reasoning (*logos*) for the development and adjudication of law (*nomos*).[3]

## 2.1 Establishing the distinctive nature and potential of positive obligations in the current reasoned phase of the jurisprudence

The study of positive obligations should cover the technical principles by which their content can be determined in the wide range of circumstances in which private individuals interact. The legal principles of the earlier case-law (which are still in circulation) will be discussed and juxtaposed with recent developments in the Court's legal reasoning. The discussion revolves around the judgments of *Hatton and Others* in 2001 and 2003, which mark the beginning of the modern jurisprudence[4] that has coincided with or has psychologically been influenced by the advent of the new century/millennium and the ever-increasing dynamism of European societies in the current era of the advanced internationalisation of human rights movements.[5] The main purpose of this section is to establish the distinctive nature and potential of positive obligations in order to secure the perspective of the active protection of human rights (i.e. the substance of positive obligations) in the determination of the content of positive obligations in various circumstances.

### 2.1.1 The merging of positive and negative obligations: the fair balance test

In most of the case-law relating to violations of human rights by private parties, the positive obligations of the state have usually been merged with negative obligations under the so-called 'fair balance test'. A case in which the fair balance test was elaborated and has since been widely cited as an authority for its application is *Rees* dated in 1986. The applicant, a postoperative transsexual, had been experiencing embarrassment and humiliation whenever his birth certificate had to be produced. He complained

3  M. de Blois, 'The Fundamental Freedom of the European Court of Human Rights', in R. Lawson and M. de Blois (eds), *The Dynamics of the Protection of Human Rights in Europe, Essays in Honour of H.G. Schermers* (Dordrecht: Martinus Nijhoff, 1994), pp. 35–59, p. 37: 'This has to do with what I would like to call the quest for rationality which is a predominant factor in the theory of law. Judicial decisions are not acceptable only because the judge is invested with the power to decide.'

4  *Hatton and Others* v. *the United Kingdom* [2001] and [2003] (Grand Chamber) no. 36022/97.

5  *Giuliani and Gaggio* v. *Italy* [2009] no. 23458/02; *Kop* v. *Turkey* [2009] no. 12728/05. For earlier insights, see statement by Prime Minister Olof Palme before the UN General Assembly on the occasion of the commemoration of the Fortieth Anniversary of the United Nations (21 October 1985), available at www.olofpalme.org.

that his full integration into social life had been constrained by the state's refusal to take steps that would legally constitute him as a male (his new apparent sexual identity) on the birth certificate.[6]

Accepting the government's readily-given admission of its positive obligations, the Court laid down the legal test of positive obligations under Article 8, as follows:

> In determining whether or not a positive obligation exists, regard must be had to the fair balance that has to be struck between the general interest of the community and the interests of the individual, the search for which balance is inherent in the whole of the Convention [...]. In striking this balance the aims mentioned in the second paragraph of Article 8 (art. 8–2) may be of a certain relevance, although this provision refers in terms only to "interferences" with the right protected by the first paragraph – in other words is concerned with the negative obligations flowing therefrom (see, mutatis mutandis, the Marckx judgment of 13 June 1979, Series A, no. 31, p. 15, para. 31).[7]

It is clear that a merging solution was sought when the state's failure could be seen as an act or omission and, therefore, a negative or positive obligation could be argued. In that connection, the legitimate aims of interference in paragraph 2 of Article 8 were held to be of 'a certain relevance'. In applying the fair balance test, as defined in that case, the Court recognised a wide margin of appreciation to the state to dismiss the applicant's claims.

However, in that case, none of the legitimate aims of interference of paragraph 2 justified the wide margin of appreciation, which was accorded to the state on the mere ground that a modification of public record would have to be carried out by 'detailed legislation' in order to address the implications involved.[8]

Without having to go into an analysis of how it is ever possible for detailed legislation to be the sole ground for refusing protection of a

---

6 *Rees* v. *the United Kingdom* [1986] no. 9532/81, para. 34. The *Rees* case is one of the classic authorities that has widely been cited in subsequent case-law for the application of the fair balance test, see, e.g., *Powell and Rayner* v. *the United Kingdom* [1990] no. 9310/81, para. 41; *Lopez Ostra* v. *Spain* [1994] no. 16798/90, para. 51; *Hokkanen* v. *Finland* [1994] no. 19823/92, para. 55; *O'Reilly and Others* v. *Ireland* (dec.) [2002] no. 54725/00; *Hatton and Others* v. *the United Kingdom* [2001] no. 36022/97, para. 96; *Fadeyeva* v. *Russia* [2006] no. 55723/00, para. 99. These cases serve in turn as authorities for the fair balance test, see, e.g. *Hatton and Others* v. *the United Kingdom* [2003] no. 36022/97, para. 98 citing *Powell and Rayner*; *Giacomelli* v. *Italy* [2006] no. 59909/00, para. 78 citing *Powell and Rayner*; *Ledyayeva and Others* v. *Russia* [2006] nos 53157/99,..., 53695/00, para. 101 citing *Fadeyeva*; *Oluic* v. *Croatia* [2010] no. 61260/08, para. 46 citing *Hatton and Others*.
7 *Rees* v. *the United Kingdom*, ibid., para. 37.
8 Ibid., para. 44.

human right, and by extension, the very development of law,[9] we proceed to discuss wider technical issues that have ensued from the application of the merging balance test.

The main technical problem with the fair balance test comes down to the simple point that, since that test is not categorically conditioned on the justification of paragraph 2's legitimate aims of interference, its assessment is not clear, and hence the application of law is far from certain to be 'fair'. To put it straightforwardly, which are exactly the 'general interests of the community' for which the state is accorded a margin of appreciation?

In scholarly commentary, informed criticism on the merging of the fair balance test, as that made by Caroline Forder, is rare. Her point is as follows:

> apart from the "general interest" aims laid down in paragraph 2 of Article 8, a second, more ill-defined "general interest" test, or reference to the "due regard to the needs and resources of the community" is emerging to apply to those cases to which Article 8 (2) does not apply. Apart from the obvious illogicality of creating a second general interest test in addition to an existing statutory one, these developments present a formidable threat to the protection offered by Article 8. There is a danger that the "general interest" test which is emerging is much wider than the aims prescribed in Article 8 (2) the pursuit of which may justify restriction of the rights protected and thus that restriction may be permitted in cases of positive obligations when it would not be permitted in cases of negative obligations. In conjunction with the possibility, explained above, that some claims may be described as positive *or* negative the circumscribed restriction permitted under Article 8 (2) is in danger of being converted into an unlimited one.[10]

What in essence is highlighted is that a balance test (*Rees* style) has been allowed to operate through the state's margin of appreciation in the absence of concrete, and more importantly, binding legitimate aims. Consequently, that test constitutes an arbitrary deviation from the express provisions of the Convention and the predictability of its codified norms.

It is worth reiterating that in its classical form, the state's margin of appreciation is connected to the principle of proportionality. Proportionality presupposes 'a pressing social need' and mitigating measures or

---

9 Unlike the majority of the Court in *Rees*, the dissenting judges, Bindschedler-Robert, Russo and Gersing, considered alternatives and mitigating measures vis-à-vis certain contextual settings that would be affected if the applicant's claim were upheld.

10 C. Forder, 'Legal Protection under Article 8 ECHR: *Marckx* and Beyond' (1990) 37(2) *NILR* 162–181, p. 179.

alternatives in order to justify an interference as being 'necessary' in a democratic society,[11] under paragraph 2 of the Convention rights. In other words, the state's margin, which is *a* part of the proportionality assessment, cannot arbitrarily be elevated to autonomous status and operate independently of the very purpose for which it was originally invented and justified.

Additionally, the fair balance test is said to balance the 'interests of the individual'. But how are the 'interests of the individual' balanced without examining what is at stake under the circumstances? Of course, as the case passes the admissibility examination, it can be assumed that there should be a negative impact on the applicant. However, the full extent of what is at stake for the individual concerned may not be reflected by the degree of severity of the admissibility threshold. In that respect, the impact assessment may not be exhausted with general estimations, for circumstances vary considerably, and it is often necessary to involve expert opinion to establish the exact degree of severity of the negative consequences. Such considerations did appear in the Court's judgment in *Rees*, in which it was stated that

> the Court is conscious of the seriousness of the problems affecting these persons and the distress they suffer. The Convention has always to be interpreted and applied in the light of current circumstances (see, mutatis mutandis, amongst others, the Dudgeon judgment of 22 October 1981, Series A, no. 45, pp. 23–24, paragraph 60). The need for appropriate legal measures should therefore be kept under review having regard particularly to scientific and societal developments.[12]

This passage recognises that the impact assessment should also rely on scientific opinion so as to incorporate objective elements in the judicial examination. It remains, however, an *obiter dicta* statement that is given after a decision of non-violation of Article 8 has already been concluded in the immediately previous paragraph of the judgment.

### 2.1.2 The proposal to determine positive obligations under the paragraph 2 provisions

The uncertainty and unpredictability surrounding the 'fair balance test' was addressed in the concurring opinion of judge Wildhaber in the otherwise unanimous decision of the case of *Stjerna*.[13] In that case, the applicant

---

11 L. Loucaides, *Essays on the Developing Law of Human Rights* (Dordrecht: Martinus Nijhoff, 1995), chapter 9, sec. 10: 'The Principle of Proportionality'; Y. Arai-Takahashi, *The Margin of Appreciation Doctrine and the Principle of Proportionality in the Jurisprudence of the ECHR* (Antwerp: Intersentia, 2002).
12 *Rees* v. *the United Kingdom* [1986] no. 9532/81, para. 47.
13 *Stjerna* v. *Finland* [1994] no. 18131/91.

complained that the state's refusal to allow him to change his surname violated the right to respect for private life, as guaranteed by Article 8 of the Convention. The judge pointed out the difficulty for the Court to distinguish between positive and negative obligations. He stated that 'the dividing line between negative and positive obligations is not so clear-cut' and in the cases, such as that of *Gaskin,*

> the refusal by the British authorities to grant a former child in care unrestricted access to child-care records could be considered as a negative interference, whereas a duty on the State to provide such access could arguably be viewed as a positive obligation.[14]

With regard to the more pertinent question about the determination of positive obligations through the fair balance test, the concurring judge found that 'the Court has in effect applied only the first paragraph (art. 8–1) in such cases'. In the interests of avoiding an 'incoherent jurisprudence', and relying on the statements of the Court in *Keegan,*[15] and *Hokkanen*[16] for a 'striking similarity between the applicable principles', he proposed a merging approach that defies a 'negative/positive dichotomy', stating that

> it would be preferable to construe the notion of "interference" so as to cover facts capable of breaching an obligation incumbent on the State under Article 8 para. 1 (art. 8–1), whether negative or positive. Whenever a so-called positive obligation arises the Court should examine, as in the event of a so-called negative obligation, whether there has been an interference with the right to respect for private and family life under paragraph 1 of Article 8 (art. 8–1), and whether such interference was 'in accordance with the law', pursued legitimate aims and was "necessary in a democratic society" within the meaning of paragraph 2 (art. 8–2).[17]

There are some points that need to be analysed and highlighted, as the proposal of judge Wildhaber for a complete merging of positive and

14 Ibid., citing the concurring opinion of judge Wildhaber; *Gaskin* v. *the United Kingdom* [1989] no. 10454/83.
15 *Keegan* v. *Ireland* [1994] no. 27229/95, para. 49.
16 *Hokkanen* v. *Finland* [1994] no. 19823/92, para. 55.
17 *Stjerna* v. *Finland* [1994] no. 18131/91. P. van Dijk, ' "Positive Obligations" Implied in the European Convention on Human Rights: Are the States Still the "Masters" of the Convention?', in M. Castermans-Holleman *et al.* (eds), *The Role of the Nation-State in the 21st Century: Essays in Honour of Peter Baehr* (The Hague: Kluwer Law International, 1998), pp. 17–33, p. 32: 'there is no reason not to use here, also by analogy, the same criteria borrowed from the limitation clauses of other provisions.'

negative obligations under the notion of interference has attracted particular attention and support in the scholarly commentary.[18]

It has first to be noted that the fair balance test is often evaluated under
the state's margin of appreciation, which arises in the third stage of the
examination of paragraph 2. In addition, the first paragraph of the Convention rights does not relate to justifiable acts of interference by state
actors. Therefore, it cannot be said that 'only the first paragraph' of a
Convention right was applied in the earlier case-law.

At times, there is confusion with the term 'margin' when it is used to
describe a 'choice' of measures to guarantee the active protection of
human rights under paragraph 1, as opposed to examining the necessity/
proportionality of the interference under paragraph 2 to which the principle of margin of appreciation is connected. In the passage of *Rees* quoted
above, the fair balance test and the certain relevance of the legitimate
aims of paragraph 2 have been justified with reference *mutatis mutandis* to
the earlier case of *Marckx*.[19] However, as we have seen in the discussion of
*Marckx* in the previous chapter, the Court expressly stated that 'the State
has a choice of various means, but a law that fails to satisfy this requirement violates paragraph 1 of Article 8 without being any call to examine it
under paragraph 2.'[20] The 'choice of various means' is a choice from a
range of measures that can be taken to actively protect the human rights
of the individuals under paragraph 1 of a Convention right. This 'choice',
which may have been worded as a 'margin of appreciation' in subsequent
case-law or used to make an easy connection to the authority of *Marckx*,
has nothing to do with the entrenched principle of margin of appreciation that arises exclusively under the third stage of the examination of paragraph 2 to assess the proportionality of the state's interference.

Admittedly, judge Wildhaber's proposal for a complete merging of
positive and negative obligations under the perspective of 'interference'
aims at a 'coherent jurisprudence' through the certainty and predictability
of the codified provisions of paragraph 2 of the Convention rights. In that
regard, the fair balance test will no longer be considered *in abstracto*, as
seen in *Rees* above. Instead, only the exhaustively listed legitimate aims, the
express stages and well-entrenched principles of paragraph 2 examination
will have to be applied. It should be noted that under this proposal, the

18 P. van Dijk, ibid., p. 25: 'it would seem justified to bring the non-fulfilment of a positive
 obligation under the notion of "interference".' Referring to the opinion of judge Wildhaber in *Stjerna*, he added that 'it would be preferable "to construe the notion of interference" so as to cover facts capable of breaching the obligation incumbent on the State
 under Article 8 § 1, whether negative or positive.'; F. Sudre, 'Les "Obligations Positives"
 dans la Jurisprudence Européenne des Droits de l'Homme', in P. Mahoney *et al.* (eds),
 *Protecting Human Rights: The European Perspective: Studies in Memory of Rolv Ryssdal* (Köln:
 Carl Heymanns Verlag, 2000), pp. 13591–1376, p. 1374.
19 *Marckx* v. *Belgium* [1979] no. 6833/74.
20 Ibid., para. 31.

fair balance test adds nothing to the balance that is inherent in the proportionality principle.[21]

But with regard to the active protection of human rights that is the core meaning of positive obligations, paragraph 2 is not automatically relevant. In that respect, in the proposal for a complete merging of the state's obligations under the perspective of paragraph 2, the first criterion that the interference must be 'prescribed by law' (or 'in accordance with law') needs particular attention. Pieter van Dijk has suggested that '[i]n those cases one must conclude that the "interference" which consists in the non-fulfilment of an implied positive obligation, finds its cause in the law and is, therefore, provided by law.'[22] It should be reiterated, however, that the standard of this criterion has long been interpreted as being very strict and qualitatively sophisticated so as to guarantee a satisfactory level of foreseeability and certainty of the content of law, and hence of the level of human rights protection, for the benefit of all interested parties.[23] More importantly, the issue of the active protection of human rights concerns a content of positive obligations that is first directed at the regulatory level.[24] Accordingly, what needs to be prescribed by law are not simply the conditions that justify the 'non-fulfilment' of a positive obligation.

### 2.1.3 The stages before the balance test

In recent jurisprudence, the fair balance test has increasingly being subjected to an objective assessment of evidence to guarantee an informed process for the merits examination of human rights claims. To the extent that specific intermediate steps (i.e. of public administration) have to be taken in order to produce the requisite evidence, these steps become in turn an indispensable part of the judicial examination. Although the discussion in this section is still placed within the structure of paragraph 2, the shift in focus towards an objective legal reasoning influences comparatively the development of positive obligations.

The opportunity to improve the fair balance test arose with the case of *Hatton and Others*, in which the applicants complained of the state's failure

---

21 *Ruano Morcuende* v. *Spain* (dec.) [2005] no. 75287/01 (available in French only).
22 P. van Dijk, in M. Castermans-Holleman *et al.* (eds), *The Role of the Nation-State in the 21st Century: Essays in Honour of Peter Baehr*, p. 26.
23 See, e.g., *Sunday Times* v. *the United Kingdom* [1979] no. 6538/74.
24 See discussion in Chapter 1, p. 24, with regard to the case of *X and Y* v. *the Netherlands* [1985] no. 8978/80. C. Drögue, *Positive Verpflichtungen der Staaten in der Europaischen Menschenrechtskonvention* (Heidelberg: Springer 2003), p. 390: 'This [fair balance] test cannot be an exact replication of the test for negative obligations. Thus, positive obligations cannot fulfil the requirement of being "provided for by law" as they may indeed be obligations to enact legislative measures.'

to protect them from nuisance, which was caused by the commercial activities (night-flights) of a private corporation.[25] Although the interference with the human right of the applicants was directly attributed to a private party, it was the state's planning administration that had authorised the operation and expansion of the corporation's business. Before the Court, the state's endorsement of the corporation's activities was confirmed in the submission of the government, which expressly invoked the legitimate aim of 'the economic well-being of the country', as listed in paragraph 2, to justify its indirect involvement in the interference complained of.

What will be looked at here is not a conclusive legal reasoning – given the two judgments of that case (the Chamber's finding of violation of Article 8 was reversed by the Grand Chamber) and the considerable number of influential concurring and dissenting opinions – but the occasion that has signalled an informed debate among the judges on the quality and intensity of their examination. The principal consideration is to achieve an objective legal reasoning and a more expansive review of the state's system in order to produce judgments, whose effects set standards that can apply to the wide context of private parties' activities (e.g. commerce or industry) to which the given individual case relates.

The Court's examination in the case of *Hatton and Others* revolves around the fair balance test that is used as a unifying principle, whether the state's failure is approached as an act of its agents or an omission to protect individuals from the activities of a private party.[26] From the application of the balance test in that case, it is clear that the legitimate aims of paragraph 2 do not have a 'certain' or abstract relevance, since the Court examines exclusively the legitimate aim of the 'economic well-being of the country.'[27] What changes in the judicial examination is that well before a margin of appreciation arises for the state under the fair balance test, it should be established that the competing interests of litigant parties meet the applicable thresholds of significance in order to qualify for competing status. Thus, on one hand, the impact suffered (or to be suffered) by the individual should reach the threshold of severity that engages a Convention right. Analogously, on the other hand, the economic well-being of the country should be significant (the entrenched 'pressing social need' threshold) in order to limit legitimately the scope

---

25  *Hatton and Others* v. *the United Kingdom* [2001] and [2003] (Grand Chamber) no. 36022/97. A similar complaint had been examined in the earlier case of *Powell and Rayner* v. *the United Kingdom* [1990] no. 9310/81.

26  *Hatton and Others* v. *the United Kingdom* [2001] no. 36022/97, para. 96; *Hatton and Others* v. *the United Kingdom* [2003] (Grand Chamber) no. 36022/97, para. 98.

27  *Hatton and Others* v. *the United Kingdom*, ibid., paras 97, 100, 102, 106–107; *Hatton and Others* v. *the United Kingdom* (Grand Chamber), ibid., paras 121–122, 126.

of human rights protection.[28] As this information has to be known in order to balance objectively, and hence 'fairly', the competing interests, it conditions whether the balance test or the state's margin can arise under the circumstances. Accordingly, the legal examination does not start from the balance test, but from the administrative structures (i.e. to conduct investigations and studies) from which the requisite evidence emerges.[29]

The exact content of such administrative structures is assessed by the standard of effectiveness, whose examination targets those critical details affecting the quality of evidence that is finally produced. What accounted for the different outcome reached in the judgments of Chamber and Grand Chamber was the different weight that was given to the critical importance of the public administration's failure to: (1) examine sleep prevention when assessing the negative impact on the applicants and (2) commission an independent (as opposed to industry-produced) evaluation of the benefits for the economic well-being of the country.[30]

In the scholarly commentary of the post-*Hatton and Others* period, the evidence that is required to prove the relevance or legitimacy of the state's margin of appreciation and the public administrative framework from which that evidence derives, are conveniently termed as 'proceduralisation' or 'proceduralisation movement'. In commenting on the changing legal environment and the current technical approach of the Court in various key stages of its judicial examination, Françoise Tulkens (a judge of the Court acting in personal capacity) and Sébastien Van Drooghenbroeck have explained that

28 Loucaides, *Essays*, chapter 9, sec. 10, p. 197: 'The Principle of Proportionality', who notes: '[t]he case-law uses the test of proportionality in conjunction with the requirement of "pressing social need". The organs of the Convention must first be satisfied that there was a pressing social need for the measure under examination and then examine whether the particular measure was proportionate to that need.' See also the joint dissenting opinion of judges Costa, Ress, Türmen, Zupančič and Steiner in *Hatton and Others* v. *the United Kingdom* [2003] no. 36022/97: 'The margin of appreciation of the State is narrowed down because of the fundamental nature of the right to sleep, which may be outweighed only by the real, pressing (if not urgent) needs of the State.' On the threshold of 'pressing social need', see e.g., *Smith and Grady* v. *the United Kingdom* [1999] nos 33985/96; 33986/96; *Colaço Mestre and SIC-Sociedade Independente de Comunicaçao S.A.* v. *Portugal* [2007] nos 11182/03 and 11319/03; *Enerji Yapi-Yol Sen* v. *Turkey* [2009] no. 68959/01.

29 *Hatton and Others* v. *the United Kingdom* [2003] no. 36022/97, paras 104, 128. See also *Giacomelli* v. *Italy* [2006] no. 59909/00, paras 83–84.

30 H. Post, '*Hatton and Others*: Further Clarifications of the "Indirect" Individual Right to a Healthy Environment' (2002) 2 *N-SAIL* 259–277, p. 273: 'Here, the Court [Chamber] presumes that the UK has the duty to prove that no interference with the rights mentioned in Article 8.1, has taken place, and was not impressed by the quality of the research into the complaints of the applicants that the UK Government presented.' A. Clack, 'Heathrow Case Challenged', *Guardian*, (23 May 2005). S. Greer, *The European Convention on Human Rights: Achievements, Problems and Prospects* (Cambridge: Cambridge University Press, 2006), p. 265: 'The key controversy in *Hatton*, therefore is how the substantive issue is to be approached procedurally.'

the benefits rest on the objectivity and credibility that the procedural approach brings to the controlling function of the Court.... Under this perspective, the proceduralisation movement can explain the postponement of the margin of appreciation by inserting a preliminary condition: Before examining the issue of the States' appreciations, it has to be established that the chances of reaching a "good decision" have been multiplied by using a formal methodological framework through which the whole set of pertinent interests can be taken into account in an equitable and impartial manner. In that way, the development of procedural guarantees and the control that is exercised on them can appear as the natural and fruitful corollary of the doctrine of the states' margin of appreciation, and through which, of the subsidiary function that is assumed by the European Court of Human Rights. [translation][31]

The shift in emphasis on the qualitative assessment of the administrative framework that secures the necessary evidence and which alone guarantees the objective evaluation of the merits involved, has been confirmed in the subsequent case of *Goodwin*, which concerned a complaint similar to that seen in *Rees*. In reversing its previous reasoning, as applied in *Rees*, the Court held that the respondent government can no longer claim that the matter falls within their margin of appreciation, save for the choice of appropriate means to guarantee the human rights interests of the individuals concerned (as in *Marckx*).[32] The reason that the state's margin did not arise in that case, compared with the approach taken in *Rees*, was the importance that was placed on the examination of evidence. The judges relied on evidence contained in a report of the Interdepartmental Working Group indicating that the number of potential applicants (i.e. post-operative transsexuals) is between 2,000–5,000 and, therefore, it could not be said that they 'pose the threat of overturning the entire system.'[33] As '[n]o concrete or substantial hardship or detriment to the public interest has indeed been demonstrated [by the state] as likely to flow from any change to the status of transsexuals',[34] the state could not be said to have either engaged a legitimate aim for its interference or established the threshold of a pressing social need (or, as stated: 'substantial hardship or detriment to the public interest'). In the absence of the requisite evidential proof, the Court was able to conclude unanimously

31  F. Tulkens and S. Van Drooghenbroeck, 'L'Évolution des Droits Garantis et l'Interprétation Jurisprudentielle de la CEDH' (Lecture speech at the University of Grenoble on 27 September 2002), available at http://webu2.upmf-grenoble.fr/espace-europe/acad2002/textes/tulkens.htm (accessed October 2010).
32  *Goodwin* v. *the United Kingdom* [2002] no. 28957/95, para. 93. See also discussion at pages with note 20 above.
33  Ibid., para. 87, see also para. 92.
34  Ibid., para. 91.

that the state's assertions were 'framed in general terms' and, therefore, it could not find that 'any real prospect of prejudice has been identified as likely to arise if changes were made to the current system.'[35] In such circumstances, the stage for the margin of appreciation of the state could not be reached.

The efforts of the European judges to restore certainty and predictability in the development and application of European human rights law are increasingly concentrating on the structures of the domestic public administration,[36] which is responsible for furnishing the necessary evidence[37] by which the state authorities will be able to objectively appreciate the necessity (i.e. pressing social need and proportionality) of limiting the scope of human rights protection in pursuit of a legitimate aim of interference.[38]

### 2.1.4 A firm distinction between positive and negative obligations

Positive obligations are imposed on the state by virtue of paragraph 1 of the Convention rights. Accordingly, the cases discussed above, namely *Rees, Gaskin, Powell and Rayner, Stjerna, Hatton and Others, Goodwin*, in which positive obligations have been examined through a merging approach or otherwise, are not positive obligations cases.

In *Rees*, the applicant's complaint concerned the state's express refusal to alter his birth certificate that would reflect his new gender post-operation status. In *Gaskin*, the Commission found that the refusal of the state authorities to allow the applicant access to his birth file was an interference with the right to respect for his private life and, therefore, its justification had to be made under paragraph 2 of Article 8.

In all these cases, it is clear that the applicants did not argue on the state's positive obligations. That their complaints were examined as positive or positive and negative (in a merging fashion) obligations cases is due to the willingness of the Court to adopt the governments' readily-given admission of their positive obligations. The substance of law, however, does not change by whichever way or from whichever angle one chooses to argue a legal case.

---

35 Ibid., para. 87.
36 See also E. Dubout, 'La Proceduralisation des Obligations Relatives aux Droits Fondamentaux Substantiels par la Cour Européenne des Droits de l'Homme' (2007) 70 *RTDH* 397–425, p. 402: 'One of the notable consequences of extending the examination of procedural obligations is to "objectivise" – in a sense of rendering more objective – the judicial control of respect of fundamental rights which, to some extent, is left dedramatised [to be conducted in neutral terms]. The judge of liberties moves progressively to become judge of procedures.', (translation).
37 *Fadeyeva* v. *Russia* [2006] no. 55723/00, para. 128: 'the Court reiterates that the onus is on the State to justify, using detailed and rigorous data, a situation in which certain individuals bear a heavy burden on behalf of the rest of the community.'
38 *Ruano Morcuende* v. *Spain* (dec.) [2005] no. 75287/01.

When an individual can establish entitlement to a human right – for example, by meeting the threshold of negative impact engaging a Convention right – then the state is under a positive obligation to guarantee human rights protection to that individual by virtue of paragraph 1 of the relevant provision. If the state fails to guarantee protection and, as a result, the individual is not able to enjoy it in the particular circumstances concerned, then the state's liability is raised under paragraph 1 of that right. In *Stjerna*, a human right could not be engaged in the applicant's circumstances (see further discussion below, pp. 71, 95) and, therefore, it is preposterous to examine positive obligations on something that is not there in the first place.

The issue of perspective of the active protection of human rights can be seen in the Commission's opinion in *Gaskin*, in which it stated that

> respect for private life requires that everyone should be able to establish details of their identity as individual human beings and that in principle they should not be obstructed by the authorities from obtaining such very basic information without specific justification.[39]

To put it simply, the applicant in that case had sought access to his birth record, the claim fell squarely within the scope of private life under Article 8 and, therefore, the state's first reaction would be to accord the individual access to his record due to his entitlement to a constitutional human right.

The issue of perspective is in essence the constitutional perspective that imposes the priority of protection of human rights. Most human rights are not absolute and, thus, appropriate limitations are also provided. It is, however, of crucial importance to establish the perspective and priority of protection of human rights, as they affect the order from which the legal examination is undertaken.

The importance of the constitutional perspective can more easily be seen in the debate about the constitutionality of some rights. In discussing the protection of privacy (as linked to the general interest of private life within the meaning of Article 8), David Feldman argued: '[b]ecause claims to privacy-related rights can be deleterious to public life, or to individuals within a group, any attempt to exclude an area of human activity from public scrutiny needs justification.... Rights in the private sphere are best justified, from the point of view of the community, by reference to people's obligations when acting in different capacities.'[40] This kind of informed argumentation is clearly valuable before the right to privacy is included in a constitutional document. On acquiring constitutional status, the perspective is automatically reversed, namely that 'any attempt' to

---

39 *Gaskin* v. *the United Kingdom* [1989] no. 10454/83, para. 39.
40 D. Feldman, 'Privacy-Related Rights and their Social Value', in P. Birks (ed.), *Privacy and Loyalty* (Oxford: Oxford/Clarendon Press, 1997), pp. 15–50, pp. 25–26.

interfere with one's privacy needs justification, thereby securing a process of prior examination whose burden of proof lies primarily with the party that pursues the limitation of a constitutional right.[41]

Analogously, in the system of the Convention, the state can pursue a limitation to the scope of a human right under one of the legitimate aims that are exhaustively listed in paragraph 2 (where available) of the Convention rights. In all cases mentioned above (save for *Stjerna* which could have been resolved at the admissibility stage), the Court could have looked at the justifications argued by the state for not according human right protection to the individuals concerned. In that regard, the legitimate aims of paragraph 2 do not have a 'certain' relevance, but they constitute categorical criteria for strict observance. Accordingly, the connection that is made, in the judges' dissenting opinions in *Hatton and Others*,[42] between the state's margin and the principle of proportionality to assess the 'necessity' of the interference aims at re-asserting the express criteria and structures of the Convention provisions (i.e. necessity).[43] The same applies with the 'pressing social need' threshold engaging a legitimate aim of interference which was only reiterated in dissenting opinions, despite being well-entrenched in the jurisprudence.[44] If it is not already clear from the foregoing analysis, and in order to remove any doubts, positive obligations are argued and are readily assumed by the governments' counsels in order to take advantage of the loose standards of the fair balance test, which has so far been allowed to compromise the express direction of the very text of the Convention in paragraph 2 provisions.[45]

41 *Stjerna* v. *Finland* [1994] no. 18131/91, para. 37; see also *K.H. and Others* v. *Slovakia* [2009] no. 32881/04, in examining a complaint similar to that seen in *Gaskin* v. *the United Kingdom* [1989] no. 10454/83 (i.e. access to one's personal medical records), para. 48, the Court made clear that it 'does not consider that data subjects should be obliged to specifically justify a request to be provided with a copy of their personal data files. It is rather for the authorities to show that there are compelling reasons for refusing this facility.'

42 See the joint dissenting opinion of judges Costa, Ress, Türmen, Zupančič and Steiner in *Hatton and Others* v. *the United Kingdom* [2003] (Grand Chamber) no. 36022/97.

43 As explained by the Commission in the *Sunday Times* v. *the United Kingdom* [1979] no. 6538/74: 'no other criteria than those mentioned in the exception clause itself may be at the basis of any restrictions and these criteria in turn must be understood in such a way that the language is not extended beyond its ordinary meaning.', Series B, vol. 28, p. 9, quoted by Loucaides, *Essays*, chapter 9, sec. 5: 'Strict Interpretation of Limitations', pp. 185–186.

44 See the quoted passage from the dissenting opinion of the judges at note 28 above.

45 Forder, 'Legal Protection under Article 8 ECHR: *Marckx* and Beyond'; F. Sudre, in P. Mahoney *et al.* (eds), *Protecting Human Rights: The European Perspective: Studies in Memory of Rolv Ryssdal*, p. 1373: 'In general, the [judicial] control of positive obligations lacks rigour and appears more uncertain than the control of negative obligations.', (translation); Post, '*Hatton and Others*: Further Clarifications of the "Indirect" Individual Right to a Healthy Environment', pointing out that '[t]his gave them more leeway than in the case of direct interference by a public authority', p. 264; D. Spielmann, 'Obligation Positives et Effet horizontal des Dispositions de la Convention', in F. Sudre (ed.), *L'Interprétation de la Convention Européenne des Droits de l'Homme* (Brussels: Nemesis/Bruylant, 1998), pp. 133–174, p. 151.

It should also be mentioned that there are circumstances where the failure of the state to provide for the protection of a human right may not be attributed to a conscious and deliberate attempt to justify an act or omission (e.g. refusal), but to the mere fact of inaction or impracticality of protection. Impracticality may be a pragmatic and inherent limit to human rights protection that will be discussed in more detail below. It suffices to say here that impracticality is often considered in relation to the extent of protection, rather than protection as such. By contrast, the failure of the state to guarantee protection, because of inaction, to an individual who is able to engage a human right, will automatically raise the state's liability under paragraph 1 of the Convention rights, meaning that the evaluative principles of paragraph 2 do not come into play.

### 2.1.5 The perspective of human rights protection: the rule or the exception – the contextual or the ad hoc response?

The issue of perspective concerns the fundamental point from which the scope and content of human rights protection is determined. If the potential of positive obligations is to target a system of human rights, as opposed to some reactive responses so as to guarantee the active protection of human rights, then the content of these obligations should be looked at before the incident of interference and in connection with the wide context of private interactions to which the given isolated case relates.

In *Hatton and Others*, the positive obligation to regulate the protection of human rights in the whole context of industry had already arisen for the state under paragraph 1 of Article 8, that is prior to the decision of the planning authorities to grant a private corporation permission to extend its activities to the detriment of the applicants' human rights interests.[46] In such circumstances, any decision to pursue a legitimate aim of interference is an isolated issue of ad hoc nature[47] and, therefore, paragraph 2 of the Convention rights cannot be allowed to set the perspective from which the content of positive obligations can be determined. As pointed out by judge Costa, in his dissenting opinion in the Grand Chamber

---

46 Post, ibid., pp. 269–270: 'The present judgment seems to contain all these elements, but not always in a very transparent format.' and p. 273: '[t]he *Hatton and Others* judgment can be said to have further clarified what is required under Article 8.1: the State must carefully research and assess, previous to decision making, whether policies might have adverse effects on the environment to the extent of violating the right to respect for privacy and family rights.'

47 K. Done, 'Farborough Faced to Turned Away Business', *Financial Times* (11 February 2008): 'The airport applied in 6 October 2005 to double the weekend limit to 5,000 flights within the 28,000 quota. That was refused by the local authority.'

judgment, the negative impact on the applicants' private life could well have reached the level of severity contemplated by Article 3, for which no limitation exists. As far as other industrial activities are concerned, the right to life under Article 2 is also relevant.[48] It follows that a system of human rights protection cannot be taken seriously when constitutional protection is only available through the process of justifying an isolated interference.

The perspective of positive obligations is that of *front door* under which the protection of human rights is actively arranged as a whole system of protection that is built in relation to the given context of activities of private parties (e.g. industry), rather than as a collection of ad hoc responses to individual complaints (e.g. the expansion of a corporation's activities). It is the contextual approach that allows the holistic reading of the Convention rights (as discussed in Chapter 1) so as to identify all relevant human rights interests, whose protection has to be guaranteed before the circumstantial issue of interference, in paragraph 2 terms, ever emerges. In short, the question of perspective of the active protection of human rights in the form of positive obligations is synonymous with the question of whether human rights are guaranteed by a system of protection that exists domestically or by ad hoc balances pronounced by the European judge at the occasion of isolated complaints.

## 2.2 The wider and common justification of the state's obligations: the critical element of knowledge of the need of human rights protection

Approaching the positive obligations of the state from the perspective of paragraph 1, whose effect arises first,[49] it is clear that the Convention aims at a domestic system of protection that can address 'inherent' human rights issues, while due allowances are made for legitimate limitations upon specific (listed) aims that the state may decide to pursue (the circumstantial option of 'if and when') on the condition that the requisite safeguards can be met.

However, this basic assertion has to be reconciled with the Court's repetitive statement that the 'essential object' of the Convention rights is

---

48 See, similarly, in the context of domestic violence, *A* v. *Croatia* [2010] no. 55164/08, para. 57: 'the State authorities had a positive obligation to protect the applicant from the violent behaviour of her (former) husband. This obligation might arise under all three Articles of the Convention relied upon, namely Articles 2, 3 and 8.'

49 J. De Meyer, in A.H. Robertson (ed.), *Privacy and Human Rights*, pp. 262–264.

the state authorities' non-interference with human rights.[50] Although positive obligations are reasoned additionally as 'inherent',[51] the constant reiteration of the 'essential object' of the Convention explains, to a certain extent, why some of the current practices and proposals have adopted the paragraph 2 perspective. By way of analogy, the priority and perspective of paragraph 1 can be secured if they are grounded upon the same justification of 'essentiality' that the Convention rights have always presupposed.

Looking more closely at the repetitive affirmation of the 'essential' object of the Convention rights, it can reasonably be said that the absence of an accompanying explanation indicates that its justification has always meant to be obvious. Because obvious things must be stated when important issues are concerned, the only obvious explanation is that the state, as the initiator of the act complained of, *knows* of the likely interference with the human right of an individual. Whether or not the act of interference can be justified, knowledge of the very act automatically engages the state's obligation to abstain from interfering either at all or without the appropriate safeguards (as generally set out in paragraph 2 provisions and further detailed in the jurisprudence). In that connection, it is the element of that knowledge that exposes the state's involvement in all circumstances, marking as 'essential' the issue of human rights protection in the eyes of European human rights law.

By contrast, the state's involvement is not clearly present when positive obligations are claimed. It has already been seen in the important article of Jan De Meyer in the early 1970s (discussed in Chapter 1) that the international liability of the state can be engaged when its responsibility is indirectly 'involved' in human rights violations that are caused by private parties.[52] Since a claim for a positive obligation to actively protect human rights can be raised almost everywhere, the state may not be said to be

---

50 See, e.g., the *Belgian Linguistic* case [1968] nos 1474/62,..., 2126/64, para. 7; *Marckx* v. *Belgium* [1979] no. 6833/74, para. 31; *Stubbings and Others* v. *the United Kingdom* [1996] nos 22083/93; 22095/93, para. 62; *Passannante* v. *Italy* (dec.) [1998] no. 32647/96; *Clunis* v. *the United Kingdom* (dec.) [2001] no. 45049/98; *Oneryildiz* v. *Turkey* [2002] no. 48939/99, para. 144; *Craxi (No. 2)* v. *Italy* [2003] no. 25337/94, para. 73; *Van Kuck* v. *Germany* [2003] no. 35968/97, para. 70; *Surugiu* v. *Romania* [2004] no. 48995/99, para. 59, *Moreno Gomez* v. *Spain* [2004] no. 4143/02, para. 55; *Adali* v. *Turkey* [2005] no. 38187/97, para. 267; *Maurice* v. *France* [2005] no. 11810/03, para. 114; *Sorensen and Rasmussen* v. *Denmark* [2006] nos 52562/99,..., 52620/99, para. 57; *Uçar* v. *Turkey* [2006] no. 52392/99, para. 133; *Associated Society of Locomotive Engineers & Firemen (ASLEF)* v. *the United Kingdom* [2007] no. 11002/05, para. 37; *Tysiac* v. *Poland* [2007] no. 5410/03, para. 109; *Dickson* v. *the United Kingdom* [2007] no. 44362/04, para. 70.

51 See, e.g., *Marckx* v. *Belgium*, ibid., para. 31; *Airey* v. *Ireland* [1979] no. 6289/73, para. 32; *Guerra and Others* v. *Italy* [1998] no. 14967/89, para. 58; *McGuinley and Egan* v. *the United Kingdom* [1998] no. 21825/93, para. 98; *Van Kuck* v. *Germany* [2003] no. 35968/97, para. 70; *Von Hannover* v. *Germany* [2004] no. 59320/00, para. 57; *Siliadin* v. *France* [2005] no. 73316/01, para. 58; *Oluic* v. *Croatia* [2010] no. 61260/08, para. 46.

52 J. De Meyer, in A.H. Robertson (ed.), *Privacy and Human Rights*, p. 273.

'involved' if knowledge of the need of human rights protection does not lie with its agents. Accordingly, the element of knowledge has to be established to prove that the state remains silent and passive to human rights violations, actual or potential, of which its agents have had prior knowledge.

The element of knowledge in international law and in scholarly bibliography is not quite new. Various views have been worded advocating either a subjective element for a guilty 'psychological' aspect of an expressly intentional act or negligent omission,[53] or an 'objective' element assessed by an obligation of result.[54] For the purposes of the current study, as exclusively concerned with the Convention, we admit the usefulness of these insights in inserting an objective factor in the determination of the state's liability, but we proceed to adopt a less strict approach for the Convention, which aims, as a 'living instrument', at constantly developing and homogenising European human rights standards.[55] In that regard, a flexible examination of the element of knowledge will be taken below so as to allow intermediate and on-the-spot developments (i.e. standards developed at the very occasion of the adjudication of the applicant's claims). The main consideration is to justify and control the extended scope of the international liability of the state, while preserving the dialectics of justice in the law-making mission of the Convention.[56]

The existence of this objective element narrows considerably the apparently infinite scope of positive obligations. In this respect, the perspective of the active protection of human rights under paragraph 1 is secured by the practical and manageable scope of positive obligations. In addition, to the extent that the element of knowledge conditions the state's liability, it is not only employed to engage the state's positive obligations in the circumstances concerned but remains pertinent in whichever stage and level their content is determined.

In general terms, the element of knowledge is evaluated in relation to two separate identity types that reflect two corresponding conditions of proximity which are critical in the determination of the state's obligations.

---

53 G. Perrin, 'Le Problème de la Faute dans la Responsabilité Internationale de l'Etat', in W. Haller *et al.* (eds), *Im Dienst an der Gemeinschaft* (Basel: Helbing & Lichtenhahn, 1989), pp. 127–133.

54 Loucaides, *Essays*, chapter 6: 'Responsibility Under the European Convention on Human Rights: Objective or Subjective Test?'

55 C. Tomuschat, 'What is a "Breach" of the European Convention on Human Rights?', in R. Lawson and M. de Blois (eds), *The Dynamics of the Protection of Human Rights in Europe: Essays in Honour of H.G. Schermers* (Dordrecht: Martinus Nijhoff, 1994), pp. 315–337.

56 *Wemhoff* v. *Germany* [1968] no. 2122/64, para. 8: 'Given that it [the Convention] is a law-making treaty, it is also necessary to seek the interpretation that is most appropriate in order to realise the aim and achieve the object of the treaty, not that which would restrict to the greatest possible degree the obligations undertaken by the Parties.'

1   The identity of the individual(s) in need of human rights protection (the first condition of proximity); and/or
2   The source of the threat to human rights (the second condition of proximity).

In recognition that the element of knowledge of the need of human rights protection operates as an objective criterion of preliminary importance, it has first to be analysed as to its general application. As that element constitutes the common justification of the 'essential object of the Convention rights' for both positive and negative obligations, its relevance and application have to be discussed under both headings.

### 2.2.1  The element of knowledge in negative obligations cases

#### 2.2.1.1  Express knowledge from direct interference with known results

Knowledge of the need of human rights protection reasonably lies with the state, when it is its agents that initiate the very act of interference. Such a situation can be seen from the facts of the case of *McCann and Others*, which concerned a lethal operation of special anti-terrorist units to arrest and apprehend suspected terrorists. The applicants complained that the killing of their relatives by state agents violated the right to life under Article 2. In such circumstances, an element of pre-meditation and intentional infliction of harm goes without saying from the very nature of the operation of the state officers.[57] The Court expressly described the use of lethal force as 'deliberate', a clear finding that has been highlighted in subsequent cases. In *Ilhan*, in which the applicant complained of a life-threatening assault by state agents, the judges particularly noted:

> [the] situations where the initiative [for an effective investigation under Article 2] must rest on the State for the practical reason that the victim is deceased and the circumstances of the death may be largely confined within the knowledge of State officials.[58]

Therefore, in circumstances in which the state agents are the main actors interfering intentionally with the human rights of an individual, prior knowledge of that interference is presupposed. It is the express and specific knowledge of the upcoming interference that makes it absolutely 'essential' for the state to protect the individual by making sure that appropriate safeguards have existed and are duly implemented in conformity with the requirements of paragraph 2. Every premeditated act of interference automatically raises the obligation of human rights protection, given

---

57   *McCann and Others* v. *the United Kingdom* [1995] no. 18984/91, para. 150.
58   *Ilhan* v. *Turkey* [2000] no. 22277/93, para. 91.

that, at its early stage, an act of interference is about to violate the human rights interests of some individuals.[59] The justifiable nature of such acts connotes an additional element of knowledge about the content of safeguards, which is determined in relation to the criteria of paragraph 2 and the attached principles and standards of the relevant jurisprudence.

In such settings, the issue of protection is strictly confined to the justification of the state's interference under the applicable safeguards of the Convention. Thus, although an actual violation of a human right occurs (as assessed by the harm sustained), a legal violation cannot be established against the state when the interference complained of has been justified under the legitimate limitations of paragraph 2. All in all, the 'essentiality' of the negative obligations of the state concerns the process by which the relevant standards are observed.

In *Andronicou and Constantinou*, which also concerned a lethal operation by the state agents, the Court's main task was to check whether the safeguards, laid down previously in *McCann and Others*, had been complied with by the state agents. As these standards had been met, a violation of Article 2 could not be found, despite the fact that the applicants' relatives were killed during the lethal operation.[60] In these circumstances, the issue of protection of human rights arises only in relation to a very narrow framework in which an express act of an otherwise justifiable interference has already been initiated (or is about to) by state agents and concerns a content of measures to comply with the required safeguards.

Thus, contrary to what has been suggested elsewhere, cases such as *McCann and Others* cannot be classified as positive obligations cases, because the obligation to guarantee and implement some positive measures relates to the required safeguards that justify an interference and, therefore, this obligation arises, if (and only if) an act of interference has been exercised or is about to.[61] In that connection, the issue of protection of human rights does not concern active protection, but the due implementation of the requisite legal safeguards that justify a legitimate limitation to the applicable scope of a human right.

The state's compliance with entrenched standards of a justifiable interference in the context of lethal operations of the police has also been

---

59 For potential human rights violations, see, e.g., *Klass and Others* v. *Germany* [1978] no. 5029/71; *Dudgeon* v. *the United Kingdom* [1931] no. 7525/76.

60 See, e.g., *Andronicou and Constantinou* v. *Cyprus* [1997] no. 25052/94.

61 For analysis of the case-law on the lethal operations of state agents (especially *McCann and Others*) and the reinforced content of safeguards under paragraph 2, see F. Ni Aolain, 'The Evolving Jurisprudence of the European Convention Concerning the Right to Life' (2001) 1 *NQHR* 21–42. See also C. Warbrick, 'The European Convention on Human Rights and the Prevention of Terrorism' (1983) 32 *ICLQ* 82–119. Cf. F. De Sanctis, 'What Duties Do States Have with Regard to the Rules of Engagement and the Training of Security Forces under Article 2 of the European Convention on Human Rights?' (2006) 10(1) *IJHR* 31–44, p. 39.

examined in *Makaratzis*, in which the applicant complained about excessive use of firepower by the police officers who tried to stop him while he was dangerously driving his car to escape from their control. In that case, the Court made, for the first time, some statements on positive obligations, courting the view of the Institut de Formation en Droits de l'Homme du Barreau de Paris, which was allowed as *amicus curiae*.[62] Admittedly, the first sentence of paragraph 1 of Article 2 can be interpreted as giving rise to a positive obligation for the state to put in place an adequate legislative and administrative framework to guarantee the right to life.[63] However, in the context of the lethal operations of the police, the content of the state's obligation concerns the entrenched standards of organisation and control of the police operation which are required in order to justify the state's legitimate interference under paragraph 2. In that respect, the content of these obligations has developed and develops independently of the general application of positive obligations.

It is important to maintain a firm approach on these issues, because every positive measure of compliance with human rights standards could be classified as a positive obligation, a fact that would lead to the gradual dilution of positive obligations or to situations of conflict between positive and negative obligations.[64]

### 2.2.1.2 Implied knowledge from incidental interference with known or predictable results

Human rights complaints are not always clear-cut, and an act of deliberation can be disputed on the ground that harm occurred unintentionally or accidentally. In the case of *Ergi*, the applicant complained that an innocent woman (his sister) was killed in the cross-fire between security forces against

---

62 *Makaratzis* v. *Greece* [2004] no. 50385/99, paras 45 and 71. Such combined approaches have not been repeated in subsequent cases, *Celniku* v. *Greece* [2007] no. 21449/04 (available in French only); *Leonidis* v. *Greece* [2009] no. 43326/05.
63 *Makaratzis* v. *Greece*, ibid., paras 50 and 71.
64 See also the partly dissenting opinion of judge Wildhaber joined by judges Kovler and Mularoni in *Makaratzis* v. *Greece*, ibid. (cited cases omitted): 'Our Court's case-law states that a State may have a positive obligation to protect the life of individuals from third parties (cf. §50). Concretely, this may mean that the police had to protect the lives of pedestrians, car drivers and their colleagues from the applicant. The Court's case-law states at the same time that in exceptional circumstances, physical ill-treatment by State officials which does not result in death may disclose a violation of Article 2... If these two strands of case-law are overextended, they may ultimately overlap and come into conflict. The State might then paradoxically violate both its positive duty to protect the life of individuals from third parties and its obligation to curb the use of force by the police. Obviously, such an overlap would be unfortunate. In extreme cases it can place the competent authorities in an impossible situation'. See also Warbrick, 'The European Convention on Human Rights and the Prevention of Terrorism', p. 118.

PKK in the south-east of Turkey in violation of Article 2. From the evidence submitted it was not possible to prove that the applicant's sister was killed by state agents, let alone to show their intention to inflict harm.[65] The Government denied its responsibility by distinguishing *McCann and Others* on the absence of premeditation from the part of its agents to harm the deceased.[66] The Court held that the state's liability for violation of Article 2 could not be established in this part of the complaint.

However, the European judges did not confine their examination to evidence of express intention, but looked at the issue of 'incidental loss of civilian life' in lethal operations to define the applicable safeguards in the form of 'precautions' against accidental harm.[67] Thus, the state officers may not have intended to kill the deceased, but it was clear that their acts may result in accidental harm, and hence their knowledge of such a likely incident is reasonably presumed. To argue otherwise would exclude the state's liability in circumstances where, for example, in order to stop an armed fugitive running away on a crowded street, police officers could start firing indiscriminately and later assume that they did not know of any harm that could be caused to innocent bystanders. Therefore, the safeguards developed in *McCann and Others* include, in addition, precautionary measures to protect the life and limb of innocent bystanders.

Moreover, precautions have also to be taken in relation to the lives of state officers, viewed as individuals/employees, who participate in dangerous operations. That issue arose in *Halit Dinç*, in which a chief-sergeant had been killed by other members of security force during a night operation against rebels in a frontier zone. The Court reiterated that, according to the provisions of paragraph 2 of Article 2, the use of lethal force could only be justified if it was 'absolutely necessary' under the circumstances. In examining the state's liability under a 'strict interpretation' of proportionality of its agents' response, the Court found *inter alia* that the instruction to shoot did not provide for any guarantees to safeguard against arbitrary acts of state agents.[68]

From the analysis of the case-law in this section, it is clear that when an intentional interference is initiated by state agents, safeguards have to be provided to cover all categories of individuals who can be exposed to any perceivable risk of harm, either directly or indirectly. Knowledge of the likely risks and of the categories of individuals to whom these risks apply can reasonably be implied from the nature of the activities concerned. For the

---

65 *Ergi* v. *Turkey* [1998] no. 23818/94.
66 Ibid., para. 75.
67 Ibid., para. 79. *Abdurashidova* v. *Russia* [2010] no. 32968/05, para. 79.
68 *Halit Dinç* v. *Turkey* [2006] no. 32597/96, paras 49, 55–56 (available in French only). See also R. Norton-Taylor, 'Sending Troops into Battle Without Proper Equipment Could Breach Rights, Says Judge', *Guardian* (12 April 2008); M. Hickley, 'Negligence over Soldier Son's Death in Iraq', *Daily Mail* (19 August 2008).

lethal operations of security forces, the content of safeguards is assessed in relation to those individuals who are likely to be exposed to known threats, namely innocent bystanders, security officers and alleged suspects.

### 2.2.1.3 Express or implied knowledge by context and comparative examples

The state indirectly interferes with human rights when it is its agents that have permitted the activity of a private party which causes the violation of the human rights of identifiable individuals. We have already seen in *Hatton and Others* that the private lives of some individuals were adversely affected when the private corporation controlling the nearby airport increased the quota of night flights. However, the private party's interference was made possible by the decision of the state's planning authority to grant permission for an extension of night flights in that airport.[69]

The element of knowledge can be imputed on the state if it is shown that the state authorities are aware that their dealings with private parties can negatively affect the human rights of other private individuals. Such will be the case when similar complaints have been reported in the past at both national and European levels (empirical knowledge by context).[70] The element of knowledge can also be deduced from international reports and documents that have been adopted to raise awareness about the negative effects of some activities of the private sector and to set minimum standards for their operation (comparative and contextual knowledge).[71]

### 2.2.1.4 Express knowledge from express complaints

A great number of laws and administrative orders are adopted by the state with the aim to organise, and better organise, the society of its citizens. Given the diversity and large quantity of various measures that are produced by the state machinery, it can reasonably be argued that some

---

69  *Hatton and Others* v. *the United Kingdom* [2001] and [2003] (Grand Chamber) no. 36022/97. See also *Giacomelli* v. *Italy* [2006] no. 59909/00; *Van Kuck* v. *Germany* [2003] no. 35968/97.

70  M. de Salvia, 'Ambiente e Convenzione Europea dei Diritti dell'Uomo' (1997) 10(1) *RIDU* 78–83; M. Demerieux, 'Deriving Environmental Rights from the European Convention for the Protection of Human Rights and Fundamental Freedoms' (2001) 21 *OJLS* 521. For cases arising from the same factual situation/context establishing an awareness at both national and European level, see, e.g., *Powell and Rayner* v. *the United Kingdom* [1990] no. 9310/81 and *Hatton and Others* v. *the United Kingdom*, ibid. (industrial activities, airport noise); *Ergi* v. *Turkey* [1998] no. 23818/94 and *Isayeva* v. *Russia* [2005] no. 57950/00 (innocent bystanders in lethal operations).

71  See, e.g., the Buttarelli Report on Protection of Personal Data with regard to Surveillance [CJ-PD (2001) 11 rev.], Council of Europe (for the Project Group on Data Protection).

negative effects on human rights may not always be known until an express complaint is raised. In other words, it may not always be possible for the state to contemplate the negative effects of all of its acts if no reaction is reported by the individuals concerned.

In such circumstances, the element of knowledge of the need to protect human rights is present when an express complaint has been communicated to the competent administrative authority, either for the first time by the given applicant or by another individual in similar circumstances in the past. It would be unfair to automatically engage the international liability of the state without allowing the domestic administrative system a reasonable time to address a human rights complaint. This is the logic behind the provision of Article 35.1, which requires that domestic remedies be exhausted by the affected individuals so as to allow the state an opportunity to rectify any wrongs or failures.[72]

To the extent that 'effective' remedies must exist within the state's legal system in order for the individual to have access to an 'arguable' human rights claim, as required under Article 13 and the ensuing jurisprudence,[73] the very act of an individual's complaint in pursuit of domestic remedies amounts to an express knowledge of a likely interfering effect of the state's practices. Such an example is the case of *Rees*, in which the applicant had expressly requested that the state's administrative authorities modify the public registration system with regard to post-operative transsexuals due to serious embarrassment and prejudice that was suffered when a birth certificate had to be produced. On such a notification, the state becomes expressly aware of the negative effect that its administrative practices have on the human rights of some individuals, and it can choose to:

1   Question that the harm complained of exists or reaches the threshold of seriousness that engages the human right relied upon (the admissibility question).
2   Modify its practice accordingly so as to remove the effect complained of either completely or, at least, below the actionable degree of severity.
3   Uphold the practice in pursuit of the legitimate aims that are listed in paragraph 2 (if available) and establish the legal criteria justifying an act of interference.[74]

---

72  *Selmouni* v. *France* [1999] no. 25803/94, paras 74–77.
73  P. Mertens, *Le Droit de Recours Effectif devant les Instances Nationales en cas de Violation d'un Droit de l'Homme* (Brussels: Editions de l'Université de Bruxelles, 1973); R. Sapienza, 'Il Diritto ad un Ricorso Effettivo nella Convenzione Europea dei Diritti dell'Uomo' (2001) 2 *RDI* 271–297. See detailed discussion of Article 13 in Chapter 4.
74  The 'prescribed by law' stage of paragraph 2 in entirely new claims may be reduced to the basic safeguard of 'access to an arguable claim'. See discussion in Chapter 4 on what constitutes an 'arguable' human rights claim.

*2.2.1.5 Express knowledge from previous decisions of non-justifiability of the interference*

The element of knowledge has to be re-assessed when a subsequent judicial examination, in closely similar circumstances, concludes that an act of interference cannot be justified.

Taking again the example of *Rees*, it can be said that the unfavourable outcome of that case has been felt across the member states by all those individuals being in the same circumstances with the applicant. In the subsequent case of *Goodwin*, in which the Court reversed its position in *Rees*, a new human rights standard has been set under Articles 8 and 12 making clear that the public records of post-operative transsexuals have to be modified to reflect their new sexual identity, unless an insurmountable burden can be proved by the state. Provided that there is no change in the critical parameters upon which that conclusion was reached, it follows that the state is directly and expressly informed of both the negative effect and the non-justifiability of its practices in such circumstances.

When a Court's decision sets a pan-European standard, knowledge of it does not solely lie with the respondent state, but with all member states, given that the human rights standards of the Convention constitute the common *acquis* of European human rights law (see also p. 80  with note 70). In essence, previous decisions of the Court, in which the issue of non-justifiability of interference has conclusively been resolved, amount to an express form of knowledge from the point of view of European judicial examination.[75]

### 2.2.2 The element of knowledge in positive obligations cases

*2.2.2.1 Implied knowledge from a known context of private parties' interactions*

The element of knowledge can be assumed when the protection of human rights is examined in a context of private parties' interactions in which known human rights issues exist. Empirical social experience can be relied upon to confirm this knowledge under the circumstances concerned. In other words, a violation of a human right is just another case waiting to happen.

Violence against the person is a known context with respect to which the Court has stressed in *Osman* that

> [i]t is common ground that the State's obligation in this respect extends beyond its primary duty to secure the right to life by putting in place effective criminal-law provisions... Article 2 of the Convention

75 See, e.g., *L.* v. *Lithuania* [2007] no. 27527/03.

may also imply in certain well-defined circumstances a positive obligation on the authorities to take preventive operational measures to protect an individual whose life is at risk from the criminal acts of another individual.[76]

Known human rights issues also exist in the context of healthcare. The Court has equally made clear in *Calvelli and Ciglio* that 'positive obligations therefore require States to make regulations compelling hospitals, whether public or private, to adopt appropriate measures for the protection of patients' lives.'[77]

Industrial activities also pose threats to human rights. In *Oneryildiz*, which concerned a fatal industrial accident that was caused by an explosion in a waste-treatment factory (the case is also discussed below), the Court has seized the opportunity to highlight the contextual reach of positive obligations. It emphasised the element of knowledge with reference to 'the potential risks inherent' in the activity in question, as well as to 'the context of any activity, whether public or not, in which the right to life may be at stake, and *a fortiori* in the case of industrial activities, which by their very nature are dangerous'.[78]

Other known contexts are certainly those that are codified in the text of the Convention, such as family life (Article 8), correspondence (Article 8) and peaceful assemblies (Article 11).

Often, when the element of knowledge is established from the presence of a known context of private parties' interaction, then both the source of the threat to human rights and the individuals who are likely to be affected can reasonably be identified, whereby establishing the relevant conditions of proximity. Thus, to know that an industrial activity is dangerous easily identifies the individuals to whom a positive duty is owed, namely the factory's personnel and those living in the nearby area.[79]

---

76 *Osman* v. *the United Kingdom* [1998] no. 23452/94, para. 115; *Mahmut Kaya* v. *Turkey* [2000] no. 22535/93, para. 85.

77 *Calvelli and Ciglio* v. *Italy* [2002] no. 32967/96, para. 49.

78 *Oneryildiz* v. *Turkey* [2004] (Grand Chamber) no. 48939/99, paras 65 and 71. See also section titles of the 'General Principles' of the Court: 'Principles relating to the prevention of infringements of the right to life as a result of dangerous activities: the substantive aspect of Article 2 of the Convention', before para. 89. For similar application in other contexts, see *Kilinc and Others* v. *Turkey* [2005] no. 40145/98, para. 41: 'Similar regulation can require the taking of practical measures in order to provide effective protection of those who are exposed to the inherent dangers of military life.', (translation) (available in French only).

79 Special attention should be given to children whose behaviour is not as predictable as those of adults, see, e.g., *Pasa and Erkan Erol* v. *Turkey* [2006] no. 51358/99 (available in French only).

## 2.2.2.2  Implied knowledge from previous incidents or comparative examples

When the issue of protection of human rights, as described in the applicant's complaint, is examined with reference to the wide context of private parties' activities to which the isolated case relates, it may be possible to rely on comparative examples to determine the dual issues of *if* and, if so, to what *extent*, positive obligations can be imposed.

The element of knowledge can be sought in previous incidents,[80] or in the practices of member states (or even those of non-member states), in which similar human right issues have already been dealt with under a proven record of effectiveness.[81] The same applies where relevant national or international documents exist in the form of recommendations, resolutions or scientific studies and reports that have usually contextual targets.[82]

It has also been observed that in the development of European human rights standards, the quality of practice rather than the quantity of similar approaches may be preferred. In analysing the Court's reasoning in the case of *Siliadin*,[83] which concerned the issue of slavery in private relationships, Holly Cullen has pointed out that, despite the fact that only one state had at the time ratified the Council of Europe's new convention on people trafficking, member states have been presented with a challenge to adopt clearer and stronger laws to criminalise trafficking for forced labour.[84]

The influence of comparative examples can be traced as early as the case of *Marckx*, in which the Court expressly referred to two international conventions in order to point to the principle of *mater semper certa est*, as applied

---

80  See, e.g., *Powell and Rayner* v. *the United Kingdom* [1990] no. 9310/81 and *Hatton and Others* v. *the United Kingdom* [2003] (Grand Chamber) no. 36022/97. See also *Guerra and Others* v. *Italy* [1998] no. 14967/89; *Tatar* v. *Romania* [2009] no. 67021/01/01 (available in French only); *Hajduova* v. *Slovakia* [2010] no. 2660/03.

81  See, e.g., *Pretty* v. *the United Kingdom* [2002] no. 2346/02.

82  *Guerra and Others* v. *Italy* [1998] no. 14967/89, para. 34; *Oneryildiz* v. *Turkey* [2004] no. 48939/99, paras 58–59; *Tatar and Tatar* v. *Romania* (dec.) [2007] no. 67021/01, paras 44–45, in which the following documents are quoted: Resolution no. 1430/2005 of the Parliamentary Assembly of the Council of Europe on industrial hazards; European Parliament's Resolution on 5 July 2001 (OJ C 65 E, 14 March 2002, p. 382); Council Directive 85/337/EEC as amended by Council Directive 97/11/EC on the assessment of the effects of certain public and private projects on the environment; the UNECE Espoo Convention on Transboundary Environmental Impact Assessment; Council Directive 96/82/EC of 9 December 1996 on the control of major-accident hazards involving dangerous substances (Seveso II Directive) and UNECE Convention on the Transboundary Effects of Industrial Accidents; Council Directive 96/61/EC of 24 September 1996 concerning integrated pollution prevention and control (IPPC Directive). See also *Tatar* v. *Romania* [2009] no. 67021/01, paras 26, 28, 32, 91, 95.

83  *Siliadin* v. *France* [2005] no. 73316/01.

84  H. Cullen, '*Siliadin v. France*: Positive Obligations under Article 4 of the European Convention on Human Rights' (2006) 6 *HRLR* 585–592, p. 592. For human trafficking (sexual exploitation), see *Rantsev* v. *Cyprus and Russia* [2010] no. 25965/04.

in the applicant's circumstances.[85] The 'currently small number' of member states that had ratified these conventions at that time did not prevent the Court from reasoning that 'the existence of these two treaties denotes that there is a clear measure of common ground in this area amongst modern societies.'[86] Although this statement was made in the examination of Article 8 taken in conjunction with Article 14 (the anti-discrimination provision), it should normally have also appeared in the preceding examination of Article 8 in which only some in-passing references were given to international instruments. Perhaps this is due to the fact that the discrimination issue virtually overlapped with or was closely connected to the complaint under Article 8 taken alone. In addition, the use of some principles in Latin points to some millennia-old and tired issues that reinforce the argument of prior knowledge of the need of human rights protection.

It should be noted, however, that the determination of the element of knowledge through comparative examples is not always exercised consistently. In *Colak and Tsakiridis*, the applicant complained that the state failed to adequately regulate the duty of care of the medical practitioners so as to require them to disclose patients' infections (i.e. HIV-positive condition) to those who can be affected (i.e. relatives, companions). In favouring the government's argument, the Court treated the case as being a new issue and, therefore, 'it was not possible for the legislator to issue stricter rules'.[87] It did not find it necessary to explain why its comparative study had not be employed in that case. Probably, a possible explanation may be found in the fact that a domestic appeal court agreed in principle with the disclosure of medical records in such circumstances. But new standards of medical negligence could not be of any use to the applicant due to the difficulty of applying developments in law retrospectively.[88] In the future, however, it is reasonably expected that the element of knowledge can be established in such circumstances at the respondent state's level, because, as the Court acknowledged:

> a higher standard would have to be applied to a physician's diligence in cases which might arise after [the appellate court's] judgment given in the instant case, which clarified the physician's professional duties in these specific circumstances, had been published.[89]

85 *Marckx* v. *Belgium* [1979] no. 6833/74, para. 20, citing the Brussels Convention on the Establishment of Maternal Affiliation of Natural Children, which was prepared by the International Commission on Civil Status (entered into force on 23 April 1964), and the Convention on the Legal Status of Children born out of Wedlock, which was concluded within the Council of Europe (entered into force on 11 August 1978).
86 *Marckx* v. *Belgium*, ibid., para. 41; P. Duffy, 'The Protection of Privacy, Family Life and Other Rights under Article 8 of the European Convention on Human Rights' (1982) 2 *YbkEL* 191–238, p. 238.
87 *Colak and Tsakiridis* v. *Germany* [2009] nos 77144/01 and 35493/05, para. 31.
88 For the problem of retroactivity in human rights disputes between private parties, see discussion in Chapter 1, section: 'The *drittwirkung* proposal', p. 44.
89 *Colak and Tsakiridis* v. *Germany* [2009] nos 77144/01 and 35493/05, para. 34.

### 2.2.2.3 Express knowledge of an identifiable threat

Although positive obligations can arise contextually, more personal issues can reasonably be addressed when an individual in need of human rights protection can be identified. There are, however, circumstances in which knowledge of the specific threat (i.e. the second condition of proximity is present) suffices by itself to engage the state's positive obligations vis-à-vis non-identifiable individuals (i.e. the first condition of proximity is absent).[90]

An example of such a circumstance is when a dangerous individual is found guilty for acts of violence and, therefore, a positive obligation arises automatically for the state to sentence and detain the convicted individual in order to protect the people at large. It is the known identity of the source of a threat that gives rise to a positive obligation to protect all members of the society against the dangerous individual by means of a prolonged detention. Indeed, detention of convicted criminals is the corollary obligation of enforcing a sanction that the state is under a positive obligation to regulate in advance in the context of violence against the person. The appropriate deterring effect of a regulated measure is considered in relation to the type and intensity of the regulated sanctions.[91]

In such a known context, a question is raised about the implications of granting prison leaves to serving offenders. Without having to go into discussion of the justifiability or merits of the prison leave scheme,[92] it can be asserted that when a decision is made to grant prison leave to a dangerous offender, the initial positive obligation of the state to protect innocent individuals at large against a known (identified) threat can never be negated.[93] In this respect, it can reasonably be expected that when a sanction is not fully enforced, and innocent individuals are harmed, a strict liability principle can apply to examine the state's response.

It is observed, however, that in some case-law the identification or foreseeability of a potential victim has been required in order to engage the positive obligations of the state (i.e. the first condition of proximity should be present). In the case of *Bromley*, the applicant's daughter was killed by a psychopath and dangerous offender who had been released temporarily on prison leave, while he was serving a sentence for a serious offence.

---

90  See discussion above, p. 76.
91  On the intensity of sanctions, see, e.g., *X and Y* v. *the Netherlands* [1985] no. 8978/80; *Oneryildiz* v. *Turkey* [2004] no. 48939/99; *Calvelli and Ciglio* v. *Italy* [2002] no. 32967/96; *Ilhan* v. *Turkey* [2002] no. 32967/96; *Siliadin* v. *France* [2005] no. 73316/01, etc. Cullen, '*Siliadin* v. *France*: Positive Obligations under Article 4 of the European Convention on Human Rights', p. 589. See also discussion in Chapter 1, p. 23 and Chapter 4, pp. 192–198.
92  Ν. Παρασκευόπουλος και Ε. Φυτράκη, 'Η «Αυστηροποίηση» και οι Άδειες των Κρατουμένων' *Ελευθεροτυπία* (16 November 2007).
93  *A* v. *Croatia* [2010] no. 55164/08, para. 78: 'The Court stresses that the main purpose of imposing criminal sanctions is to restrain and deter the offender from causing further harm. However, these aims can hardly be achieved without the sanctions imposed being enforced.'

In her application, the mother claimed that there was 'a positive duty on the State to protect her daughter's life, which included the duty not to release prematurely those who constituted a risk to the life and limb of the public in general'.[94] In examining the state's positive obligations in such circumstances, the Court limited its reasoning to the domestic civil law criteria that condition liability on the foreseeability or proximity of an identified individual, rather than of the people at large.

Similar issues were dealt with in the case of *Mastomatteo*, in which the Court found again that there was no breach of the state's obligations when its authorities permitted a temporarily release of a convicted criminal who subsequently murdered the applicant's son.[95] Judge Bonello dissented, reasoning:

> [a] State, I submit, does not adequately ensure to everyone the enjoyment of the right to life when it puts in place machinery which benefits society and criminals if it works properly and, when it does not, overlooks the fate of its victims.[96]

Progress has been made with the finding of violation of Article 2 in the case of *Maiorano and Others*, in which the Court intensified its review and found that, in the circumstances concerned, the public officials had been negligent in releasing a dangerous offender and, therefore, it established that there had been a causal link between the death of innocent individuals and the state authorities' involvement in the offender's premature release.[97]

## 2.2.2.4 Express knowledge from express complaints

In most cases, a positive obligation for a more narrow and personal protection of human rights will arise for the state when the identity of an individual in need of protection is known. Whenever an individual expressly notifies the state about a threat to their human rights, the element of knowledge is established. As a result, a positive obligation is imposed on the state to actively protect that individual, provided, of course, that a Convention right has been engaged under the circumstances.[98]

Before going on to discuss relevant case-law, it should be clarified that here we do not concern ourselves with the element of knowledge that is indirectly established under Article 35.1, which conditions the individual petition upon the exhaustion of domestic remedies, and hence knowledge

94 *Bromley* v. *the United Kingdom* (dec.) [1999] no. 33747/96.
95 *Mastromatteo* v. *Italy* [2002] no. 37703/97, para. 95.
96 Ibid., para. 9 of the dissenting opinion of judge Bonello.
97 *Maiorano and Others* v. *Italy* [2009] no. 28634/06 (available in French only).
98 See discussion on the scope of the Convention rights below (section 2.3.1).

of a human right issue surfaces somehow, mostly *ex post facto* at the trial stage. The content of positive obligations that is looked at in this sub-section regards the active protection of human rights before harm is suffered. In general, it should be stressed that the active protection of human rights is not disputed as such. What is argued is that protection has not been provided in the end because the state authorities could not possibly have known the identity of the individual in need of human rights protection.

An important case is *Osman* whose facts concerned an express notification to the police about the threats that a family had been receiving from another individual.[99] The Court found that upon the applicant's notification, the police complied fully with their positive obligations, as could reasonably be required of them in such circumstances, namely to investigate incriminating evidence in order to proceed with an arrest or provide manned protection to the applicant's family.[100] Since such incriminating evidence (added knowledge) was not produced in the end, the content of the state's positive obligation was exhausted with the implementation of the core administrative practices of investigation (see further discussion below, pp. 111–112).

In the subsequent case of *Kilic*, a journalist had informed the state's authorities about death threats against the staff of a newspaper.[101] The applicant's claim was examined against a background of serious incidents of killings and attacks of the newspaper's employees.[102] The Commission's findings *in situ* made specific reference to a 'pattern of attacks',[103] as confirmed by a statutory report pointing to the seriousness of the situation in a region of the country.[104] In that case, and unlike *Osman*, there was no need to establish incriminating evidence (the added knowledge) in order to define the content of the state's positive obligations in the form of: a) manned protection of the newspapers' employees and b) further investigation to identity and apprehend the source of threat to the individual's life.[105]

Similar considerations apply when the state's authorities are alerted to the disappearance of an individual that occurs against a background of killings of the people who disappear.[106] In such circumstances, the operational measures that are examined concern measures of investigation to locate criminal suspects and the whereabouts of the victims.[107]

---

99  *Osman* v. *the United Kingdom* [1998] no. 23452/94.
100  Restraints are imposed on the powers of the police due to competing human rights under Articles 5 and 8, see *Osman* v. *the United Kingdom*, ibid., para. 116.
101  *Kilic* v. *Turkey* [2000] no. 22492/93.
102  Ibid., para. 66. The Court recalled previous case-law concerning the same factual situations.
103  Ibid., para. 55.
104  Ibid., para. 68.
105  Ibid., paras 76, 132.
106  See, e.g., *Koku* v. *Turkey* [2005] no. 27305/95; *Osmanoglu* v. *Turkey* [2008] no. 48804/99. See further discussion in Chapter 4.
107  *Kilic* v. *Turkey* [2000] no. 22492/93, paras 128, 133.

In exceptional circumstances, such as those characterised by specific patterns, an express notification may not be required. In *Mahmut Kaya*, the Court held that a positive obligation had arisen for the state's authorities to protect the life of a doctor in the south-east region of Turkey where a Kurdish minority lives, despite the fact that there was no express request for protection. It was found that the doctor's life was in danger due to previous incidents against individuals who had supported the cause of the Kurdish minority in that region. As the deceased doctor was known for such a support, it could reasonably be said that the state's authorities had knowledge of the need for human rights protection in relation to an identifiable individual.[108]

There are also situations in which threatening acts have ulterior aims – for example, to intimidate individuals from freely expressing their opinions, as seen in *Plattform 'Arzte fur das Leben'*, in which the applicants had informed the police that a counter demonstration from an opposing group would cross their scheduled route.[109] In *Ozgur Gundem*, the applicants, owners and staff of a newspaper, had expressly requested protection from the state authorities against repetitive attacks that clearly aimed at preventing them from publishing.[110] Other examples in which express notification establishes the element of knowledge of the individual's identity include the case of *Moreno Gomez*, in which an express call was made to the police to protect the applicants from noise emanating from an adjoining bar.[111]

By way of contrast, such an element of knowledge of the individual's identity could not be established in the case of *Gungor*. The applicant complained about the state authorities' failure to protect his son who was murdered by unknown individuals in a high-profile residential establishment. The Court could not find that there was any specific threat of which the state's authorities 'had or ought to have had knowledge' so as to move expeditiously and offer practical protection to the individual concerned.[112] As a result, the state's liability under the substantive aspect of the right to life could not be engaged.

In the case of *Opuz*, an express complaint to the state authorities that was subsequently withdrawn did not negate the element of knowledge. The applicant complained that the state's inadequate response to the threats and incidents of violence by her abusive husband violated Article 2 (for the death of her mother) and Article 3 (for severe and repetitive physical abuse of the

---

108 *Mahmut Kaya* v. *Turkey* [2000] no. 22535/93; see also the high-profile case of *Dink* v. *Turkey* [2010] nos 2668/07,..., 7124/09 (available in French only).

109 *Plattform 'Arzte fur das Leben'* v. *Austria* [1988] no. 10126/82.

110 *Ozgur Gundem* v. *Turkey* [2000] no. 23144/93; *Dink* v. *Turkey* [2010] nos 2668/07,..., 7124/09. M. Champion, 'Court Faults Turkey Over Editor's Murder', *The Wall Street Journal* (14 September 2010).

111 *Moreno Gomez* v. *Spain* [2004] no. 4143/02; see also *Tatar and Tatar* v. Romania (dec.) [2007] no. 67021/01, para. 46.

112 *Gungor* v. *Turkey* [2005] no. 28290/95, para. 60 (available in French only).

applicant herself). The withdrawal of complaints to the domestic authorities did not absolve the state of its positive obligation to protect identifiable individuals, because knowledge of the threats involved could be established by previous incidents of violence and reported allegations for death threats.[113] In finding a violation of Article 2 the Court reasoned that

> once the situation has been brought to their attention, the national authorities cannot rely on the victim's attitude for the failure to take adequate measures which could prevent the likelihood of an aggressor carrying out his threats against the physical integrity of the victim.[114]

### 2.2.3 The autonomy of the element of knowledge

The element of knowledge of the need of human rights protection reaches an autonomous status when its presence alone suffices to engage the positive obligations of the state.

In the case of *Budayeva and Others*, the Court, for the first time in its jurisprudence, imposed positive obligations on the state to protect the lives of individuals from natural disasters of which its authorities had (or ought to have had) prior knowledge.[115] The applicants complained under Article 2 that the state authorities had failed to comply with their positive obligations to take appropriate measures to mitigate the risks to their lives against natural hazards.

In establishing whether a positive obligation can arise in such a context, the Court has relied on the authority of the case of *Osman* to reiterate that 'this positive obligation entails above all a primary duty on the State to put in place a legislative and administrative framework designed to provide effective deterrence against threats to the right to life'.[116] To reinforce this position, it quoted from its judgment in *Oneryildiz*, that '[t]his obligation must be construed as applying in the context of any activity, whether public or not, in which the right to life may be at stake'.[117]

Looked at more closely, however, 'effective deterrence' or to protect individuals against 'any activity' does not apply to the facts of *Budayeva and Others*, in that there is no issue of deterrence against threats of private parties, or any private/public 'activity' involved in the protection of individuals' lives from natural hazards. It is only the element of

---

113  *Opuz* v. *Turkey* [2009] no. 33401/02, paras 147, 173.
114  Ibid., para. 153 (cited case omitted). See also paras 168, 173 (under Article 3).
115  *Budayeva and Others* v. *Russia* [2008] nos 15339/02,…, 15343/02. See also *Beru* v. *Turkey* [2011] no. 47304/07, para. 46 (protection against stray/wild animals) (available in French only).
116  Ibid., para. 129.
117  Ibid., p. 130.

knowledge of the incoming natural disaster and the corresponding need of human rights protection that engages the state's positive obligations to actively protect individuals in such circumstances. The main question examined in that case was the extent of protection that relates to the more specific content of positive obligations that we cover in the following section.

## 2.3 The content of positive obligations under paragraph 1 of the Convention rights

Positive obligations are imposed by virtue of paragraph 1 of the Convention rights. Whether or not the state authorities decide to pursue a legitimate aim of interference, positive obligations may have already arisen contextually, engaging the state in the active protection of human rights.

The content of positive obligations can be determined in various interconnected and prioritised stages under which the active protection of human rights is organised contextually, as a system, and ad hoc, as a personal form of assistance.

In every stage, the evaluative principle that is employed is that of effectiveness that cuts across the board.[118] The way by which this principle applies or the exact occasion of its application varies from case to case depending on the focus of the judicial examination.[119] In the interests of predictability and exactness,[120] the principle of effectiveness is approached as an objective factor to guide the determination of the content of positive obligations.[121]

In this section, the examination of the content of positive obligations is organised by addressing the following issues: (1) the scope of the Convention rights against which positive obligations can only arise, (2) the scope of protection under paragraph 1 of the Convention rights, (3) limits of practically

---

118 *Airey* v. *Ireland* [1979] no. 6289/73, para. 24: 'The Convention is intended to guarantee not rights that are theoretical or illusory but rights that are practical and effective'; *Marckx* v. *Belgium* [1979] no. 6833/74, para. 31; *Golder* v. *the United Kingdom* [1975] no. 4451/70, para. 35.

119 Warbrick, 'The European Convention on Human Rights and the Prevention of Terrorism', p. 96, who argues that '[t]he utility of the principle of effectiveness for the interpretation of the Convention is rooted in the constitutional nature of its provisions – general prescriptions of indeterminate extent – but the other qualifying conditions are absent.'

120 Cf. P. van Dijk, in M. Castermans-Holleman *et al.* (eds), *The Role of the Nation-State in the 21st Century: Essays in Honour of Peter Baehr*, p. 22: 'First of all, there are no clear-cut criteria for determining whether and when effectiveness will have been achieved.'

121 See Mertens, *Le Droit de Recours* quoting, at pp. 81–82, M.J. Touscoz: 'It is mainly about the quality of a judicial principle that fulfils objectively its social function' (translation) and R.J. Dupuy: 'Effectiveness is not about a legal principle, it comes before it. It is a primordial rule, an inherent justification of the reality of a norm or that of an institution.', (translation), both passages from M.J. Touscoz, *Le Principe d'Effectivité dans l'Ordre International* (LGDJ, 1964), preface and p. 1, respectively.

implied in paragraph 1, (4) the core content of protection (the contextual level), (5) the practical measures of protection (the ad hoc level).

It should be recalled that the study of positive obligations in this chapter concentrates on their substantive content. The additional and concurring content of positive obligations that concerns effective remedies is examined separately in Chapter 4. The content of positive obligations in circumstances where limitations to the scope of human rights are justified under paragraph 2 of the Convention provisions, or where a conflict of rights gives rise to a conflict of positive obligations is addressed subsequently in section 2.4 below.

### 2.3.1  The preliminary question of the scope of human rights: assessing the negative impact involved

The protection of human rights arises as a legal issue over the specific rights that are enshrined in the text of the Convention. Accordingly, positive obligations can be imposed on the state in so far as a Convention right can be engaged, at least, in 'arguable' terms.[122] If a Convention right cannot be engaged in the applicant's circumstances, the petition will be rejected as 'manifestly ill-founded' under Article 35.3–4. In such a case, the question of the state's positive obligation is not reached.

In spite of its preliminary relevance, the question of the scope of a human right has sometimes been overlooked or not given the necessary weight that it deserves. Alpha Connelly has earlier highlighted that this question has to be approached consistently and be considered first, rather than 'jumping' the express stages of the Convention provisions and examining the impact question under paragraph 2.[123]

The scope of a Convention right concerns mainly the conceptual meaning of a human right that can be discerned from the literal reading of the relevant provisions and their judicial interpretation.[124] Under that

---

122  The qualifying adjective 'arguable' is inserted by the requirements of Article 13, as interpreted by the Court. See discussion in Chapter 4, section 4.2.1.

123  For a study of earlier decisions of the Commission, see A. Connelly, 'Problems of Interpretation of Article 8 of the European Convention on Human Rights' (1986) 3 *ICLQ* 567–593, pp. 580, 590. See also C. Warbrick, 'The Structure of Article 8' (1998) 1 *EHRLR* 32–44, p. 43: '[i]ncoherence arises when the Court collapses the examination of whether there is a positive obligation under Article 8(1) with the question of whether it has been breached, an Article 8(2) matter. The approach is analytically misfounded because of the lack of substantive distinction between positive and negative obligations.'

124  Duffy, 'The Protection of Privacy, Family Life and Other Rights under Article 8 of the European Convention on Human Rights', p. 204, who points out that '[i]t will also be recalled that the Article 8(1) rights are subject to limitations in their very definition, or, as the Court put it in *Golder*, there are "bounds delimiting the very content of any right"'. In *Marckx* v. *Belgium* [1979] no. 6833/74, it was found, in relation to a parallel claim, that 'it is not a requirement of Article 8 that a child should be entitled to some share in the estate of his parents or even of other near relatives', para. 53.

process, thresholds of negative impact are set in relation to each of the Convention rights in order to define the actionable level of applicability.[125] Wherever the human rights interests of Articles 2 and 3 are engaged, a greater content of protection has to be prescribed due to their semi-absolute and absolute status, respectively.

In order to explain that the scope of a human right is a preliminary question for the determination of the positive obligations of the state, relevant case-law has to be discussed and analysed in relation to the two pertinent issues: the conceptual aspect of the Convention rights and their threshold of negative impact.

Important issues about the conceptual meaning of the Convention rights were dealt with in the case of *Abdulaziz, Cabales and Balkandali*. The applicants complained about the state's practice, as authorised by statutory law, of not granting residence permit to their foreign husbands (and fiancé for the second applicant, Mrs Cabales). All applicants were also foreigners themselves who had acquired indefinite residential status in the respondent state before entering into a marital relationship at a later point in their lives. In addition, in the case of Mrs Balkandali, the applicant had a son (who had the right to abode in the state concerned) with Mr Balkandali. In examining the applicants' complaints under Article 8 (the 'family life' component), the majority of the Court asked whether the state met its positive obligation to respect family life in such circumstances. The applicability of Article 8 was easily established in relation Mrs Abdulaziz and Mrs Balkandali, as 'whatever else the word "family" may mean, it must at any rate include the relationship that arises from a lawful and genuine marriage.'[126] Applicability was also recognised with regard to Mrs Cabales for a genuinely committed cohabiting relationship (ended subsequently in marriage).

However, the *real* issue of the applicability of Article 8 was determined, as follows:

> The duty imposed by Article 8 (art. 8) cannot be considered as extending to a general obligation on the part of a Contracting State to respect the choice by married couples of the country of their matrimonial residence and to accept the non-national spouses for settlement in that country.[127]

125 See, e.g., the *Greek Case*, Commission's Report of 5 November 1969, Yearbook XII (1969), p. 501; *Ireland* v. *the United Kingdom* [1978] no. 5310/71, para. 162; *Fadeyeva* v. *Russia* [2006] no. 55723/00, paras 69, 70. For a study of the decisions of the Commission, see Loucaides, *Essays*, p. 181: 'Interpretation of the scope of the right is to some extent influenced by the facts of the cases, especially by the degree of severity of the consequences of the particular situation to which the complaint refers.' See also discussion in Chapter 3, section 3.2.1.1.

126 *Abdulaziz, Cabales and Balkandali* v. *the United Kingdom* [1985] nos 9214/80,…, 9474/81, para. 62. The relevance of Article 12 was also noted by the Court.

127 Ibid., para. 68.

This conclusion should be contrasted with the concurring opinion of judge Bernhardt, who reasoned:

> According to the present judgment, Article 8 para. 1 (art. 8–1) is applicable but, if taken alone, is not violated because there is no "lack of respect" for family life. This reasoning excludes the application of Article 8 para. 2 (art. 8–2), and it in fact places inherent limitations upon the rights guaranteed in paragraph 1 of Article 8 (art. 8–1). In my opinion, the measures in question can only be, and indeed are, justified by the application of Article 8 para. 2 (art. 8–2).[128]

The point that there cannot be 'inherent limitations upon the rights guaranteed in paragraph 1 of Article 8 (art. 8–1)' is also confirmed by the Court's admission that a marital relationship is, in every circumstance encountered, 'family life' within the meaning of Article 8. In essence, the inclusion of 'family life' in the wording of Article 8.1 serves as a contextual specification of the broader right of respect for private life, so as not to re-argue and re-discover the core aspects of private life in every given case.[129]

To decide that the scope of Article 8 does not extend to the applicants' circumstances negates the very substance of Article 8. Another way to put it, the question of negative impact regards the non-enjoyment of a family life to which the applicants are already entitled by definition under the very wording of paragraph 1 of Article 8. This also transpires from the arguments of the government in relation to one of the applicants for whom indefinite leave was granted 'essentially on the ground that [the applicant] was an unmarried woman with little prospect of marriage'.[130] Therefore, it is unthinkable, even for the state officials, that the state can impose limitations on the choice of marriage partners. That some public officials with the task of examining an indefinite leave application betted the marriage chances of the applicant is not an issue that should concern the European community. The states are absolutely free to shape their own immigration policies, as 'the right of a foreigner to enter or remain in a country was not as such guaranteed by the Convention,

---

128 Ibid., para. 1 of the concurring opinion of judge Bernhardt. See also the concurring opinion of judge Thór Vilhjálmsson, who pointed to the legitimate aim of economic well-being of the country. The concurring judges did not elaborate much on the justifiability of that aim under the circumstances.

129 The emphasis is reasonably put on marriage rather than co-habitation. The former reassures the state of a genuine and strong commitment, while the latter can be seen as ephemeral and temporary. From the viewpoint of Article 12, see *O'Donoghue and Others* v. *the United Kingdom* [2010] no. 34848/07, para. 82: 'Article 12 secures the fundamental right of a man and woman to marry and found a family. […] It is subject to national laws of the Contracting States but the limitations thereby introduced must not restrict or reduce the right in such a way or to such an extent that the very essence of the right is impaired' (cited cases omitted).

130 *Abdulaziz, Cabales and Balkandali* v. *the United Kingdom* [1985] nos 9214/80,…, 9474/81, para. 39.

but immigration controls had to be exercised consistently with Convention obligations.'[131] To put it straightforwardly, either immigrants are not welcome or, if they are, they have to be admitted with full respect of their human rights (the whole package), as guaranteed by the basic level of the Convention.

The question of the conceptual meaning of a human right has mostly been encountered in relation to Article 8 due to the broadness of the term 'private life'. For reasons of consistency, it should be recalled from the discussion in Chapter 1 (section 1.3.3) that, since early jurisprudence, the Court has connected this term to the notion of development of one's personality. In appropriate circumstances, in order to manage the application and development of positive obligations in a more certain and realistic manner, it may also seem useful to frame the question in negative terms, namely to look at those critical conditions without which the personality of an individual cannot develop.

In the current phase of the jurisprudence, the preliminary question of the scope of a human right is likely to be more pressing in the examination of the threshold of negative impact that engages a Convention right. Such a question arose in the case of *Costello-Roberts,* in which the applicant complained that the corporal punishment inflicted on him as a disciplinary measure in a private school was a treatment that gave rise to a violation of Articles 3 and 8. The Court reiterated first that, although the treatment complained of was the act of a headmaster of a private school, the state's responsibility may be engaged if private acts were allowed to violate human rights. It specified also that in order for the punishment to be 'degrading' within the meaning of Article 3, 'the humiliation or debasement involved must attain a particular level of severity and must in any event be other than that usual element of humiliation inherent in any punishment'.[132] The particular facts of the case were pertinent to the assessment of negative impact, but other factors were also taken into account, such as 'the nature and context of the punishment, the manner and method of its execution, its duration, its physical and mental effects and, in some instances, the sex, age and state of health of the victim'.[133] In the end, the Court found that, in the particular circumstances of the case, the minimum threshold of severity had not been reached. A similar conclusion was made in relation to the applicant's parallel claim under Article 8. It is worth pointing out that if the Article 8 threshold cannot be engaged in the applicant's circumstances, this finding will also suffice to negate the parallel claim under Article 3 due to the higher threshold of negative impact that applies to its provisions.

Similar issues have been underlined in subsequent jurisprudence, such as the case of *Stjerna,* in which a proposal for a complete merging of positive

---

131  Ibid., para. 59. *East African Asians* v. *the United Kingdom* (dec.) [1970] nos 4403/70, ..., 4530/70, para. 184: 'No right to enter and to reside in a particular country is, as such, guaranteed by the Convention.'

132  *Costello-Roberts* v. *the United Kingdom* [1993] no. 13134/87, para. 30.

133  Ibid. See also *Ledyayeva and Others* v. *Russia* [2006] nos 53157/99, ..., 53695/00, para. 90.

and negative obligations has been argued in a separate opinion of the judgment. With reference to our discussion above (section 2.1.2), it is recalled that the case concerned a complaint about the state's refusal to allow the applicant to change his surname. The Court could not find 'that the sources of inconvenience the applicant complained of are sufficient to raise an issue of failure to respect private life under paragraph 1 (art. 8–1)'.[134] A reference was also made to the similar assessment of the Commission that the inconvenience suffered was 'not significant enough'.[135] It is clear, therefore, that since the Commission had already reached this conclusion, the whole case could well have been rejected as manifestly ill-founded at the admissibility stage.[136] As far as the general conceptual question is concerned, it was held that the applicant's claim was 'sufficient to raise an issue of failure to respect private life under paragraph 1 (art. 8–1)',[137] or 'an individual's name does concern his or her private and family life'.[138] It was, however, the critical parameter of the actionable threshold of the negative impact involved that determined the real applicability of Article 8 in that case.[139]

If the negative impact in the applicant's circumstances was actionable, then with his claim the individual had 'notified' the state's authorities of a human right issue (the element of knowledge). In that respect, a positive obligation arises by virtue of a personal entitlement to a legal right under paragraph 1 of the relevant provision.[140]

From the discussion of the case-law in this section, it is clear that there is a great need for consistency in the application of legal principles and their prioritisation in judicial examination. A firm approach in the examination of the scope of human rights[141] and, especially, of the critical determinative of the threshold of negative impact, will benefit the development and application of positive obligations in the system of the Convention.

---

134  *Stjerna* v. *Finland* [1994] no. 18131/91, para. 42.

135  Ibid., paras 41, 42.

136  Ibid., para. 41.

137  Ibid., para. 42.

138  Ibid., para. 37.

139  See also *Ledyayeva and Others* v. *Russia* [2006] nos 53157/99,…, 53695/00, para. 100.

140  Connelly, 'Problems of Interpretation of Article 8 of the European Convention on Human Rights', p. 572.

141  A more firm approach is now expected due to the new admissibility provisions of Article 35.3.b, mainly the criterion of 'a significant disadvantage' which has, however, a more restricted application given that it applies only where its evaluation is possible without the need for a merits examination. The Court has so far relied on the general principle of *de minimis non curat praetor* to reject applications on account of their trivial nature, see, e.g., *Korolev (II)* v. *Russia* (dec.) [2010] no. 25551/05; *Rink* v. *France* [2010] no. 18774/09 (available in French only); *Peretyaka and Sheremetyev* v. *Ukraine* [2010] nos 17160/06 and 35548/06. See also Explanatory Report to Protocol No. 14, CETS No. 194 (adopted on 7 April 2004), paras 78–80; Practical Guide on Admissibility Criteria (2010), pp. 92–95, available at www.echr.coe.int/NR/rdonlyres/91AEEEBC-B90F-4913-ABCC-E181A44B75AD/0/ Practical_Guide_on_Admissibility_Criteria.pdf (accessed January 2011).

The two principal questions of knowledge of the need of human rights protection that conditions the state's liability (as discussed in section 2.2), and the scope of the Convention rights against which positive obligations arise (as discussed in this sub-section), form the general preliminary framework of technical principles that can manage objectively and also flexibly the broad nature of positive obligations. Having secured the basic foundations, we move on to discuss the more specific content of positive obligations.

### 2.3.2 The scope of protection: the underlying aim of prevention of human rights violations

The active protection of human rights, as is required by positive obligations under the Convention, does not simply mean some *ex post facto* relief to the victim. Even if we assume that the admissibility criterion for a victim status under Article 34 is interpreted very strictly (which it is not),[142] there is nothing to prevent the Court, in its *ex post* judicial examination, from targeting an *ex ante* system of human rights protection. From whichever angle the state's positive obligations are approached, it is inescapable to conclude that the quintessence of protection concerns the *prevention* of human rights violations.

The most basic level of prevention, as evaluated by the minimum standard of effectiveness, is to regulate appropriate sanctions that will be enforced *ex post* in the event of a violation. Under this content of positive obligations, prevention is realised through the deterring effect of the regulated sanctions.[143]

Beyond the (absolutely) basic *ex post* level, the issue of prevention concerns mainly the protection of individuals before an actual violation of a human right occurs. Under this aim, the effectiveness of protection is evaluated in relation to precautionary measures and human rights standards that condition the activities of private parties. Compliance with such regulatory measures is guaranteed by the positive involvement of public administration in all those feasible stages in which the activities of private parties can reasonably be subjected to their supervision and control.

---

142 *Monnat* v. *Switzerland* [2006] no. 73604/01, para. 31: 'the word "victim" in the context of Article 34 of the Convention denotes the person directly affected by the act or omission in issue, the existence of a violation of the Convention being conceivable even in the absence of prejudice (see *Brumărescu* v. *Romania* [GC], no. 28342/95, § 50, ECHR 1999–VII). An applicant cannot claim to be a "victim" within the meaning of Article 34 of the Convention unless he is or has been directly affected by the act or omission in question or runs the risk of being directly affected by it', (cited case omitted).

143 *Osman* v. *the United Kingdom* [1998] no. 23452/94, para. 115; *Mahmut Kaya* v. *Turkey* [2000] no. 22535/93, para. 85.

The meaning of the active protection of human rights as the actual prevention of human rights violations has boldly been affirmed in the case of
*E and Others*. The applicants were children who suffered repetitive sexual
abuse by another individual in their family environment. They complained
that the state, through its local social services department, failed to protect
them from inhuman and degrading treatment within the meaning of
Article 3 and from damage to their private life under Article 8. The argument of the government under Article 8 was that 'deterrent sanctions
against sexual and physical abuse and the statutory system of child protection fulfilled any positive obligation imposed by this provision to protect
the applicants from abuse by W.H.'[144] This is the formal submission of the
government's counsels on the scope of the state's liability for violations of
human rights by private parties. The fact that the Court ignored it in its
entire judgment confirms the point that the serious meaning of the active
protection of human rights under paragraph 1 of the Convention rights is
the actual prevention of sexual abuse and its reoccurrence. Indeed, the
Court pointed to the finding of violation of Article 3, whose scope is absolute and its threshold degree of negative impact is higher than that under
Article 8.

In that case, the state was held responsible because, although incidents of sexual and physical abuse of the children by the same individual
had occurred in the past, the social services failed to take practical steps,
as could reasonably be required in such circumstances. In particular, it
was found that the authorities did not monitor the perpetrator's behaviour in the aftermath of his conviction for the past abuse, neither talked
individually to the children despite the recorded disturbed behaviour of
some of them. It should also be noted that the argument of the government's counsels on the *ex post facto* framework of deterring sanctions did
not reflect the actual practice in the state's system. It is clear from the
facts that the social services had not been inactive and regular visits had
been arranged to review the well-being of the family. However, their
positive duty of care was assessed against a specific, and yet basic, content
of precautionary measures that had to be implemented as obligations of
means in the circumstances concerned (see further discussion below,
pp. 113–114).

The issue of prevention of human rights violations arising under paragraph 1 of the Convention rights has also been seen in the Grand
Chamber judgment of the case of *Oneryildiz*.[145] In that case, the Court has
made unequivocally clear that the principal content of positive obligations
is directed at all those stages of protection before a human rights violation
occurs. Although statements on prevention have appeared in previous

---

144  *E and Others* v. *the United Kingdom* [2002] no. 33218/96, para. 104.
145  *Oneryildiz* v. *Turkey* [2004] no. 48939/99.

case-law,[146] in *Oneryildiz*, prevention is the starting point that is highlighted in the section titles of the judgment.[147]

The facts of that case concerned the death of thirty-nine people following an explosion at a waste-treatment factory. The applicant lost nine of his close relatives who were living in the nearby area. According to the information contained in the judgment, the factory in question had operated with technical problems since its early years. The state's authorities had failed to check the safety of the factory and enforce compliance with the appropriate technical standards. They also allowed inhabitants to settle on the adjoining land. It was also proved that, although public officials had been made aware of the existence of a recent experts' report pointing to serious dangers for the local population, no measures were taken within the scope of their powers to prevent fatal harm being inflicted upon innocent individuals.

The applicant complained about the state's failure to protect his relatives in violation of Article 2, pointing to negligent omissions from the part of the state authorities. In finding a violation of Article 2, the Court examined the state authorities' negligence against a specific content of positive obligations (as in *E and Others*) which concerned measures, whose scope was both contextual (i.e. industrial sector) and specific (i.e. the particular activity of waste-treatment).

The contextual determination and application of positive obligations is justified by the fact that, often, more than one human right may be threatened from a given activity. The applicant's complaint about the death of his relatives was brought under Article 2, but precautionary measures in the form of warning information were defined with reference to the earlier authority of *Guerra and Others*, in which the applicants, who were potential victims, had their claim examined under Article 8.[148]

These issues have also been exemplified in the cases of *Taskin and Others* and *Ockan and Others*, both arising from the same facts. The applicants complained about the state's decision to authorise a private gold mine, whose operation was posing known risks to the physical integrity of the local population.[149] The applicants were not actual victims of a human rights violation

---

146 *Ireland* v. *the United Kingdom* [1978] no. 5310/71, para. 239; *Osman* v. *the United Kingdom* [1998] no. 23452/94, paras 103, 107, 115; *L.C.B.* v. *the United Kingdom* [1998] no. 23413/94, para. 36; *Mahmut Kaya* v. *Turkey* [2000] no. 22535/93, para. 101.

147 See, subsequently, *Fadeyeva* v. *Russia* [2006] no. 55723/00, para. 89: 'the Court's first task is to assess whether the State could reasonably be expected to act so as to prevent or put an end to the alleged infringement of the applicant's rights.'

148 *Guerra and Others* v. *Italy* [1998] no. 14967/89, discussed in Chapter 1, pp. 50–51.

149 *Taskin and Others* v. *Turkey* [2004] no. 46117/99, para. 48; *Ockan and Others* v. *Turkey* [2006] no. 46771/99 (available in French only). The main difference between these two cases is in the number of applicants that joined the petition that corresponded to 10 and 314 individuals, respectively. See also *Lemke* v. *Turkey* [2007] no. 17381/02 (available in French only).

and, therefore, their complaints concerned pre-emptive actions about a future violation.[150] Their complaints about physical harm were based on both Articles 2 and 8. The Court had only to examine the lowest threshold of negative impact that could potentially be involved in the applicants' circumstances, which was that under Article 8.[151] Relying on the evidence submitted, the European judges were able to easily establish that the potential negative impact was actionable under Article 8, and as a result, a positive obligation has arisen for the state to prevent a human rights violation.

Therefore, it can be said that the content of positive obligations can be determined by various means, but the maximum potential of protection is the actual prevention of human rights violations. In the analysis of the case-law, it has been shown that prevention is not an abstract notion but regards a specific content of positive obligations that has first to be determined contextually. In that account, the issue of the active protection of human rights moves beyond ad hoc responses to target a whole system of protection that is organised and implemented before the isolated issue of interference ever emerges. Such a system should cover all human rights interests that can potentially be involved in the given context of activities of private parties. It has been explained in various instances above, that the scope of Article 8 entails a lower degree of negative impact on individuals' physical and psychological integrity than those contemplated by Articles 2 and 3. It is reasonable therefore to expect that the organisation of prevention of human rights violations starts with lowest threshold of negative impact that can potentially be actionable in the contextual circumstances concerned.

### 2.3.3  Limits of practicality in the protection of human rights

Inherent limitations to positive obligations under paragraph 1 of the Convention rights are recognised in relation to the states' capabilities (i.e. public funds and administrative resources) to practically realise the protection of human rights. Contextual differences exist and must be taken

---

150  In *Taskin and Others* v. *Turkey*, ibid. para. 104, the government's submission on the non-applicability of Article 8 was that 'the risk referred to by the applicants was hypothetical, since it might materialise only in twenty to fifty years. This was not a serious and imminent risk. In addition, the applicants could not point to any specific fact concerning an incident directly caused by the gold mine in question.' The Court did not accept this argument. See also *Tatar* v. *Romania* [2009] no. 67021/01, paras 97, 106–107.

151  See also *Tatar and Tatar* v. *Romania* (dec.) [2007] no. 67021/01, para. 47. For the threshold of severity under Article 8, see *Lopez Ostra* v. *Spain*, para. 51: 'Naturally, severe environmental pollution may affect individuals' well-being and prevent them from enjoying their homes in such a way as to affect their private and family life adversely, without, however, seriously endangering their health.' *Fadeyeva* v. *Russia* [2006] no. 55723/00, para. 88: 'Even assuming that the pollution did not cause any quantifiable harm to her health, it inevitably made the applicant more vulnerable to various diseases.'

into account, because limits of practicality do not attract the same justifications everywhere. Accordingly, the general position of the Court that positive obligations should be interpreted in a way which does not impose an impossible or disproportionate burden on state authorities[152] should be examined under the following division of sections:

### 2.3.3.1 Protection against acts of interference by private parties

ACTS TAKEN IN ACCORDANCE WITH THE LAWS OF THE STATE

When human rights are violated by acts of private parties, it is often the case that although the violation is actually caused by a private party, it is the state that allows the interference complained of through a direct and conscious endorsement[153] or inaction[154] or various combinations of both.[155] In such circumstances, the causal link is no longer confined to the relationship between the activity of the private party and the ensuing violation of a human right, since that activity operates legally within the state's legal order. In *Hatton and Others*, the private corporation increased the quota of night flights causing unbearable noise problems to some local residents, but in no circumstances did its directors pursue the maximisation of the corporation's profits in defiance of the state's legal standards and procedures.

Limitations to the liability of the state due to its limited resources cannot easily be accepted when human rights are violated by an activity of a private party operating lawfully within the established legal order. This is because the financial cost of protection is mainly borne by the private party. The positive obligation to prevent a human rights violation can be discharged by such measures, as (1) refusing the setting up of a private activity during the licensing stage; (2) denying expansion plans; (3) requiring the closure of business premises for as long as human rights standards have not been complied with; (4) enforcing the withdrawal of dangerous products or services; etc. All these measures constitute absolutely basic steps for which no serious argument of an unnecessary or insurmountable burden on the state's resources can be raised.

In principle, the fact that the protection of human rights may incur a considerable financial burden on a private party does not negate per se the binding effect of these rights. Of course, this does not mean that a

---

152 *Osman* v. *the United Kingdom* [1998] no. 23452/94, para. 116; *Edwards* v. *the United Kingdom* [2002] no. 46477/99, para. 55; *Bone* v. *France* (dec.) [2005] no. 69869/01 (available in French only).

153 *Hatton and Others* v. *the United Kingdom* [2001] and [2003] (Grand Chamber) no. 36022/97.

154 *Guerra and Others* v. *Italy* [1998] no. 14967/89; *Oneryildiz* v. *Turkey* [2004] no. 48939/99.

155 *Oneryildiz* v. *Turkey*, ibid.; *Taskin and Others* v. *Turkey* [2004] no. 46117/99.

very high cost of protection should always be imposed, for a great range of daily activities involve various risks to human rights.[156] It is reiterated that the protection of human rights is objectively evaluated by the standard of effectiveness (effective protection) that is employed to define the content of various measures against which the financial cost of protection arises. The content of protection is usually evaluated by contemplating the end result, namely not to suffer a violation of human rights by a given activity. The end result examination is a helpful tool to determine what is below or in excess of what is required to ensure human rights standards in the operation of the activities of the private sector.

It should be noted that, although our discussion is placed in section 2.3 that covers 'the content of positive obligations under paragraph 1 of the Convention rights', the points raised here are also relevant where the activities of private parties can be justified by the state in pursuit of the economic well-being of the country, which is a limitation to the scope of Article 8 expressly recognised in the provisions of its paragraph 2. In such circumstances, all financial issues involved (i.e. benefits or burdens) have to be taken into account.

Where the state takes a decision to allow the interference of a private party in pursuit of the economic well-being of the country, this does not change the fact that it is still the activity of a private party that directly causes harm to some individuals and it is private rather than public funds that are required to cover the cost of human rights protection.

Both these parameters reasonably influence the examination of proportionality of the state's indirect interference. If the state fails the proportionality stage, then, at that very moment, public authorities will remain under a positive obligation to guarantee the protection of human rights against the activities of a private party. For this reason, it is important to know what the current standards of proportionality are.

One of the most relevant contexts of private interactions, in which the economic well-being of the country can be engaged as a legitimate limitation to the scope of protection under Article 8, concerns the activities of industry and commerce. The standard of proportionality test (or its other name: fair balance) can be seen in the case of *Fadeyeva*, in which the applicant successfully complained of a violation of Article 8 as a result of the state's failure to protect her private life and home from severe environmental nuisance that was caused by the activities of a private steel plant.[157]

The government was able to establish easily the applicability of the economic well-being of the country as the legitimate aim for the interference of the private company.[158] In that case, the economic benefit derives from

---

156 *Kalender* v. *Turkey* [2009] no. 4314/02, para. 49 (available in French only).
157 *Fadeyeva* v. *Russia* [2006] no. 55723/00.
158 For the 'pressing social need' threshold of a legitimate aim of interference, see note 28.

a mega-scale steel plant (the main employer of approximately 60,000 people), as opposed to unfounded arguments on the country's well-being from some night flights (within the meaning of the 'pressing social need' threshold) and the industry-produced evidence that we saw in *Hatton and Others*.[159]

In examining the necessity of the interference, the Court first noted that the state authorities had applied a sanitary security zone and, thus, 'the existence of such a zone is a condition sine qua non for the operation of a dangerous enterprise – otherwise it must be closed or significantly restructured.'[160] The standard of proportionality that applied in establishing the necessity of the interference has involved two options for the state: helping the applicant move from the dangerous area or taking effective measures to reduce industrial pollution to acceptable levels.[161] It is clear, in *Fadeyeva*, that although the state succeeded in engaging the economic well-being of the country under the paragraph 2 limitations, the protection of human rights was not excluded because of the financial burden that was imposed on the operation of the industrial plant in question.[162]

It can, therefore, be said that when we examine limitations to the cost of human rights protection under the legitimate aim of the economic well-being of the country, in practice we are mainly concerned with the extent of protection. Protection cannot be excluded because:

1    A positive obligation has already arisen for the state to guarantee the active protection of individuals under paragraph 1 of a Convention right, that is before the incidental decision of a public authority to pursue the legitimate aim of the economic well-being of the country.

159 For the quality of evidence submitted by the government in *Hatton and Others* v. *the United Kingdom* [2001] and [2003] (Grand Chamber) no. 36022/97, see note 30.

160 *Fadeyeva* v. *Russia* [2006] no. 55723/00, para. 116; see also para. 119.

161 Ibid., paras 133,142. The Court's approach in *Fadeyeva* can be traced in the separate opinion of judge Costa in the Chamber judgment of *Hatton and Others* in 2001, that is a dissenting opinion, since the Grand Chamber reversed the Chamber's decision in 2003. In particular, the current president of the Court reasoned that 'it has to be one thing or the other: either the number of potential victims of night flight noise is limited and the "beneficiaries" of those flights can compensate them, or it is too high for the level of compensation to be financially viable for the beneficiaries, whereupon night flights need to be reviewed in their entirety.'

162 The same reasoning applied in the subsequent case of *Ledyayeva and Others* v. *Russia* [2006] nos 53157/99,…, 53695/00, which arose from the same facts. Reiterating that in *Fadeyeva*, the European judges 'considered two alternative avenues that could have been employed by the authorities in order to solve the applicant's problem: the resettlement of the applicant outside the zone and the reduction of the toxic emissions', the Court concluded on the violation of Article 8 offering the same options for the state, paras 103, 110, 117. In addition, due to the continuous effect of the interference, the state's response will be monitored by the Committee of Ministers, para. 117.

2   In view of the high threshold of the 'pressing social need' engaging a legitimate aim of interference and the equally high standards of proportionality, the state remains under the positive obligation described in (1) above, until its indirect interference can be justified.

3   If a justification can be made under paragraph 2, it will mean that substantial protection of human rights has been provided to meet the proportionality standard.

ACTS TAKEN IN DEFIANCE OF THE LAWS OF THE STATE

Limitations to the protection of human rights where a disproportionate financial burden on the state's resources is involved can more easily be recognised in circumstances where human rights are violated by private parties acting in defiance of the standards prescribed in domestic law. Admittedly, it is not expected that the state should prevent the actual violation of human rights in the infinite range of relationships between private parties. Although the scope of the state's liability is controlled by the element of knowledge of the need of human rights protection, such as, for example, when a specific request for protection is made to state authorities (the element of express knowledge), there are still limits to public funds and administrative resources that influence the scope of positive obligations.

Acts taken in defiance of law will usually require a reactive response by the enforcement authorities (e.g. the police), whose efficiency has limits and a predefined operational budget. It is with reference to this context that statements on the limited availability of the state's resources have mostly been seen in the jurisprudence. In the *Osman* case, the applicant had notified the police about threats of violence to his family by another individual. On such an express notification, a positive obligation was imposed on the state authorities to investigate the applicant's call for help, but 'such an obligation must be interpreted in a way which does not impose an impossible or disproportionate burden on the authorities.'[163]

Importantly, it should be noted that limits of practicality relate to the extent of protection, rather than to the general issue of protection as such. In contexts where there are known human rights issues, a core content of positive obligations is presupposed to exist in the form of regulations and enforcement procedures (see discussion in sections 2.3.4–6 below). In *Osman*, it was not disputed that there was a core positive obligation on the state agents to gather incriminating evidence through operational steps of investigation, but rather which and how extensive these steps should be to guarantee the effectiveness of the investigation.[164] The same reasoning can be seen in the earlier case of *Plattform 'Ärzte für das Leben'*, in which the

163  *Osman* v. *the United Kingdom* [1998] no. 23452/94, para. 116; *Mahmut Kaya* v. *Turkey* [2000] no. 22535/93, para. 86; *Mastromatteo* v. *Italy* [2002] no. 37703/97, para. 68.
164  Ibid., paras 104–105.

police were called to intervene in order to protect the applicants' demonstration from an opposing counter-demonstration. The applicant (an association) complained before the Commission that it had not had sufficient police protection during its demonstrations. However, the decisive issue, as seen in the Court's examination, was not simply that the police were under a positive obligation to intervene in order to protect the applicant's Art. 11 interests, but rather the number of police officers that had to be summoned and being present on the ground.[165] Based on the facts, the Court found that the state authorities did not fail to take reasonable and appropriate measures.

### 2.3.3.2 Protection when an act of interference is absent

It has been seen in the case of *Budayeva and Others* above that positive obligations are imposed on the state to protect individuals from natural disasters, provided that knowledge of the risks involved can be established under the circumstances. In such a context, the issue of the active protection of individuals is not examined in relation to a previous act of interference that is attributed to the activities of a private party.[166]

More notable are the cases in which various individuals claim direct assistance from the state because they are not able to enjoy human rights due to their own circumstances of personal vulnerability (physical and psychological condition). An example from the jurisprudence is the case of *Zehnalova and Zehnal*, in which the applicants complained unsuccessfully about the lack of access to various buildings open to the public that facilitate social relationships, and hence the development of personality within the meaning of Article 8.[167]

In such a context, the protection of human rights is mostly dependent on direct monetary contribution by the state. In view of the non-uniform landscape of financial resources of member states, the financial cost of human rights protection constitutes an inherent limitation to positive obligations.[168] Where this cost is considerable, the Court will have first to justify the legitimacy of its intervention before determining the content of positive obligations. Chapter 3 is devoted entirely to the state's positive obligations to protect vulnerable individuals in circumstances where a prior act of interference is absent.

---

165  *Plattform 'Arzte fur das Leben'* v. *Austria* [1988] no. 10126/82, paras 35–39.
166  In *Budayeva and Others* v. *Russia* [2008] nos 15339/02 ... 15343/02, para. 135, the Court noted that the consideration of the burden imposed on the state authorities 'must be afforded even greater weight in the sphere of emergency relief in relation to a meteorological event, which is as such beyond human control, than in the sphere of dangerous activities of a man-made nature.'
167  *Zehnalova and Zehnal* v. *the Czech Republic* (dec.) [2002] no. 38621/97 discussed in Chapter 3.
168  See, e.g., *Pentiacova and 48 Others* v. *Moldova* (dec.) [2005] no. 14462/03.

### 2.3.3.3  Conditioning positive obligations on a minimum scope of protection: the bottom-up justification

The scope of positive obligations under paragraph 1 of the Convention rights relates to a content of protection that can realistically be secured by the state's resources. Where the protection of a human right cannot be guaranteed by the state, positive obligations may not arise for reasons of impracticality. If, however, some form of protection is possible, then provided that it satisfies the minimum level of effectiveness, a positive obligation will arise in relation to that form of protection. Thus, although the extent of protection may vary from one context to another and with the circumstances of each particular case, it is important to establish a minimum content of protection in order to deal with positive obligations in a non-theoretical manner.

The active protection of human rights in any given circumstance can be realised through a content of measures that can be illustrated as follows:

$$\text{Extent of Protection} = Measure_1 + Measure_2 + \ldots + Measure_n$$

If the state's resources cannot cover all these measures, it does not mean that positive obligations are not imposed. If only $Measure_1$ is possible, then positive obligations can arise and be accordingly imposed in relation to this measure alone, provided that the effectiveness of protection is guaranteed.

Specific examples have to be discussed following the categorisation of limits of practicality set out in the previous subsections. When the protection of human rights is examined against natural disasters (the non-interference context), it can reasonably be said that to inform the local population promptly of any risks to their safety and how to proceed in an emergency situation is a measure that does not impose an impossible burden on the state's resources.[169] To the extent that this measure offers effective protection, albeit basic, it amounts to $Measure_1$ of a realistic and manageable content of protection, which alone gives rise to a corresponding positive obligation under paragraph 1 of the relevant Convention rights. By contrast, if no measure can be taken that has some effective contribution to the human rights issue concerned, then positive obligations may not arise for reasons of impracticality.

Analogous considerations apply to the protection of human rights against acts taken in defiance of the laws of the state. By way of example, if there are likely incidents of violence on the occasion, say, of a football match, which cannot be controlled by a reasonable expedition of police force ($Measure_1$), then effective protection in such circumstances can be guaranteed by cancelling the activity in question ($Measure_2$). Because to cancel an activity, or

---

169 *Budayeva and Others* v. *Russia* [2008] nos 15339/02,…, 15343/02, para. 152. See also *Albekov and Others* v. *Russia* [2008] no. 68216/01, para. 88.

postpone it until safety standards are implemented, amounts to an effective protection, which does not impose an unrealistic burden on the state, positive obligations can legitimately arise in relation to $Measure_2$.

The same factual example also falls within the category of lawful activities of private parties. Because a sports event concerns an activity which is run as a lawful business (whether or not it is funded by public or private money), positive obligations are asserted against a greater extent of protection for which the financial cost involved is not borne of the state's resources. In that regard, a more enhanced content of protective measures can be imposed to implement health and safety standards in premises open to the public (i.e. stadiums), such as medical units ($Measure_3$), emergency exits ($Measure_4$), etc.

### 2.3.4 The core content of human rights protection: the legislative framework

In most circumstances, a regulatory framework can be imposed as a core content of positive obligations under paragraph 1 of the Convention rights. Regulations of human rights standards to educate the behaviour of private parties or to condition the operation of their activities are the first and most basic content of positive obligations. Their implementation is guaranteed through a parallel regulation of sanctions of an appropriate deterring effect. The legislative framework arises as a core positive obligation when the element of knowledge of the need of human rights protection can be established contextually.

Such a context in which the interaction of private parties involves known risks to human rights is of course that of violence against the person. Positive obligations in the form of sanctions of an appropriate deterring effect (e.g. jail sentences) and due enforcement procedures have long been recognised in the Court's jurisprudence. It has been seen in the discussion of *X and Y* in Chapter 1 that a criminal rather than civil law remedy should first be available to the victims of rape under Article 8.[170] The issue of protection is particularly pressing when innocent life is threatened. The Court repeatedly reiterates that the state's positive obligation

> involves a primary duty on the State to secure the right to life by putting in place effective criminal-law provisions to deter the commission of offences against the person, backed up by law-enforcement machinery for the prevention, suppression and punishment of breaches of such provisions.[171]

170 *X and Y* v. *the Netherlands* [1985] no. 8978/80. See also *M.C.* v. *Bulgaria* [2003] no. 9272/98.
171 *Osman* v. *the United Kingdom* [1998] no. 23452/94, para. 115; *Mahmut Kaya* v. *Turkey* [2000] no. 22535/93, para. 85; *Kilic* v. *Turkey* [2000] no. 22492/93, para. 62; *Kontrova* v. *Slovakia* [2007] no. 7510/04, para. 49.

Another example of a known context of private interactions in which a positive obligation arises for the state to regulate human rights standards is that of trade union representation. The actions of a trade union have long been recognised as a special aspect of freedom of association that is guaranteed by paragraph 1 of Article 11.[172] A relevant case in this context is *Wilson, the National Union of Journalists and Others*, in which the applicants complained that the state has allowed employers to use financial incentives in order to induce employees to surrender important trade union rights. In addition, they could even discriminate (e.g. constructive dismissals) against those employees who have chosen to pursue the advantages of union membership (e.g. collective representation). In that case, there was no argument about the legitimate aims of interference under paragraph 2. For the government, this was an issue of collective bargaining to be resolved between the interested parties, leaving 'each side to persuade the other'.[173] However, although the state has not directly been involved in labour disputes, it has failed in its positive obligation to protect the Article 11 interests of the applicants, since '[i]t is the role of the State to ensure that trade union members are not prevented or restrained from using their union to represent them in attempts to regulate their relations with their employers.'[174]

Regulations of human rights standards as core positive obligations have also been seen in the *Oneryildiz* case that concerned, as discussed above (p. 98), a fatal industrial accident in which 39 individuals lost their lives. In the context of industrial activities in which well-known hazards exist, the Court was able to define easily both the contextual and particular content of measures that the state is expected to regulate in advance. In what may have been one of the most comprehensive and all-encompassing statements on the content of positive obligations arising under paragraph 1, the Court (in its Grand Chamber capacity) described, first, the general content of the regulatory framework in the form of various critical administrative steps, stating that

---

172  *National Union of Belgian Police* v. *Belgium* [1975] no. 4464/70, para. 38; *Swedish Engine Drivers Union* v. *Sweden* [1976] no. 5614/72, para. 39; *Wilson, the National Union of Journalists and Others* v. *the United Kingdom* [2002] nos 30668/96, . . ., 30678/96, para. 48. In his concurring opinion, judge Gaukur Jörundsson stressed that 'the case-law has clearly concluded that a right to be heard (as a collective representation) is protected by Article 11. One can say, therefore, that this right is a minimum which should be protected.'

173  *Wilson, the National Union of Journalists and Others* v. *the United Kingdom*, ibid., para. 39.

174  Ibid., para. 46. See also *Danilenkov and Others* v. *Russia* [2009] no. 67336/01, paras 120–121 and 136; *Wojtas-Kaleta* v. *Poland* [2009] no. 20436/02. See also S. Simitis and A. Lyon-Caen, 'Community Labour Law: A Critical Introduction to its History', in P. Davies *et al.* (eds), *European Community Labour Law: Principles and Perspectives, Liber Amicorum Lord Wedderburn of Charlton* (Oxford: Oxford/Clarendon Press, 1996), pp. 1–22.

The positive obligation to take all appropriate steps to safeguard life for the purposes of Article 2 (see paragraph 71 above) entails above all a primary duty on the State to put in place a legislative and administrative framework designed to provide effective deterrence against threats to the right to life... [§] This obligation indisputably applies in the particular context of dangerous activities, where, in addition, special emphasis must be placed on regulations geared to the special features of the activity in question, particularly with regard to the level of the potential risk to human lives. They must govern the licensing, setting up, operation, security and supervision of the activity [in question]...[175]

It that passage, it is clear that administrative steps have to be regulated in advance in the context of dangerous activities, such as those of industry. The dangerousness of a given activity is assessed with reference to 'inherent risks' that establish a contextual knowledge of the need of human rights protection.[176]

Continuing from the last quoted sentence of the passage above, the Court moves on to specify practical measures that form part of the content of regulations. In particular, it has stated:

[...] and must make it compulsory for all those concerned to take practical measures to ensure the effective protection of citizens whose lives might be endangered by the inherent risks. [§] Among these preventive measures, particular emphasis should be placed on the public's right to information, as established in the case-law of the Convention institutions.[177]

The Court highlights precautionary ('preventive') measures with reference to the whole context of industrial activities and specifies the measure of warning information, which is well-entrenched in the relevant jurisprudence.[178] Additional practical measures have also to be regulated in relation to the particular nature of the activity concerned (e.g. waste-treatment).[179] The content of regulated measures and standards of human rights protection is not only addressed to the state authorities, but also to the private

---

175 *Oneryildiz* v. *Turkey* [2004] no. 48939/99, paras 89–90; *Kalender* v. *Turkey* [2009] no. 4314/02, para. 43 (available in French only); *Bacila* v. *Romania* [2010] no. 19234/04, para. 61 (available in French only).

176 *Oneryildiz* v. *Turkey*, ibid., para. 71.

177 Ibid., para. 90.

178 See, e.g., *Guerra and Others* v. *Italy* [1998] no. 14967/89 and, more recently, *Tatar* v. *Romania* [2009] no. 67021/01.

179 *Oneryildiz* v. *Turkey* [2004] no. 48939/99, paras 58, 108.

parties, who are directly responsible for the human rights violations.[180] A more detailed discussion of administrative and practical measures is presented below (sections 2.3.5–6).

From the foregoing analysis of the case-law, it can generally be asserted that in contexts of private interactions in which known human rights issues are involved, a positive obligation arises for the state to regulate in advance individual conduct and the operation of the activities of private parties, as well as the duties of the state authorities in relation to the acts of the former. The exact content of regulations may vary from one context to another, but a common denominator exists in the form of the standard of effectiveness.

### 2.3.5  The core content of human rights protection: the administrative framework

The core content of positive obligations also includes administrative structures to implement and enforce the human rights standards that have been regulated by the state in advance. As in previous sections, the content of administrative structures is examined under the prism of prevention of human rights violations.

Although the content of administrative measures varies with context due to the wide range of private activities, a common approach can be discerned. For reasons of consistency, it should be reiterated that positive obligations raise the state's liability in circumstances in which its agents are not directly involved. As discussed above (pp. 73–76), the state's involvement can only be exposed when the element of knowledge of the need of human rights protection lies with its agents. In this connection, the content of administrative measures should include the procedural structures through which the critical element of knowledge can be established. Accordingly, the administrative framework serves as an institutionalised intermediate level of effectiveness that sits between the regulated standards and the practical measures of protection.

In the following, a common approach to the determination of the administrative framework is sought in various contexts of private interactions, such as criminal violence, children in unfavourable family environments, and industrial activities. Particular attention is drawn to the standard of effectiveness, whose application affects the scope and content of administrative structures.

---

180 See *Tatar* v. *Romania* [2009] no. 67021/01, para. 87: 'Thus, Article 8 could apply to environmental issues, whether the state has directly caused the pollution or its responsibility derives from the lack of adequate regulation of the private sector's activities.', (translation).

## 2.3.5.1 *Violence against the person*

Administrative structures as part of the core content of positive obligations have been exemplified in the case of *Osman*. As discussed above (p. 88), the applicants had called the police for help against the threats of an identifiable individual. In evaluating the content of protective measures in such circumstances, the Court has laid down a test (hereinafter, the *Osman* test) as follows:

> where there is an allegation that the authorities have violated their positive obligation to protect the right to life in the context of their above-mentioned duty to prevent and suppress offences against the person (see paragraph 115 above), it must be established to its [the Court's] satisfaction that the authorities knew or ought to have known at the time of the existence of a real and immediate risk to the life of an identified individual or individuals from the criminal acts of a third party and that they failed to take measures within the scope of their powers which, judged reasonably, might have been expected to avoid that risk.[181]

The *Osman* test revolves around the element of knowledge that is pertinent in the determination of the state's positive obligations. It contains, however, some technical parameters that can affect considerably the scope of the administrative framework and its function as a core intermediate stage of positive obligations. Therefore, the exact relevance and application of that test needs careful analysis.

According to Jeremy McBride, the passage quoted above sets a general test to examine the question of when a positive obligation has arisen under the circumstances. It could be used as a 'causal test' in every context when the right to life (Article 2) is concerned, 'because life is not less valuable in some situations than in others.'[182] The relevance of that test is examined in relation to the rejection, by a majority Court, of the applicant's submission that the police could have better assessed the threat to his family if they had taken more effective measures of investigation. In particular, it has been argued that 'it [the Court] appears to confuse the question of what the existence of a duty to act requires with whether such a duty exists; if there was no basis for believing there to be a serious threat

---

181 *Osman* v. *the United Kingdom* [1998] no. 23452/94, para. 115. A similar test had been used in the *Corfu Channel* case of the International Court of Justice (ICJ Reports, 1949, p. 4) discussed by Loucaides, *Essays*, p. 148.

182 J. McBride, 'Protecting Life: A Positive Obligation to Help' (1999) 24 *ELR* (SUPP HR) 43–54, p. 45. In addition, the adjective 'real' of the *Osman* test is interpreted as 'at least compelling', p. 46. We do not share this view, as the proposed interpretation deviates from the literal meaning of the express word used in that test. The judges, as legal scientists, could well have adopted the proposed adjective if they had thought that a more restrictive element of knowledge had to be conditioned.

then it is irrelevant that there were constraints on taking the action suggested.'[183]

The suggestion for the *Osman* test to be elevated to a status of broad applicability has to be critically evaluated. If the *Osman* test can be used as an ever-available 'causal test' that transcends context, then it affects the whole application of positive obligations. Although, undeniably, the general element of knowledge is of broad applicability, the *Osman* test contains calculating parameters of 'seriousness' and 'immediacy' that confine the scope of positive obligations to mere reactive responses. In this respect, it is not difficult to see the downgrading of the administrative framework from core intermediate stage of a system of protection to ad hoc measures of incidental relevance.

If the Court has 'confused the question' of positive obligations, as argued, then we reach a paradoxical situation in which, when the police are notified of threats against some individuals, European human rights law would merely require the officers to hold a meeting over their desks to discuss whether 'a real and immediate risk' exists, instead of going out to actively conduct their own investigation for the requisite evidence.

The passage from the *Osman* case, as quoted above, sets a test for coercive action upon incriminating evidence in the context of the police only.[184] Given that reactive 'protective policing measures'[185] go without saying,[186] it becomes clear that the judicial examination of the state's positive obligations should start with the intermediate core stage of administrative steps (i.e. investigation), because it is these steps that often condition the reactive response.[187] Indeed, in *Osman*, the main focus of the Court was on the effectiveness of the initial investigation, which looked for the requisite incriminating evidence.[188] The majority of the Court found that such an administrative step existed in the form of an entrenched procedure of various operational measures, which had sufficiently been implemented under the circumstances.

---

183  Ibid., p. 48.

184  D. Xenos, 'Asserting the Right to Life (Article 2, ECHR) in the Context of Industry' (2007) 8 *GLJ* 231–254, p. 239–241.

185  A. Mowbray, *The Development of Positive Obligations under the European Convention on Human Rights by the European Court of Human Right* (Oxford: Hart, 2004), p. 15.

186  *Osman* v. *the United Kingdom* [1998] no. 23452/94, para. 107: 'Article 2 of the Convention may imply a positive obligation on the authorities of a Contracting State to take preventive measures to protect the life of an individual from the danger posed by another individual.', (quoting the government's submission). Cf. *Opuz* v. *Turkey* [2009] no. 33401/02, para. 145.

187  There is a substantial body of jurisprudence regarding critical steps and standards of police investigations. See, e.g., the numerous cases against Turkey and Russia. See also discussion in Chapter 4, pp. 198–201.

188  See the submission of the applicant in *Osman* v. *the United Kingdom* [1998] no. 23452/94, paras 104–105, and the partly dissenting, partly concurring opinion of judge De Meyer joined by judges Lopes Rocha and Casadevall.

## 2.3.5.2 Children under social care supervision

The core relevance of the administrative framework has also been elaborated in the context of unfavourable family environments. An important case in this context is *Z and Others*.[189] The applicants were four children who were subjected to prolonged neglect and abuse in their family environment and, as a result, they suffered physical and psychological injury, whose degree of severity reached the threshold of inhuman and degrading treatment that is prohibited by Article 3. Although the state's social care authority had assumed responsibility to supervise the welfare of the children of this family, they failed to take the necessary steps to protect them. It should be noted that in such a context of private relationships, human rights issues are not unlikely to emerge.[190] Accordingly, a positive obligation arises for the state to protect the children of those families that are under the supervision of its agents. In such contextual circumstances, the first administrative step is to set up effective monitoring practices that are capable of finding evidence of any actual or potential abuse (i.e. the more specific knowledge). It is through such an administrative practice that the requisite evidence can be established so as to trigger, subsequently, a reactive response in the form of direct and personal assistance. In finding a violation of Article 3, the Court reasoned its decision on the 'failure of the [state's] system' (as opposed to some ad hoc and reactive measures) highlighting in that way the multilevel framework of positive obligations that the state has to implement in such a known context of private relationships.

The scope of the administrative framework has further been elaborated in *E and Others*, which also dealt with the issue of abuse of children in unfavourable family environments. It is recalled from previous discussion that the state was found in violation of Article 3 on the ground that its social services failed to adequately monitor a family with a recorded history of sexual and physical abuse of children.[191] In such a context of private relationships, a positive obligation arises for the state to take steps to prevent human rights violations. The (additional) positive obligation to react upon a specific threat that is 'serious' and 'immediate' (e.g. to take children into community care) was, as in the *Osman* case, beyond question.

The main focus is on the existence of a 'system' of protection that consists of core administrative steps to monitor the behaviour of suspects and

189  *Z and Others* v. *the United Kingdom* [2001] no. 29392/95.
190  N. Mole, 'Z and Others v UK and TP and KM v UK' [2001] *IFLJ* 117–123; A. Di Stefano, 'Public Authority Liability in Negligence e Diritto ad un Ricorso Effettivo nell' Ordinamento Britannico: Nota all Sentenza della Corte Europea dei Diritti dell'Uomo nel Caso Z e altri c. Regno Unito' (2003) 1 *RIDU* 97–127.
191  *E and Others* v. *the United Kingdom* [2002] no. 33218/96. See also discussion above, p. 98.

family members. In that regard, the government's argument that 'the social services did not have knowledge of any continuing abuse' at the material time is deprived of its relevance, as this knowledge derives from its agents' own work during core administrative steps that are already required as core positive obligations. Of equal irrelevance is the 'but for' causation test of *ex post facto* results that ' "but for" the failing or omission of the public authority ill-treatment would not have happened'.[192] Because the Convention is not a fourth-instance forum, the administrative steps of investigation and evaluation of findings are imposed as core positive 'obligations of means'[193] to ensure the 'proper and effective management of [the state authorities'] responsibilities' against the principal aim of prevention of human rights violations (i.e. 'to avoid, or at least, minimise the risk or the damage suffered.)[194]

### 2.3.5.3 Industrial activities

The question of positive obligations in the form of core administrative steps is particularly pertinent in the context of industrial activities, where threats to human rights may concern a great number of people. Administrative obligations have been exemplified in the *Oneryildiz* case, in which the applicant complained of the state's failure to prevent a fatal industrial accident. In the quoted passage from *Oneryildiz* above (p. 109), it is clear that a core administrative framework must be regulated and implemented in advance governing 'the licensing, setting up, operation, security and supervision' of industrial activities.

As already discussed, the starting point of the Court's examination is the prevention of human rights violations and the contextual reach of the state's obligations. However, it is worth visiting the government's main argument in order to further stress the importance of some technical details that are pertinent to the scope of the administrative framework. In the referral of the case to the Grand Chamber, the government argued that the Chamber failed to apply the 'immediacy' and 'reality' criteria of the *Osman* test when it examined the responsibility of the state authorities in the fatal industrial accident. Despite this express submission by the government, the Grand Chamber did not examine the *Osman* test, but seized the opportunity to lay down the core administrative content of positive obligations that had to be implemented well before the threats to human rights became 'immediate'.[195]

---

192 Ibid., para. 99. The government argued that 'notwithstanding any acknowledged shortcomings it has not been shown that matters would have turned out any differently', para. 99.
193 B. Hofstötter, 'European Court of Human Rights: Positive obligations in E. and others v. United Kingdom' (2004) 2(3) *I-CON* 525–560.
194 *E and Others* v. *the United Kingdom* [2002] no. 33218/96, para. 100.
195 Xenos, 'Asserting the Right to Life (Article 2, ECHR) in the Context of Industry', pp. 239–240.

In *Taskin and Others*, another important case in the context of industry (discussed in section 2.3.2), the focus of judicial examination shifts exclusively on the implementation of administrative procedures that are required in order to assess the dangerous effects of an industrial activity. In that case, the applicants were not actual victims, since their complaints concerned potential harm. In such circumstances, the positive obligation to prevent a human rights violation can only be determined by evaluating the effectiveness of the environmental impact-assessment, which establishes the specific knowledge of the gravity of the threats involved.[196] Such an administrative practice is core to the 'supervisory' role of the public administration that functions as a system of protection of human rights in the context of dangerous industrial activities.

In appropriate circumstances, it is expected that a core content of administrative steps can be regulated additionally or otherwise, against the private parties that control the operation of dangerous activities, provided that the state retains a supervisory function.[197] In order to reduce the cost of public supervision or because experts with high technical knowledge may be needed, private parties can legitimately be required to fund, either alone or collectively, the investigation and research of the negative effect of their activities on human rights. Every expert that is sub-contracted during these investigations will also be bound by legal standards of professional negligence for which a parallel framework of regulations and enforcement procedures is secured by the state.

### 2.3.5.4 The scope of effectiveness: determining the content of administrative measures

The content of the administrative framework is determined by evaluating the standard of effectiveness. Departing from the aim of prevention of human rights violations, the scope of effectiveness involves both a general and a specific level. At the general level, effectiveness justifies the administrative framework as an indispensable core stage of positive obligations and defines the main structures therein. Such administrative obligations include *inter alia* a supervisory and investigatory mechanism, which is a common requirement in various contexts of private interactions. At the specific level, effectiveness targets those critical steps and parameters upon

---

196 *Taskin and Others* v. *Turkey* [2004] no. 46117/99, para. 111. See also *Budayeva and Others* v. *Russia* [2008] nos 15339/02 ... 15343/02, para. 136; *Tatar* v. *Romania* [2009] no. 67021/01, paras 88, 101, 112, 114, 122.

197 R. Smith, 'The Public is Being Regularly Deceived by the Drug Trials Funded by Pharmaceutical Companies, Loaded to Generate the Results they Need', *Guardian* (14 January 2004); R. Evans and S. Boseley, '"Drug Firms" Lobby Tactics Revealed', *Guardian* (28 September 2006).

which the effectiveness of administrative structures depends. Accordingly, a more specific content of administrative safeguards has to be described.

The intensity of review of the exact content of administrative obligations can be seen in the cases already discussed. In *Osman*, the applicant expressly criticised the effectiveness of the investigation system of the police in order to prove that the state had failed in its positive obligations under Article 2. In a majority ruling, the Court found that the steps taken by the state agents were what could reasonably be expected under the contextual circumstances concerned. It is noted, however, that the Court did not elaborate much on the exact steps and standards of the investigation process.[198]

In *Oneryildiz*, the Court pointed out, in a more informed way, that due allowances should be made for such structures that are capable of 'identifying shortcomings in the processes concerned and any errors committed by those responsible at different levels'.[199] In this connection, individual access in the decision-making process of the administrative framework for comments, information and the right to challenge – through courts or otherwise – the effectiveness of the overall process is, as stated in *Taskin and Others*, 'beyond question'.[200]

These developments of the case-law reflect a more sophisticated and objective evaluation of the standard of effectiveness which coincide with the growing realisation that the protection of human rights is primarily secured in the domestic, rather than the European, level. In this respect, the content of positive obligations extends to the critical details of the multilevel framework of public administration. In addition, appropriate safeguards are required to circumvent cumbersome procedures and improve current practices so as to update accordingly the content of the administrative framework at the regulatory level.[201]

### 2.3.6 The content of human rights protection: the extent of protection – practical measures

The content of positive obligations includes practical measures of protection, as can be required in the applicant's circumstances. In many cases,

---

198 For dissenting and concurring opinions about the effectiveness of investigation in *Osman* v. *the United Kingdom* [1998] no. 23452/94, see note 188. See also *Opuz* v. *Turkey* [2009] no. 33401/02, para. 135.
199 *Oneryildiz* v. *Turkey* [2004] no. 48939/99, para. 90.
200 *Taskin and Others* v. *Turkey* [2004] no. 46117/99, para. 116; *Lemke* v. *Turkey* [2007] no. 17381/02, para. 41; *Tatar* v. *Romania* [2009] no. 67021/01, section E: 'Access to information and the participation of individuals in the preliminary decision-making process authorizing the operation [of these activities]' (translation), paras 20–23, 88, 101. See also discussion of *Taskin and Others* in Chapter 4, section 4.3.
201 *Fadeyeva* v. *Russia* [2006] no. 55723/00, para. 119: 'However, this proves only that the Severstal steel-plant has failed to comply with domestic environmental norms and suggests that a wider sanitary security zone should perhaps have been required.'

these measures are reactive in nature and can take the form of direct action to stop a private party from harming another. It has been seen in the foregoing analysis of case-law that the first question is whether there is an issue of human rights protection of which the state authorities should reasonably know. Knowledge of the need of human rights protection is actively looked at by the state's administrative mechanism, as a core content of the state's positive obligations.

In the cases of *Osman, Z and Others, E and Others, Oneryildiz, Taskin and Others* that are discussed above, the reactive response of the state to take practical measures of protection is dependent on the element of knowledge that conditions that response. In some cases, such as those concerning dangerous industrial activities, one of the entrenched measures of practical protection is to inform the local population of any risks to their health and safety.[202] In this context of private activities, the exclusive or partial content of such information is the very knowledge of the need of human rights protection that the state authorities are under a prior obligation to find during the administrative steps of supervision and control.[203]

In addition to reactive responses, practical protection can be defined in the form of precautionary measures where contextual knowledge suffices per se to establish the need for protection of human rights.[204] Such a content of protection is justified by the principal aim of prevention of human rights violations that is central to the nature of positive obligations.

---

202 *Guerra and Others* v. *Italy* [1998] no. 14967/89; *Oneryildiz* v. *Turkey* [2004] no. 48939/99.

203 Xenos, 'Asserting the Right to Life (Article 2, ECHR) in the Context of Industry', sub-section: 'Informing the local population', pp. 243–245. In *Tatar* v. *Romania* [2009] no. 67021/01, in finding the state in violation of Article 8, the Court held that the state authorities failed in their duty to inform the local population of any (past, present or future) risks to their health and well-being, and of any preventive measures in the event of an accident (para. 124). This conclusion is based on the Court's previous conclusion that the state's administrative authorities had failed to evaluate in advance, and in an efficient manner, the potential risks from the industrial activity in question (para. 112), see also paras 101, 113–114, 122.

204 See, generally, A. Trouwborst, *Evolution and Status of the Precautionary Principle in International Law* (The Hague: Kluwer Law International, 2002); S. Flogaitis and Ch. Petrou, 'Les Avancés du Principe de Précaution en Droit Public Grec' (2006) 59 *RHDI* 449–470. See also the case of *Tatar* v. *Romania* [2009] no. 67021/01, para. 109: 'The principle of pre-caution requires that the states should not delay to adopt effective and proportionate measures, which aim to prevent a serious and irreversible damage to the environment, because of lack of certainty in scientific or technical knowledge.', (translation). See also section B of that judgment: 'Relevant International Law and Practice': Principle 15 of the Rio Declaration on Environment and Development (3–14 June 1992); a case decided by the International Court of Justice on 27 September 1997 regarding the project *Gabcikovo Nagymaros*; Resolution no. 1430/2005 of the Parliamentary Assembly of the Council of Europe on industrial hazards; the principle of precaution in EU law (Article 174 (ex 130) of the Treaty of Amsterdam) and the jurisprudence of the European Court of Justice (5 May 1998, *The United Kingdom/Commission*, C-180/96, Rec. I-2265; 5 May 1998, *National Farmers' Union*, C-157/96, Rec. I-2211). See also discussion in sections 2.2.2.1–2 above.

In this respect, some form of warning information can often be established by the general nature of the activities in question.[205]

Practical measures of protection can be required and accordingly regulated against private parties, as well as the state officials in charge of control and supervision of the activities of the former. The exact content of practical measures will vary with context and the particular nature of the activity concerned, while the state has a general discretion over the choice of these measures.[206] As with any content of protection, the choice of measures is reviewed against the standard of effectiveness, which aims, consciously or unconsciously, at an end/complete result (*tel(e)os*). In appropriate circumstances and in order to make the most of the occasion of the applicant's complaint, the European judge, having the benefit of hindsight, can adopt a teleological approach to determine measures that set the minimum pan-European standard of human rights protection in the context concerned. The Court's reviewing task is often aided by comparative examples from the practice of member states and the recommendations or resolutions of relevant international documents.[207]

## 2.4 A synthesis of human rights protection

The distinct nature of the state's positive and negative obligations needs particular attention in circumstances in which the state assumes, directly or indirectly, the interfering acts of private parties in pursuit of the legitimate aims of paragraph 2 of the Convention rights. Any act of the state that confirms, maintains and ultimately permits a private party's interference with a human right is to be directly attributed to the state. The state's involvement can be seen in the form of a piece of legislation,[208] a judicial decision,[209] an administrative order[210] or any combination of them. Wherever an act of interference (directly caused by a private party and indirectly allowed by the state) can be justified under the criteria of paragraph 2 of the Convention rights, an entitlement to a human right is reduced either completely or to some extent. As a result, positive obligations are also reduced, as the issue of the active protection concerns a human right whose scope has legitimately been limited in the circumstances concerned. Analysing the

---

205 *Bone* v. *France* (dec.) [2005] no. 69869/01.
206 *Marckx* v. *Belgium* [1979] no. 6833/74, para. 31.
207 *Oneryildiz* v. *Turkey* [2004] no. 48939/99, paras 59–62; *Tatar and Tatar* v. *Romania* (dec.) [2007] no. 67021/01, section C: 'European Law'.
208 *Young, James and Webster* v. *the United Kingdom* [1981] nos 7601/76; 7806/77; *Sorensen and Rasmussen* v. *Denmark* [2006] nos 52562/99,..., 52620/99; *Wilson, the National Union of Journalists and Others* v. *the United Kingdom* [2002] nos 30668/96,..., 30678/96.
209 *Sunday Times* v. *the United Kingdom* [1979] no. 6538/74; *Van Kuck* v. *Germany* [2003] no. 35968/97; *Pla and Puncernau* v. *Andorra* [2004] no. 69498/01.
210 *Hatton and Others* v. *the United Kingdom* [2003] no. 36022/97; *Fadeyeva* v. *Russia* [2006] no. 55723/00.

earlier jurisprudence, Peter Duffy pointed out that 'it is inconceivable that positive obligations could ever be inherent in an effective respect for Article 8 rights under circumstances in which a State would be justified in interfering with these rights under paragraph 2.'[211]

However, the current caseload of the Court no longer reflects the small number of annual petitions of the earlier jurisprudence. In order to secure its own long-term effectiveness, the Court should make the most out of the given complaints and adjust the focus of its judicial examination on principles and standards that have a wide reach.

Although positive obligations may be restricted by a justified limitation to the scope of a human right under paragraph 2, they remain 'inherent' by virtue of paragraph 1, which will always arise for the state, unlike acts of interference that can only come into play under exhaustively listed aims, if available, if relevant, if reachable and if decided to be pursued by the state agents.[212] More importantly, it has been shown in previous sections that positive obligations have a core content, which has to be discharged in advance in order to guarantee the prevention of human rights violations. In other words, a core content of human rights protection is due for implementation much before an act of interference is ever attempted. In that account, unlike the legitimate aims of paragraph 2 that the state *may* decide to pursue, there is nothing optional about its positive obligations arising under paragraph 1 of the Convention rights.

Accordingly, where both positive and negative obligations can be relevant in a given circumstance, they have to reach a synthesis of human rights protection. The starting point is that the protection of human rights cannot be organised through incidental questions of justifiability of acts of interference, without recognising that protection has already arisen as an obligation for the state much before the isolated interference. In technical terms, the question is posed as follows: how can the core content of the state's positive obligations arising under paragraph 1 of the Convention rights in a known context of activities of private parties (the contextual level) maintain the priority of its implementation when examining the justifiability of a private party's interference that the state pursues under one of the legitimate aims of paragraph 2 (the ad hoc level)?

---

211 Duffy, 'The Protection of Privacy, Family Life and Other Rights under Article 8 of the European Convention on Human Rights', p. 200.

212 An act of interference is only permissible if it is taken within the limits specified in paragraph 2. See *Golder* v. *the United Kingdom* [1975] no. 4451/70, para. 44; *Klass and Others* v. *Germany* [1978] no. 5029/71, para. 42: 'This second] paragraph [of Article 8], since it provides for an exception to a right guaranteed by the Convention, is to be narrowly interpreted.' Connelly, 'Problems of Interpretation of Article 8 of the European Convention on Human Rights', p. 570; P. Duffy, 'The *Sunday Times* Case: Freedom of Expression, Contempt of Court and the European Convention on Human Rights' (1980) 1 *HRR* 17–53; Loucaides, *Essays*, chapter 9: 'Restrictions of Limitations on the Rights Guaranteed by the European Convention on Human Rights', sec. 5: 'Strict Interpretation of Limitation', p. 185.

### 2.4.1 The point of synthesis: positive obligations as the entrenched safeguards to be 'prescribed by law'

#### 2.4.1.1 Positive obligations as legal safeguards that condition and justify an act of interference

The state has a positive obligation under paragraph 1 of the Convention rights to implement a core content of administrative steps in order to identify and assess the negative impact that some activities of private parties (operating in a known context) can have on the human rights of individuals.

Such core administrative steps have been required in the landmark case of *Hatton and Others* to guarantee the requisite evidence that substantiates the state's margin of appreciation for the necessity of an act of interference. As already discussed, the examination of necessity is usually made by an overall proportionate (fair) balance between competing interests (exhaustively listed). It cannot, therefore, be said that the proportionality/necessity stage has the appropriate resources to impose the strict examination of the details of the core administrative structures, as well as the priority of their implementation.

If the positive obligations of the state are examined first, the reviewing task will start with the negative impact on individuals from the given activity and will focus on the administrative steps that undertake this assessment. As pointed out by judges Costa, Ress, Türmen, Zupančič and Steiner in their joint dissenting opinion in the Grand Chamber judgment of that case, the negative impact could well have reached the Article 3 threshold, whose binding effect is absolute.[213] In essence, what is stressed is a system of human rights protection that is capable of addressing in advance various effects of interference in a given context of private interactions.

One of the points that split the Court in both the Chamber and Grand Chamber judgments (including the respective separate and dissenting opinions) concerned the critical details of the administrative practice establishing the negative impact from the operation of the private activity (i.e. night flights). It was found that the state authorities had not considered sleep prevention during the evaluation process.[214] If this detail is critical for that evaluation, it means that the administrative practice concerned fails the standard of effectiveness, and the judicial examination stops there and then. Therefore, it is difficult to see how due attention can be paid to core administrative obligations, if these obligations are only examined indirectly at the overburdened, by any

213 *Hatton and Others* v. *the United Kingdom* [2003] (Grand Chamber) no. 36022/97, para. 13 of the joint dissenting opinion.
214 Ibid., para. 105.

means, proportionality stage, at which a balance for an overall justice prevails. This is evident from the majority decision of the Grand Chamber that 'in substance' the authorities did not overstep their margin of appreciation, despite the shortcomings of the administrative practice.[215]

In order to move from a collection of ad hoc decisions to pan-European standards that target a domestic system of human rights protection, it is necessary to adopt a stricter examination of the core content of the state's positive obligations, whose implementation arises in priority in known contexts of private interactions.

Accordingly, the proposal that is made here is that, provided that the state can establish the 'pressing social need' threshold to engage a legitimate aim of interference (where available), the administrative steps, which are core positive obligations under paragraph 1, can be incorporated as legal safeguards that have to be 'prescribed by law' (or 'in accordance with law' in Article 8 (2))[216] under the first criterion of paragraph 2. Thus, when such safeguards do not exist or have not been implemented to the standard of effectiveness, the question about the merits and justifiability of the given interference is simply not reached. In practice, this means that no act of interference can be considered if appropriate administrative safeguards have not been regulated and implemented in advance.

The first criterion of paragraph 2 (i e. to be 'in accordance with law' or 'be prescribed by law') regards the certainty and foreseeability of legal safeguards that all interested parties should be able to understand in various contextual circumstances.[217] In that account, the state is under an

---

215 Ibid., para. 129.
216 *Malone* v. *the United Kingdom* [1984] no. 8691/79, para. 66: 'the expression "in accordance with the law/prévue par la loi" in paragraph 2 of Article 8 (art. 8–2) should be interpreted in the light of the same general principles as were stated in the *Sunday Times* judgment of 26 April 1979 (Series A no. 30) to apply to the comparable expression "prescribed by law/prévues par la loi" in paragraph 2 of Article 10 (art. 10–2).'
217 Post, '*Hatton and Others*: Further Clarifications of the "Indirect" Individual Right to a Healthy Environment', p. 263, who has pointed out that '[the applicants] submitted that the interference was not "in accordance with the law" (as Article 8.2 demands). Domestic law did not offer adequate protection against the interference with their rights under Article 8.1. Also, the law must be accessible and its consequences foreseeable.' For earlier case-law, see *Sunday Times* v. *the United Kingdom* [1979] no. 6538/74, para. 49: 'In the Court's opinion, the following are two of the requirements that flow from the expression "prescribed by law". Firstly, the law must be adequately accessible: the citizen must be able to have an indication that is adequate in the circumstances of the legal rules applicable to a given case. Secondly, a norm cannot be regarded as a "law" unless it is formulated with sufficient precision to enable the citizen to regulate his conduct: he must be able – if need be with appropriate advice – to foresee, to a degree that is reasonable in the circumstances, the consequences which a given action may entail.' See also *Malone* v. *the United Kingdom* [1984] no. 8691/79, para. 67; *Rotaru* v. *Romania* [2000] no. 28341/95, para. 55. P. Duffy, 'The Case of Klass and Others: Secret Surveillance of Communications and the European Convention on Human Rights' (1979) 4(1) *HRR* 20–41, p. 26.

obligation to 'prescribe by law' legal safeguards that have to be implemented before an act of interference is attempted.[218] Administrative steps, which are core positive obligations under paragraph 1, are exactly those legal safeguards that the law has to prescribe in a foreseeable and certain manner and implement in practice.[219]

The 'provided by law' criterion is expressly stated first in paragraph 2 provisions and, therefore, it has to be exhausted first. It is fair to say that although this criterion has been examined in the jurisprudence, little attention has been paid to its importance and potential due to preference to the fair balance test and the state's margin of appreciation. The task, at this junction, is to discuss relevant case-law in which the lack of adequate safeguards that the law has to prescribe or the ineffectiveness of their implementation lead to a finding of a violation without having to examine the particular merits or the necessity (proportionality) of the interference.

Examples from the jurisprudence include the complaints about surveillance practices that state authorities have adopted in pursuit of a legitimate aim of interference, such as the interests of national security, public safety, the protection of health, the prevention of disorder or crime, as provided for under Article 8 (2). The particular facts of the surveillance practices will not be discussed, as what is looked at are preliminary questions of legal principles that are raised before the examination of the facts. Such questions appeared in the case of *Rotaru*, in which the Court found that 'the holding and use [by the state's intelligence service] of information on the applicant's private life were not "in accordance with the law"'. As a result, a violation of Article 8 was concluded on this ground alone without reviewing whether the aim pursued was 'necessary in a democratic society'.[220] It is important to note that the requirement of 'law', as the first criterion of paragraph 2, is examined as to the '*quality*' of legal safeguards.[221]

The content of these safeguards is constantly updated in the relevant jurisprudence. Often, a measure or practice, which the law has to 'prescribe' as a legal safeguard, has first been elaborated at the examination of the

218  *Klass and Others* v. *Germany* [1978] no. 5029/71. Duffy, ibid.
219  *Leander* v. *Sweden* [1987] no. 9248/81, para. 51: 'account must also be taken of administrative practices which do not have the status of substantive law, in so far as those concerned are made sufficiently aware of their content.' Loucaides, *Essays*, chapter 9, sec. 6: 'Prescribed by law', pp. 188–189.
220  *Rotaru* v. *Romania* [2000] no. 28341/95, para. 62. See also the concurring opinion of judge Lorenzen who reasoned his decision not to join the concurring opinion of judge Wildhaber on the ground that '[t]he reason why I have not joined it is solely that the Court has consistently held that when an interference with the rights under Article 8 is not "in accordance with the law", it is not necessary to examine whether the other requirements of Article 8 § 2 are fulfilled. I consider it essential to maintain that case-law.'
221  Ibid., paras 52, 56. See also *Liberty and Others* v. *the United Kingdom* [2008] no. 58243/00, para. 59.

proportionality criterion of paragraph 2. Thus, with regard to similar contextual circumstances, the proportionality examination can serve as a dialectic (elaborative) stage at which arguments and practices are explored.

In the case of *Klass and Others*, the content of legal safeguards for the state's surveillance measures was examined under the necessity/proportionality of the interference.[222] Some years later, in *Malone*, which concerned also surveillance practices, the Court confined exclusively its review at the 'in accordance with law' stage. In that case, 'law' was examined as to its existence, as such, and not as to its qualitative content. It was only judge Pettiti in his concurring opinion who cited comparative examples[223] to assert the point that 'a "law", within the meaning of Article 8 paras 1 and 2 (art. 8–1, art. 8–2), contains detailed rules which do not merely legalise practices but define and delimit them.' The judge went on to lay down a list of core administrative practices as 'a panoply of requirements' against which the quality of law (as the content of legal safeguards) should be assessed.[224] In *Rotaru*, the legal safeguards, which were previously seen at the necessity/proportionality stage in *Klass and Others*, have been entrenched for the examination of the 'quality' of law at the 'in accordance with law' stage, at which core administrative procedures of supervision were specified.[225]

An analogous process of moving (in order to entrench) the scrutiny of administrative practices to the earlier stages of judicial examination – from the third stage of the proportionality/necessity criterion to the first stage of the legal safeguards to 'be prescribed by law' criterion – has been seen in the context of lethal operations of the police against dangerous individuals. In such circumstances, interference has usually to be justified under Article 2 (the right to life), whose corresponding 'prescribed by law' stage is inserted in paragraph 1 as '[e]veryone's right to life shall be protected by law' which constitutes a natural point of synthesis of legal safeguards.

---

222 *Klass and Others* v. *Germany* [1978] no. 5029/71. Cf. Duffy, 'The Case of Klass and Others: Secret Surveillance of Communications and the European Convention on Human Rights', p. 24, who pointed out that '[i]n its opinion in *Klass* the Commission said that the requirement of legality "must be taken to mean that the law sets up the conditions and procedures for an interference"'.

223 The work of the Council of Europe (Orwell Colloquy in Strasbourg on 2 April 1984, and Data Bank Colloquy in Madrid on 13 June 1984); the Council of Europe Convention of 1981 (Private Life, Data Banks); Recommendation R (83) 10 of the Committee of Ministers of the Council; the approach taken by the Karlsruhe Constitutional Court vis-à-vis the concept of "informational self-determination".

224 See also the cases cited in the concurring opinion of judge Wildhaber in *Rotaru* v. *Romania* [2000] no. 28341/95; Loucaides, *Essays*, pp. 188–189. *Leander* v. *Sweden* [1987] no. 9248/81, para. 51; and the quotation in note 219.

225 The indirect influence of comparative examples and entrenched practices has also to be noted with reference to the European Data Protection Directive 95/46/EC and the joint work of the European Union and Council of Europe in this area, see, e.g., the Buttarelli Report.

In the important case of *McCann and Others* (discussed in section 2.2.1.1 above), the applicants contested the quality of 'law' on the ground *inter alia* that 'the law did not require that the agents of the State be trained in accordance with the strict standards of Article 2 para. 1'.[226] In the Court's view, these were issues to be evaluated under paragraph 2. The judges laid down core administrative safeguards for the planning and control of the lethal operations of the police to assess the proportionality of the state's response to the perceived threat.[227] Since the content of these safeguards concerned administrative practices (as opposed to ad hoc measures), they have been reaffirmed in subsequent jurisprudence to judge the proportionality of the state's interference.[228]

As the legal safeguards became entrenched, in the subsequent case of *Makaratzis* (that concerned also a lethal operation by the police), the Court was able to come full circle in favour of the applicants' submission that had been rejected in *McCann and Others* and found a violation of Article 2 on the quality of 'law' (i.e. the administrative safeguards which had been entrenched at the proportionality stage since *McCann and Others*), without having to assess the particular merits of the case or the necessity of the interference.[229] To appreciate the strictness of that approach, one has only to distinguish that, unlike *McCann and Others*, there were identifiable individuals in immediate danger from the applicant's behaviour, the applicant was not killed during the lethal operation and the police officers did not have time to plan their operation in advance.[230] It should also be said that the individual liability of a public officer who does not act in a proportionate way cannot be raised when it is the quality of the domestic 'law' with which the public officer has used to comply and complied in the given case.[231] This presumption reasonably applies in international law, since, if the individual officer had acted below the standards imposed by the domestic law, the case would have already been resolved at the state's level.[232]

From the foregoing analysis, it can be concluded that a synthesis of human rights protection can be achieved when the core positive obligations

---

226  *McCann and Others* v. *the United Kingdom* [1995] no. 18984/91, para. 151.
227  The standard of absolute necessity applies under Article 2 (2).
228  See, e.g., *Andronicou and Constantinou* v. *Cyprus* [1997] no. 25052/94. R. Crawshaw, 'International Standards on the Right to Life and the Use of Force by Police' (1999) 3 *IJHR* 67–91; Ni Aolain, 'The Evolving Jurisprudence of the European Convention Concerning the Right to Life'.
229  *Makaratzis* v. *Greece* [2004] no. 50385/99, paras 70–72.
230  A parallel point can be made with the case of *Ramsahai and Others* v. *the Netherlands* [2005] and [2007] (Grand Chamber) no. 52391/99, in which the lack of independence in the investigation sufficed per se to find a violation of the procedural limb of Article 2, despite the fact that the Court did not question the assessment of facts and the legal principles applied at the domestic level.
231  *Leonidis* v. *Greece*, [2009] no. 43326/05, para. 65.
232  Loucaides, *Essays*; Tomuschat, in R. Lawson and M. de Blois (eds), *The Dynamics of the Protection of Human Rights in Europe: Essays in Honour of H.G. Schermers*.

required under paragraph 1 of the Convention rights (e.g. administrative steps) are incorporated in the quality assessment of safeguards that the law has to 'prescribe' and implement under the first criterion of paragraph 2. Falling foul of this criterion, an act of interference becomes automatically unlawful irrespective of the merits of its necessity.

It should be clarified that this proposal is not ever-available so that it can be used to negate the dialectics of the process in which the European judges deliberate and test in practice which standards need to be entrenched in the case-law. The presence of a known context, comparative qualitative examples and common sense are always the safest principles for guidance.

### 2.4.1.2 Positive obligations as legal safeguards to maintain the initial justification of interference

A justified act of interference can create a new situation in which additional human rights issues will come to be involved. Such issues are particularly pertinent in circumstances where there is an interference with the right to liberty of an individual, who is lawfully detained by the state authorities.[233] Thus, on day one the state acts in accordance with its negative obligation not to interfere with the right to liberty and security (Article 5) without the requisite safeguards and, as a result, the authorities are entitled to detain individuals for a prescribed time. But, on day two, the previous-day interference has to be re-examined to address human rights issues that are involved in the *new* situation ensuing from the justified act of interference. Despite some views that Article 5 contains express positive obligations,[234] these obligations only arise following a prior act of direct interference by the state and, therefore, they amount to codified safeguards for a legitimate deprivation of liberty.[235] In such a context, the state's obligations are positive, in the literal meaning of word, but they should not be confused with the positive obligations under paragraph 1 of the Convention rights that require the state to actively protect human rights in order to prevent their violation.

An illustration of these points can be seen in the case of *Price*, in which a severely disabled individual complained that her detention to a police station and prison, which lacked appropriate facilities for her special

---

233  *Golder* v. *the United Kingdom* [1975] no. 4451/70, para. 45: 'To this extent, but to this extent only, lawful deprivation of liberty within the meaning of Article 5 does not fail to impinge on the application of Article 8.' For earlier discussion of case-law concerning the conflict of human rights interests under Articles 8 and 5 in the context of prisoners, see Duffy, 'The Protection of Privacy, Family Life and Other Rights under Article 8 of the European Convention on Human Rights', pp. 214–215.

234  Mowbray, *The Development*, chapter 4: 'Article 5'.

235  J. Murdoch, 'A Survey of Recent Case Law under Article 5 ECHR' (1998) 23 *ELR* (SUPP HR) 31–48.

needs, amounted to a treatment contrary to Article 3. The Court criticised the sentencing judge for not ascertaining, before ordering immediate imprisonment, whether the prison could ensure facilities adequate with the level of her disability. It was unanimously decided that Article 3 was violated on the grounds that

> to detain a severely disabled person in conditions where she is dangerously cold, risks developing sores because her bed is too hard or unreachable, and is unable to go to the toilet or keep clean without the greatest of difficulty, constitutes degrading treatment contrary to Article 3 of the Convention.[236]

In such well-known contextual circumstances, it can reasonably be asserted that additional safeguards are required to maintain or re-affirm the initial justification of the state's interference in lawfully depriving an individual of their liberty. These issues are more pertinent in relation to the right to life (Article 2) and the freedom from torture and inhuman or degrading treatment (Article 3). Both these rights are repeatedly labelled as the 'fundamental rights' of the Convention in recognition of their semi-absolute and absolute status, respectively, and their non-derogable nature.[237] If Articles 2 and 3 rights cannot be guaranteed, then the initial justification of interference should be revisited to examine additional safeguards in relation to these additional Convention rights that are implied in the new setting of circumstances. In this account, the original justification of the jailed confinement of convicted individuals is maintained and further conditioned on the understanding that the state is able to guarantee the fundamental rights of Articles 2 and 3 for which no legitimate aim of interference is available in the context of (otherwise) lawfully detained individuals.

The existence of such a known context in which the state exercises a significant control of individuals' lives presupposes an administrative mechanism that is capable of identifying particular human rights needs for each individual. Core administrative steps have been examined in the case of *Edwards*, which concerned the murder of a prisoner by a dangerously unstable inmate. The state was found in violation of Article 2 on the ground that the screening process of prisoners during their arrival to prison was not efficient under the circumstances.[238]

The same principles apply to all those contexts in which individuals are placed under an advanced, and yet lawful, control of the state, such as

---

236  *Price* v. *the United Kingdom* [2001] no. 33394/96, para. 30.
237  See, e.g., *Soering* v. *the United Kingdom* [1989] no. 14038/88, para. 88; *Pretty* v. *United Kingdom* [2002] no. 2346/02, paras 37, 49; *Solomou and Others* v. *Turkey* [2008] no. 36832/97, para. 63.
238  *Edwards* v. *the United Kingdom* [2002] no. 46477/99, para. 64.

in police custody or prisons,[239] mental institutions,[240] immigration centres,[241] military bases (during military service),[242] etc. In all these circumstances, individuals have lawfully been deprived of their liberty (Article 5) and of other concurring interests under Article 8 (i.e. family life). As these individuals are brought to a new situation in which additional human rights are involved (including other aspects of the same human right (e.g. Article 8)), the protection of these rights must be guaranteed.

If the issue of human rights protection is approached as new, then a separate action under the state's positive obligation can be pursued. In such a case, the content of a positive obligation is determined under paragraph 1 of the Convention rights. At that stage, inherent limits of practicality are also recognised. By contrast, if the issue of protection concerns simply a new situation that is already expected in a known context, then all obligations have to be addressed at the same time during the original examination of the interference. In that respect, a synthesis of protection can be adopted by incorporating positive obligations as entrenched safeguards that the law has to 'prescribe' in order to justify a legitimate interference or to maintain the initial justification (although, practically, there is no difference between the two). As the positive obligation is secured as an entrenched safeguard to

239 See, e.g., *Kotalla* v. *the Netherlands* (dec.) [1978] no. 7994/77; *Ensslin, Baader and Raspe* v. *Germany* (dec.) [1978] no. 7572/76; *X.* v. *the United Kingdom* (dec.) [1980] no. 8158/78; *Aerts* v. *Belgium* [1997] no. 25357/94; *Ilhan* v. *Turkey* [2000] no. 22277/93; *Dougoz* v. *Greece* [2001] no. 40907/98; *Papon* v. *France* (dec.) [2001] no. 6466/01; *Price* v. *the United Kingdom* [2001] no. 33394/96; *Kalashnikov* v. *Russia* [2002] no. 47095/99; *Muisel* v. *France* [2002] no. 67263/01; *Farbtuhs* v. *Latvia* [2004] no. 4672/02 (available in French only); *Vincent* v. *France* [2006] no. 6253/03 (available in French only); *Serifis* v. *Greece* [2006] no. 27695/03 (available in French only); *Huylu* v. *Turkey* [2006] no. 52955/99 (available in French only); *Tarariyeva* v. *Russia* [2006] no. 4353/03; *Istratii and Others* v. *Moldova* [2007] no. 8721/05,..., 8742/05; *Yakovenko* v. *Ukraine* [2007] no. 15825/06; *Pilcic* v. *Croatia* [2008] no. 33138/06; *Scoppola* v. *Italy* [2008] no. 50550/06 (available in French only); *Guvec* v. *Turkey* [2009] no. 70337/01; *Grori* v. *Albania* [2009] no. 25336/04; *A.B.* v. *Russia* [2010] no. 1439/06; *Logvinenko* v. *Ukraine* [2010] no. 13448/07; *Jasinskis* v. *Latvia* [2010] no. 45744/08. Recommendation *Rec(2006)2* of the Committee of Ministers of the Council of Europe on the European Prison Rules (amending *Rec(1987)3*) (adopted on 11 January 2006); Issue Paper of the Commissioner for Human Rights of the Council of Europe, 'Children and Juvenile Justice: Proposals for Improvements' CommDH/IssuePaper (2009)1. See also Mowbray, *The Development*, chapter 2: 'Article 2', sec.: 'Provision of Medical Services', and chapter 3: 'Article 3', sec.: 'Provision of Adequate Medical Treatment for Detainees', pp. 22, 52.

240 *Slawomir Musial* v. *Poland* [2009] no. 28300/06; *Mojsiejew* v. *Poland* [2009] no. 11818/02.

241 *Mubilanzila Mayeka and Kaniki Mitunga* v. *Belgium* [2006] no. 13178/03; *Riad and Idiab* v. *Belgium* [2008] nos 29787/03; 29810/03; *N.* v *the United Kingdom* [2008] no. 26565/05; *S.D.* v. *Greece* [2009] no. 53541/07 (available in French only); *Palushi* v. *Austria* [2009] no. 27900/04; *A.A.* v. *Greece* [2010] no. 12186/08. Recommendation *Rec1327(1997)* of the Parliamentary Assembly of the Council of Europe on the Protection and Reinforcement of the Human Rights of Refugees and Asylum-Seekers in Europe (adopted on 24 April 1997).

242 *Tastan* v. *Turkey* [2008] no. 63748/00; *Chember* v. *Russia* [2008] 7188/03; *Yurekli* v. *Turkey* [2008] no. 48913/99 (available in French only). Additional case-law is cited in note 245.

justify an interference under paragraph 2, its content can be determined as an obligation of results to require a higher level of protection by the state.

Another benefit of this approach is that the dual nature of the state's obligations remains distinct. As already pointed out, positive measures of protection do not necessarily concern positive obligations. Because positive obligations terminology has been used in the context of detained persons, it has led some commentators to invoke cases, such as *Price*, in order to assert general positive obligations towards disabled individuals. But no such connection can be made, simply because, in *Price*, there is a causal link between the harm complained of and the act of detaining an individual without providing appropriate facilities. Such a causal link (directly attributed to the state) is spectacularly absent in the claims of human rights protection of disabled individuals at large.

The main point presented here is that in circumstances where the state exercises an advanced control of the individuals' lives, additional human rights interests, such as those under Articles 2 and 3, can clearly be contemplated when considering the initial justification of the state's interference. To take the point made by Colin Warbrick in commenting on earlier case-law:

> [The state] did have an obligation to organise the detention of the defendants so that their health might be protected as far as possible in all circumstances ... Again, the need for constant control and review of the prisoners' conditions was a requirement of Article 3. The result, that prisoners can present almost insoluble dilemmas for the States by reason of their own conduct without sacrificing the basic protection of the Convention, is a consequence of the very idea of human rights.[243]

The obligation to protect the physical and psychological integrity of a prisoner, as guaranteed under Articles 2, 3 and 8,[244] may not mean the automatic release of detained individuals, but neither that their detention can be justified or maintained without guaranteeing safeguards in relation to other, higher or concurring human rights interests, which cannot, simply and plainly, be compromised. Thus, a detained individual may die in prison as a natural course of events, but it is the fault of the state when the loss of human life is attributed to a lack of appropriate and basic facilities or a failure to screen dangerous inmates.[245]

---

243 Warbrick, 'The European Convention on Human Rights and the Prevention of Terrorism', sec.: 'Treatment of Detained Persons', p. 107.

244 *Branduse* v. *Romania* [2009] no. 6586/03 (under Article 8).

245 See similar issues in the context of military service, *Kilinc and Others* v. *Turkey* [2005] no. 40145/98 (available in French only); *Salgin* v. *Turkey* [2007] no. 46748/99 (available in French only); *Hasan Çaliskan and Others* v. *Turkey* [2007] no. 13094/02 (available in French only); *Abdullah Yilmaz* v. *Turkey* [2008] no. 21899/02 (available in French only).

## 2.4.2  The point of synthesis – special contexts involving competing positive obligations claims

There are some circumstances in which a positive duty of protection under paragraph 1 of a Convention right can be owed to different individuals with diametrically opposing human rights interests against each other. When such a conflict of rights exists, a corresponding conflict of positive obligations is inevitable. For this reason, the text of the Convention recognises 'the protection of the rights and freedoms of others' as a legitimate aim of interference in some paragraph 2 provisions. General directions are also highlighted in Article 17 (prohibition of abuse of rights) and Article 18 (limitation on use of restrictions on rights) that serve as guiding principles in appropriate circumstances.[246]

A conflict of rights has been observed in the cases of *Keegan* and *Hokkanen*, which have been cited by judge Wildhaber in his concurring opinion in *Stjerna* to support a proposal for a complete merging of positive and negative obligations under 'the notion of interference' in paragraph 2 terms.[247] Cases that have arisen from a dispute over the custody of children, their reunion with their parents (*Hokkanen*) or their adoption (*Keegan*), concern contexts that are special due to the existence of a direct conflict of human rights. In such contexts, the Court will look at the human rights interests of the child but also those of the mother and the father (usually against each other). As Alpha Connelly has pointed out in analysing earlier case-law:

> [s]ometimes, the same complaint may be double-sided and call for the application of both [positive and negative] approaches. That the two approaches can be complementary, each tuned to providing an answer to different aspects of the same grievance, was seen above [the *Hendriks* case] in relation to the complaint of a divorced man that had been denied access to his child.[248]

Where a conflict of human rights exists, the measures that the state authorities are under a positive obligation to take in order to guarantee the human right of one individual may be seen as acts of interference with the human right of another individual. In order to manage the difficulties surrounding opposing human rights interests, a flexible approach should

---

246 Loucaides, *Essays*, chapter 9, sec. 11: 'Implied Limitations', sec. 14: 'Forfeiture of Rights under Article 17', and sec. 15: 'Abuse of Power' (Article 18); see *Garaudy* v. *France* (dec.) [2003] no. 65831/01.

247 *Keegan* v. *Ireland* [1994] no. 27229/95; *Hokkanen* v. *Finland* [1994] no. 19823/92. See discussion in section 2.1.2 above.

248 Connelly, 'Problems of Interpretation of Article 8 of the European Convention on Human Rights', p. 589, citing *Hendriks* v. *the Netherlands* (dec.) [1982] no. 8427/78 (Commission's Report).

be adopted when applying the fair balance test or the criteria of the paragraph 2 provisions. In that respect, what is required is a specialised study that accords due weight to contextual differences and combinations of rights in order to achieve a synthesis of the state's obligations under a tailor-made working framework.

In this section, our sole aim is to present examples of conflict of rights in private interactions and identify common approaches in the judicial examination. The contexts covered here are far from exhaustive and their discussion is exclusively made in order to prove the point that some case-law concerns special contexts (and yet important ones) and, therefore, legal principles that have been elaborated there cannot readily travel and be transposed to other contexts not concerning a conflict between Convention rights. The principles and content of positive obligations analysed in earlier sections may inform the legal tests where a conflict of rights exists, but not the opposite. It is for this reason alone that competing positive obligations are only discussed in the very last section of this chapter.

### 2.4.2.1 *Examples of contexts with conflict of rights*

FAMILY DISPUTES: CUSTODY AND ADOPTION CASES

Competing human rights interests are involved in circumstances where a parent seeks contact or reunion with his/her child after a decision of custody,[249] or where children of unfavourable family environments are taken into community care (including adoption arrangements). In such circumstances, the human rights of the father may conflict with those of the mother and/or with those of the children.

As discussed in *Z and Others* and *E and Others* above, the state is under a positive obligation to protect the physical and psychological integrity of children in their family environments when the element of knowledge of the need of human rights protection can reasonably be imputed on the state authorities. In *H.K.*, the state authorities had to place the applicant's daughter in public care due to suspicions of sexual abuse by her father, having evaluated evidence that the child was exhibiting signs of disturbance.[250] In *Kutzner*, the applicants' parental responsibility was withdrawn

---

249 Duffy, 'The Protection of Privacy, Family Life and Other Rights under Article 8 of the European Convention on Human Rights', p. 208; M. Buquicchio de Boer, 'Children and the European Convention on Human Rights: A Survey of Case-Law of the European Commission and Court of Human Rights', in F. Matscher and H. Petzold (eds), *Protecting Human Rights: The European Dimension, Studies in Honour of G.J. Wiarda* (Köln: Heymann, 1988), pp. 73–89; U. Kilkelly, *The Child and the European Convention on Human Rights* (Aldershot: Ashgate, 1999); H. Fenwick, 'Clashing Rights, the Welfare of the Child and the Human Rights Act' (2004) 67 *MLR* 889.

250 *H.K.* v. *Finland* [2006] no. 36065/97.

by the state on evidence showing that the children's development had become considerably retarded.[251]

Once a child is placed in public or private care, a competing positive obligation arises for the state to safeguard the parent's right of respect for private and family life by taking appropriate measures to facilitate the reunification of the family.[252] At the same time, a competing positive obligation exists to protect a child who has lived for some time with other persons. In *Hokkanen*, the reunion of the natural parent with the child was also examined in relation to preparatory measures that safeguard the interests of the latter.[253]

Where such a conflict of rights exists, opposing positive obligations can give rise to corresponding negative obligations. Thus, a measure that is taken for the protection of the right of one individual is also an act of interference with the right of another. In such circumstances, a fair balance test applies flexibly in view that '[w]hilst the boundaries between the State's positive and negative obligations under this provision do not lend themselves to precise definition, the applicable principles are similar.'[254]

FREE EXPRESSION AND DEFAMATION

Conflict of rights are often encountered when the freedom of expression that one individual exercises under Article 10 encroaches on the right of respect for private life of another individual under Article 8. In such a well-known context, the positive obligations that arise in relation to Articles 10 and 8 conflict against each other.[255] Examples from the abundant jurisprudence of expression versus reputation context have to be discussed to show the general opposing perspectives of positive obligations.

In the case of *Kanellopoulou* the applicant had criticised in a published interview the responsibility of a medical practitioner for the bodily harm she suffered. The Court found the state in violation of Article 10, because the criminal sanctions imposed on the applicant in defamation proceedings against her were disproportionate.[256] More

251  *Kutzner* v. *Germany* [2002] no. 46544/99, para. 116.
252  Ibid., para. 61; *Hokkanen* v. *Finland* [1994] no. 19823/92, para. 55; *Eriksson* v. *Sweden* [1989] no. 11373/85, para. 71.
253  *Hokkanen* v. *Finland*, ibid., para. 58.
254  Ibid., para. 55; *Kutzner* v. *Germany* [2002] no 46544/99, para. 62; *Keegan* v. *Ireland* [1994] no. 27229/95, para. 49.
255  See, e.g., *Krasulya* v. *Russia* [2007] no. 12365/03; *Gorelishvili* v. *Georgia* [2007] no. 12979/04; *Sanocki* v. *Poland* [2007] no. 28949/03; *Ormanni* v. *Italy* [2007] no. 30278/04; *Peev* v. *Bulgaria* [2007] no. 64209/01; *Chemodurov* v. *Russia* [2007] no. 72683/01; *Dyuldin and Kislov* v. *Russia* [2007] no. 25968/02. See H. Rogers and H. Tomlinson, 'Privacy and Expression: Convention Rights and Interim Injunctions' (2003) *EHRLR* (SPI) 37–53.
256  *Kanellopoulou* v. *Greece* [2007] no. 28504/05, para. 40 (available in French only). See also the joint dissenting opinion of judges Loucaides and Kovler.

common is the case when a media company is sued, directly or vicariously, for an expression that has been communicated to the public. In *Cumpana and Mazare*, a local newspaper claimed a violation of Article 10 for its conviction in defamation proceedings that concerned the publication of a satirical cartoon portraying a former legal expert of the city council. In such circumstances, the question before the Court is essentially of

> whether the domestic authorities struck a fair balance between, on the one hand, the protection of freedom of expression as enshrined in Article 10, and on the other hand, the protection of the reputation of those against whom allegations have been made, a right which, as an aspect of private life, is protected by Article 8 of the Convention [...] That provision may require the adoption of positive measures designed to secure effective respect for private life even in the sphere of the relations of individuals between themselves ...[257]

In practice, disputes often arise because the balance between the competing interests was not proportionate under the circumstances.

The conflict of positive obligations can also be appreciated from the perspective of an Article 8 complaint. In *Von Hannover*, it was the turn of a private party, whose reputation was injured in a publication, to claim protection under Article 8. Again, from this angle, 'protection of private life has to be balanced against the freedom of expression guaranteed by Article 10 of the Convention.'[258] In such circumstances, the *Keegan* case

---

257 *Cumpana and Mazare* v. *Romania* [2004] no. 33348/96, paras 91 and 113 (cited cases omitted); *Ormanni* v. *Italy* [2007] no. 30278/04, para. 67. See also *Leempoel & S.A. ED. Ciné Revue* v. *Belgium* [2006] no. 64772/01, para. 78: 'Where there is a conflict between the right to communicate the information and that of protecting the reputation and the rights of others, the Court reiterates that it has already indicated that, in certain circumstances, a person has a legitimate expectation to have his private life protected and respected.', (translation, available in French only); *Karhuvaara and Iltalehti* v. *Finland* [2004] no. 53678/00, para. 42; *Colaço Mestre and SI-Sociedade Independente de Comunicaçao S.A.* v. *Portugal* [2007] nos 11182/03; 11319/03.

258 *Von Hannover* v. *Germany* [2004] no. 59320/00, para. 58; *Gourguenidze* v. *Georgia* [2006] no. 71678/01, para. 57: '[the Court] has therefore examined the question of respect of positive obligations that are incumbent on the defendant State under the circumstances, when the publication does not originate from an activity or collective effort of the State organs.', (translation, available in French only); *Pfeifer* v. *Austria* [2007] no. 12556/03; *Marin* v. *Romania* [2009] no. 30699/02. *Schussel* v. *Austria* (dec.) [2002] no. 42409/98: 'The Court recalls that Article 8 taken in conjunction with the obligation to secure the effective exercise of Convention rights imposed by Article 1 of the Convention, may involve a positive obligation on the State to provide a measure of protection for an individual's private life in relation to the exercise by third parties of the right to freedom of expression bearing in mind the duties and responsibilities referred to in Article 10.'

can legitimately be cited as an authority for the fair balance test between the competing interests involved.[259]

There are also circumstances where the reputation of an individual, as guaranteed by Article 8, is connected to the record of their expression. This means that, in an action for defamation, there are in essence two competing expressions. In such a case, a clash of different rights (Art. 8 v. Art. 10) is also a clash of the same right (Art 10 v. Art 10) of different individuals.[260]

COUNTER-DEMONSTRATIONS/ASSEMBLIES

The right of a group of individuals to hold a demonstration or assembly, as guaranteed by Article 11, is one to which an opposing group of individuals is equally entitled to exercise, either at the same time[261] or as a continuous manifestation of expression in any given moment.[262]

A known case in this context is *Plattform 'Arzte fur das Leben'*, in which the applicant (an association) complained about the state's failure to adequately guarantee their right to demonstrate in circumstances where a counter-demonstration was also taking place. In setting out the general principle of law that should apply in such circumstances, the Court explained that individuals must be able to hold a demonstration without fearing to be subjected to physical violence by their opponents. It reasoned that

> genuine, effective freedom of peaceful assembly cannot, therefore, be reduced to a mere duty on the part of the State not to interfere... Like Article 8 (art. 8), Article 11 (art. 11) sometimes requires positive measures to be taken, even in the sphere of relations between individuals.[263]

---

259  *Von Hannover* v. *Germany*, ibid., para. 57; *Leempoel & S.A. ED. Ciné Revue* v. *Belgium* [2006] no. 64772/01, para. 78; *Karhuvaara and Iltalehti* v. *Finland* [2004] no. 53678/00, para. 42. As to the judicial evaluation of the balance of competing interests in the *Von Hannover* case, see the concurring opinion of judge Cabral Barreto about privacy, kings and queens, Monte Carlo and Monte Carlo Beach Club; *Pfeifer* v. *Austria*, ibid., para. 38. See also the dissenting opinions of judges Loucaides and Schäffer.

260  *Karman* v. *Russia* [2006] no. 29372/02, para. 35; *Sanocki* v. *Poland* [2007] no. 28949/03 (available in French only); *Azevedo* v. *Portugal* [2008] no. 20620/04; *Sorguc* v. *Turkey* [2009] no. 17089/03.

261  *Plattform 'Arzte fur das Leben'* v. *Austria* [1988] no. 10126/82; *Barankevich* v. *Russia* [2007] no. 10519/03.

262  *Ouranio Toxo* v. *Greece* [2005] no. 74989/01.

263  *Plattform 'Arzte fur das Leben'* v. *Austria* [1988] no. 10126/82, para. 32 (cited case omitted). See also *Christian Democratic People's Party* v. *Moldova (no. 2)* [2010] no. 25196/04; *Alekseyev* v. *Russia* [2010] nos 4916/07,..., 14599/09, para. 73. See also *Association of Citizens 'Radko' and Paunkovski* v. *the former Yugoslav Republic of Macedonia* [2009] no. 74651/01, para. 65: 'The role of the authorities in such circumstances is not to remove the cause of tension by eliminating pluralism, but to ensure that competing groups tolerate each other', (cited cases omitted).

More complicated appears to be the *Ollinger* case, in which the applicant complained about the state authorities' refusal to grant permission
for an assembly in a cemetery on all Saints' Day (a religious holiday) in
order to commemorate the Jews killed by the SS during the Second World
War. The assembly would coincide in place and time with the gathering
of a registered association (Comradeship IV), which, for more than forty
years, had commemorated SS soldiers killed in that war by congregating at
the municipal cemetery on that day of the year. Under statutory law, the
association's gathering is classified as a 'popular ceremony',[264] and hence
it is excepted from permission. In addition, the same Convention right
(Article 11) of those visiting the cemetery, either occasionally or on the
specific religious day in which the dead are commemorated, has also to be
taken into account. Moreover, an additional positive obligation arises
under Article 9 (freedom to manifest his/her religion) to protect the
cemetery-goers against deliberate disturbances that may result from the
gathering of opposing groups of individuals. The Court summarised the
various conflicts of the state's obligations, pointing out that

> As regards the right to freedom of peaceful assembly as guaranteed by
> Article 11, the Court reiterates that it comprises negative and positive
> obligations on the part of the Contracting State. [§] On the one hand,
> the State is compelled to abstain from interfering with that right... On
> the other hand, States may be required under Article 11 to take posit-
> ive measures in order to protect a lawful demonstration against
> counter-demonstrations... Turning finally to Article 9 of the Conven-
> tion ... the responsibility of the State may be engaged where religious
> beliefs are opposed or denied in a manner which inhibits those who
> hold such beliefs from exercising their freedom to hold or express
> them. In such cases the State may be called upon to ensure the peace-
> ful enjoyment of the right guaranteed under Article 9 to the holders
> of those beliefs ...[265]

The balancing of the state's positive obligations between different groups
of individuals with clashing human rights interests requires a careful
examination to explore various alternatives that are open to the interested parties. The need for clear evaluative principles that will dictate
priorities for taking or excluding some measures, as well as the stage(s)
at which these measures will have to determined, is particularly
pressing.[266]

---

264  *Ollinger* v. *Austria* [2006] no. 76900/01, para. 40.
265  Ibid., paras 35, 36, 37, 39.
266  Ibid. See the dissenting opinion of judge Loucaides who has focused on Article 9, while
    exploring alternatives accommodating the competing interests under Articles 10 and 11.

## 2.4.2.2 *General evaluative principles*

THE EVALUATION OF THE PRIORITY OF PROTECTION: USING A HIERARCHY OF RIGHTS

In the various contexts of private interactions in which a clash of rights is observed, the determination of positive obligations may need a hierarchy of interests to guide the organisation of human rights protection. The idea for a hierarchy of rights is evident in the Court's frequent labelling of the right to life (Article 2) and the prohibition of torture and inhuman or degrading treatment (Article 3) as 'the most fundamental provisions in the Convention' for which no derogation is permitted during wartime.[267] This idea has also increasingly been advocated in scholarly commentary, proving the growing perception, or common sense, that some rights are more important than others.[268] This is particularly obvious with regard to the right to life, as it is life that conditions the relevance of the rest of human rights.[269] In these terms, a hierarchy of rights can generally be deduced following the higher degree of negative impact that is involved in the particular circumstances,[270]

267 See, e.g., *Soering* v. *United Kingdom* [1989] no. 14038/88, para. 88; *Pretty* v. *United Kingdom* [2002] no. 2346/02, paras 37, 49; *Kakkoulli* v. *Turkey* [2005] no. 38595/97, para. 106; *Estamirov and Others* v. *Russia* [2006] no. 60272/00, para. 98; *Salah Sheekh* v. *the Netherlands* [2007] no. 1948/04, para. 135; *Isaak* v. *Turkey* [2008] no. 44587/98, para. 103; *Solomou and Others* v. *Turkey* [2008] no. 36832/97, para. 63: 'The Court reiterates that Article 2, which safeguards the right to life and sets out those circumstances in which deprivation of life may be justified, ranks as one of the most fundamental provisions in the Convention, to which no derogation is permitted. Together with Article 3, it also enshrines one of the basic values of the democratic societies making up the Council of Europe.'

268 Loucaides, *Essays*, chapter 9, sec. 3: 'Rights Subject to Special Protection', p. 182; F. Sudre, 'Droits Intangibles et/ou Droits Fondamentaux: Y a-t-il des Droits Prééminents dans la Convention Européenne des Droits de l'Homme?', in G. Cohen-Jonathan *et al.* (eds), *Liber Amicorum Marc-André Eissen* (Brussels: Bruylant, 1995), pp. 381–398; Greer, *The European Convention*, p. 242. See also Warbrick, 'The European Convention on Human Rights and the Prevention of Terrorism', p. 85, who has noted: '[t]he 'fundamental' rights clash one with another and a balance needs [sic] must be struck between them in particular cases. Neither the enumerated rights themselves nor the balance which must be struck between them are "neutral" between possible ways of organising society or values which may be pursued.'

269 *Pretty* v. *the United Kingdom* [2002] no. 2346/02, para. 37: 'The Court's case-law accords pre-eminence to Article 2 as one of the most fundamental provisions of the Convention [...]. It safeguards the right to life, without which enjoyment of any of the other rights and freedoms in the Convention is rendered nugatory.', (cited case omitted); *K.-W.* v. *Germany* [2001] no. 37201/97, para. 75: 'the right to life is ... the supreme value in the hierarchy of human rights.', *Streletz, Kessler and Krenz* v. *Germany* [2001] nos 34044/96,..., 44801/98, para. 94.

270 *Opuz* v. *Turkey* [2009] no. 33401/02, para. 147: 'In any event, the Court would underline that in domestic violence cases perpetrators' [Article 8 rights, i.e. family life] cannot supersede victims' human rights to life and to physical and mental integrity' (cited case omitted).

including circumstances of conflict between Articles 2 and 3[271] and even where only one individual is concerned.[272]

To take the examples of the case-law above, the right to demonstrate is legitimately exercised under Article 11, but when the physical integrity of some individuals are threatened in the course of events, Article 2 and Article 8 (as guaranteeing the physical and psychological integrity of a person) come into play to override Article 11, in appropriate circumstances, due to the higher degree of negative impact that is contemplated by their scope.[273]

In principle, the same process of evaluating the higher negative impact can apply when conflicts arise in relation to the same right that can be engaged by different individuals against each other.[274] In such circumstances, the assessment of the actual or potential negative impact on all individuals concerned can guide the priority or exclusion of protection. Thus, in the family context under Article 8, what is best for the interests of the child takes precedent over competing rights of the parents, simply because the negative impact on the child is greater.[275]

Where conflicts involve the freedom of expression, additional considerations apply. In general, unless Articles 2 and 3 can be engaged, due weight is accorded to the collective value of freedom of expression (i.e. Articles 10, 11) that guarantees democracy that guarantees the rest of the human rights.[276] Different types of expression attract greater or lesser protection depending on the collective benefit to the public interest that is underlined.[277] Political speech is revered in the

---

271 P. Vegleris, '"Twenty Years" Experience of the Convention and Future Prospects', in A.H. Robertson (ed.), *Privacy and Human Rights* (Manchester: Manchester University Press, 1973), pp. 341–412, p. 350: 'The fact remains that this limitation [of death penalty under paragraph 1 of Article 2] is out of keeping with the prohibition of torture and inhuman treatment or punishment, to which no reservation or exception is allowed (Article 3).' *Al-Saadoon & Mufdhi* v. *the United Kingdom* [2010] no. 61498/08: 'The Court does not consider that the wording of the second sentence of Article 2 § 1 continues to act as a bar to its interpreting the words "inhuman or degrading treatment or punishment" in Article 3 as including the death penalty.'

272 *Pretty* v. *the United Kingdom* [2002] no. 2346/02.

273 *Plattform 'Ärzte für das Leben'* v. *Austria* [1988] no. 10126/82.

274 See, e.g., *Hendriks* v. *the Netherlands* (dec.) [1982] no 8427/78 (Commission's Report); *H.K.* v. *Finland* [2006] no. 36065/97.

275 *Hendriks* v. *the Netherlands*, ibid., para. 124: '[the Commission] notes that feelings of distress and frustration because of the absence of one's child may cause considerable suffering to the non-custodial parent. However, where, as in the present case, there is a serious conflict between the interests of the child and one of its parents which can only be resolved to the disadvantage of one of them, the interests of the child must, under Art. 8 (2), prevail.' See also *Hokkanen* v. *Finland* [1994] no. 19823/92, para. 58; *Kutzner* v. *Germany* [2002] no. 46544/99, para. 76.

276 *Steel and Morris* v. *the United Kingdom* [2005] no. 68416/01; *Gorelishvili* v. *Georgia* [2007] no. 12979/04.

277 *Saygili and Falakaoglu* v. *Turkey* [2008] no. 39457/03.

jurisprudence and usually takes priority over interests of personal reputation in opposing human rights claims under Article 8.[278] In that respect, the type of expression serves as an additional criterion for the balance and prioritisation of the competing human rights.[279] If speech is not political and has, for example, to do with religious issues, the disruption of public order may be valued more, although there is no definite standard due to the evaluation of various ad hoc parameters that can be present in any given situation.[280]

## A CONTENT OF DUE PROCESS

In the contexts of private interactions in which known issues of conflict of interests exist, the protection of human rights cannot solely be guaranteed by some positive reactive responses and ad hoc balances. As already discussed, the content of positive obligations is determined as a system of protection. In that respect, a competent administrative mechanism may be required to undertake the necessary evaluation assessment within a framework of due process. The procedural steps by which this assessment is undertaken constitute a core content of obligations of means.[281]

The exact content of due process emerges gradually with the development of the Court's jurisprudence. In *Keegan*, the examination of the state's obligations was not confined to a balance of interests at the time of the guardianship and custody. The Court particularly stressed 'the fact that Irish law permitted the applicant's child to have been placed for

---

278 *Lingens* v. *Austria* [1986] no. 9815/82, para. 42: 'Freedom of the press affords the public one of the best means of discovering and forming an opinion of the ideas and attitudes of political leaders. More generally, freedom of political debate is at the very core of the concept of a democratic society which prevails throughout the Convention. The limits of acceptable criticism are accordingly wider as regards a politician as such than as regards a private individual.'; *Feldek* v. *Slovakia* [2001] no. 29032/95, para. 74; *Lyashko* v. *Ukraine* [2006] no. 21040/02, para. 41; *Dabrowski* v. *Poland* [2006] no. 18235/02, para. 28; *Gorelishvili* v. *Georgia* [2007] no. 12979/04, para. 35; *Lombardo and Others* v. *Malta* [2007] no. 7333/06, para. 54; *Dlugolecki* v. *Poland* [2009] no. 23806/03.

279 *TV Vest As & Rogaland Pensjonistparti* v. *Norway* [2008] no. 21132/05, para. 59: 'there is little scope under Article 10 § 2 of the Convention for restrictions on political speech or on debate on questions of public interest' (cited case omitted); *Dink* v. *Turkey* [2010] nos 2668/07, ..., 7124/09, para. 133.

280 *Otto-Preminger-Institut* v. *Austria* [1994] no. 13470/87; Cf. *Ollinger* v. *Austria* [2006] no. 76900/01.

281 *Kutzner* v. *Germany* [2002] no. 46544/99, para. 56: 'whilst Article 8 contains no explicit procedural requirements, the decision-making process leading to measures of interference must be fair and such as to afford due respect to the interests safeguarded by Article 8'; *H.K.* v. *Finland* [2006] no. 36065/97, para. 111.

adoption shortly after her birth without his knowledge or consent.'[282] In this regard, there was a procedural failure on the critical step of informing the parent when the child was taken from his custody. In *Scozzari and Giunta*, the content of due process concerned safety standards when children are placed into community care institutions. Such steps included *inter alia* monitoring child-related convictions of staff and informing the parents in full of any incidents or malpractices encountered.[283]

An indispensable part of due process is the administrative practice through which a hierarchy of competing interests is established for the purposes of the prioritisation of protection. As long as due process has been observed, it is primarily for the state's authorities to strike the fair balance of competing interests, due to their better position to evaluate in detail the plethora of ad hoc information of each case.[284]

THE PARAGRAPH 2 PERSPECTIVE

The justification for examining the paragraph 2 structures in positive obligations claims, whose binding force is grounded on paragraph 1, is the co-existence of competing positive obligations that turn the active protection of a human right to an interference with an opposing right. However, the interfering effect of a given measure does not automatically impose the typical negative obligation approach. Even if it is assumed that the state acts in order to guarantee the 'rights of others' (these 'rights' being necessarily other or the same Convention rights),[285] as a legitimate aim of interference under paragraph 2 of

282  *Keegan* v. *Ireland* [1994] no. 27229/95, para. 55. In *Kosmopoulou* v. Greece [2004] no. 60457/00, para. 49, the Court stated that 'it is of paramount importance for parents always to be placed in a position enabling them to put forward all arguments … and to have access to all relevant information which was at the disposal of the domestic courts'. A standard of promptness is also an indispensable part of due process, *Keegan* v. *Ireland*, para. 55.

283  *Scozzari and Giunta* v. *Italy* [2000] nos 39221/98; 41963/98. See also *Saviny* v. *Ukraine* [2008] no. 39948/06.

284  *Ignacollo-Zenide* v. *Romania* [2000] no. 31679/96, para. 94; *Kosmopoulou* v. *Greece* [2004] no. 60457/00, para. 45; *Chassagnou and Others* v. *France* [1999] nos 25088/94,…, 28443/95, para. 113: 'Where these "rights and freedoms" [of others] are themselves among those guaranteed by the Convention or its Protocols, it must be accepted that the need to protect them may lead States to restrict other rights or freedoms likewise set forth in the Convention. … The balancing of individual interests that may well be contradictory is a difficult matter, and Contracting States must have a broad margin of appreciation in this respect.'

285  Greer, *The European Convention*, p. 266: 'The only rights which can legitimately limit express or implicit Convention rights are other express or implicit Convention rights. If it were otherwise, the privileged position of Convention rights would be undermined by rights which those who drafted the Convention chose not to include.'; A. Connelly, 'The Protection of the Rights of Others' (1980) 5(2) *HRR* 117–140.

some Convention rights, this does not mean that a negative obligation is involved. Although in negative obligations cases the state always has a free choice of whether or not to pursue a legitimate aim of interference, the state's positive obligation to intervene in order to guarantee the protection of human rights is not optional.

In short, competing human rights interests give rise to positive obligations, whose compliance appears as interference with opposing human rights. In that regard, the measures of protection have to be justified under the three-stage structure of paragraph 2. The 'prescribed by law' stage can serve to entrench administrative practices that form the core content of due process in the context concerned.[286] It is also expected that a certain degree of discretion should be allowed to the state organs in order to strike a fair balance between the competing human rights interests involved, in recognition of the great number of ad hoc parameters that are usually present in any given complaint.[287]

## 2.5 Conclusion

Positive obligations arise under paragraph 1 of the Convention rights engaging the state in the active protection of human rights. The main justification of positive obligations is the presence, actual or potential, of an act of interference with a human right (as with negative obligations), with the difference that that interference originates from a private individual (including a state actor when operating as a private party). If a violation of a human right occurs, the state becomes indirectly responsible for failing to protect the individuals concerned, as could reasonably be required under the circumstances.

For the most part, the Court has approached the application and development of positive obligations by merging positive and negative obligations through a fair balance test that has loosely been based on paragraph 2 provisions of the Convention rights. Thus, it is not only that positive obligations do not originate from or are not related to paragraph 2, but clear complaints on the state's negative obligations have not been examined under the strict criteria of paragraph 2 provisions and the entrenched principles of the jurisprudence. As a result, the potential of positive obligations is clearly undermined by a jurisprudence that is built up as a collection of ad hoc balances of justice.

---

286 *Keegan* v. *Ireland* [1994] no. 27229/95, para. 53; *Hokkanen* v. *Finland* [1994] no. 19823/92, para. 64.

287 *Leempoel & S.A. ED. Ciné Revue* v. *Belgium* [2006] no. 64772/01, para. 59: 'In this regard, the Court reiterates that it is perhaps difficult, in the context concerned, to draft laws with total precision and a certain flexibility may prove to be desirable in order to allow the domestic courts to develop the law according to what they judge as being the necessary measures in the interests of justice ... and the changing conceptions of the society.', (translation, cited case omitted).

If paragraph 1 has not so far been accorded due weight in judicial examination, it is because of the open-ended scope of positive obligations. It is argued that the distinctive nature of positive obligations, reflecting the active protection of human rights, can be secured by the same ground justifying the essentiality of negative obligations, namely the element of knowledge of the need of human rights protection. The presence of such knowledge reinforces the legitimacy of positive obligations by 'involving' the indirect responsibility of the state in the human rights violation of private parties. Such an objective element becomes a condition *sine qua non* of the state's liability that narrows considerably the apparently open-ended scope of positive obligations.

In addition to the element of knowledge, positive obligations can be managed through a flexible interpretation of the Convention rights against which these obligations only arise. Actionable thresholds of negative impact that define the scope of the Convention rights can be adjusted to the level at which positive obligations are manageable within the system of the Convention. Accordingly, the planning of the development and application of positive obligations is organised strategically through the most important and preliminary questions.

Having established the foundations for the planning and control of positive obligations, the determination of the specific content of these obligations is made in accordance with their potential to improve and further expand the protection of human rights. When the applicant's complaint relates to a context of private parties' interactions in which known human rights issues exist, positive obligations concern a whole system of protection. Such a contextual reach reinforces the permanence and priority of paragraph 1 and, by extension, of the state's positive obligations. A core content of positive obligations can reasonably be identified in the form of a legislative and administrative framework. Their particular structures are organised around the critical element of knowledge of the need of human rights protection that is required in both the general and specific levels of protection. In that way, the more specific form of protection is determined through core interconnected steps that are implemented in intermediate levels.

Both the general and specific content of positive obligations is organised against the ultimate aim of the actual prevention of human rights violations, which is what real protection means under paragraph 1 of the Convention rights. Thus, whether or not the examination of an applicant's complaint takes place *ex post facto* at the European level, the state's liability is assessed against a content of measures that have to be taken before a violation occurs. This position further confirms the potential of positive obligations to target a system of protection, rather than some ad hoc responses.

In all circumstances, positive obligations are evaluated by the standard of effectiveness that provides an objective base to determine both the general and more specific content of positive obligations in whichever level and stage they are examined. This standard serves to set the minimum level of protection that can reasonably be required under the circumstances in view of the limited availability of the state's resources. In this connection, limits of practicality are also recognised as inherent in paragraph 1 of the Convention rights. The application and justification of such limits is divided in accordance with critical contextual differences. Limits of practicality are calculated differently where a prior act of interference exists (establishing an element of causation) and where it is absent. The former is further subdivided between acts taken in conformity with the applicable domestic legal standards and those taken in defiance of these standards.

The subdivision of contexts is also required in order to test the applicability of various legal principles or the exact manner or stage of their relevance. Such issues are particularly pertinent where an act of interference of a private party is indirectly pursued by the state under the legitimate aims of paragraph 2. When such a situation emerges, it is important to distinguish between the ad hoc and contextual levels of human rights protection. If a known context of private interactions is concerned, the core content of positive obligations may be due for implementation before the isolated decision of the state authorities to justify the interference of a private party. In such circumstances, a synthesis of human rights protection can be achieved by incorporating the core content of positive obligations that pre-exist, as the quality of safeguards that the domestic law has 'to prescribe' and implement under the first criterion of paragraph 2 provisions. The proposed synthesis applies also in circumstances in which a justifiable interference by a state actor creates a new situation in which positive obligations are involved (e.g. the medical care of prisoners) or where conflicting positive obligations arise in relation to various individuals (e.g. free expression and defamation). Differences in critical contextual parameters induce a narrower examination of positive obligations to guarantee an informed determination of the general and more specific content of human rights protection.

# 3   Protection in the absence of interference

The positive obligations of the state have been extended to cover issues of human rights protection that do not concern acts of interference directly or indirectly attributed to the state. The Convention is now relied upon by various individuals to assert a state's assistance in circumstances of their own personal vulnerability (physical and/or mental conditions). The economic status of a vulnerable individual may or may not be relevant, depending on the contextual circumstances in which human rights are considered. Where it is relevant, the lack of monetary resources may be directly attributed to the personal conditions that describe vulnerability and classify accordingly the individual concerned. From the cases that have so far been dealt with by the Court, we note claims that relate *inter alia* to housing accommodation, medical care and access facilities for the disabled, for which the state has been called to defend alleged failures of its positive obligations to assist vulnerable individuals to enjoy human rights.

It should be clarified from the outset that such claims are diametrically different from those of earlier jurisprudence in which the state's positive obligations are examined over the failure of its agents to protect 'everyone' (hence including also vulnerable individuals) from acts of interference by a non-state actor,[1] or in those exceptional circumstances in which individuals are legitimately put under the control of the state (i.e. detained persons, asylum seekers, individuals during military service,

---

1  See, e.g., *Airey* v. *Ireland* [1979] no. 6289/73; *X and Y* v. *the Netherlands* [1985] no. 8978/80; *Costello-Roberts* v. *the United Kingdom* [1993] no. 13134/87; *A.* v. *the United Kingdom* [1998] no. 25599/94; *Z and Others* v. *the United Kingdom* [2001] no. 29392/95; *Ivison* v. *the United Kingdom* (dec.) [2002] no. 39030/97; *E. and Others* v. *the United Kingdom* [2002] no. 33218/96; *A* v. *Croatia* [2010] no. 55164/08. B. Hofstötter, 'European Court of Human Rights: Positive obligations in E. and others v. United Kingdom' (2004) 2(3) *I-CON* 525–560; H. Cullen, '*Siliadin v France*. Positive Obligations under Article 4 of the European Convention on Human Rights' (2006) 6 *HRLR* 585–592.

etc.).[2] It is established jurisprudence that in such contexts the state is directly or indirectly responsible due to its sovereign ability to regulate and sanction all activities within its jurisdiction and ultimately to set up an effective system to prevent human rights violations.

The extension of the state's positive obligations in the form of direct assistance to actively protect individuals in circumstances arising out of their own personal vulnerability reinforces the constitutional imperative of human rights as free-standing minimum priorities that the society as a whole aims to realise. It is important to note the willingness of the Court to entertain the human rights claims of vulnerable individuals, which, at times, it amplifies on its own initiative under a self-asserted autonomy couched in *jura novit curia* terms.[3] In essence, the expansion of the Convention, as effectuated by the dynamic perspective of the active protection of human rights – representing a new generation of human rights claims that correspond to developments in civil society in various corners of Europe – has meant, in practice, that the source of the threat to human rights, be it a state or non-state actor, is no longer the categorical determinative of the state's international liability, although it remains unchallenged that to abstain from interfering is the essential object of the Convention provisions.[4]

More notable is the provision of prohibition of torture and inhuman and degrading treatment, as guaranteed by Article 3, given the express reference to a 'treatment', and therefore a prior act of interference from a particular source is reasonably implied. In this respect, the clarification by the Court of the scope of Article 3 in the case of *L.* is of particular relevance. In responding to an Article 3 claim concerned with the possibility of securing medical treatment (see further discussion below, pp. 164–165), the Court pointed out:

---

2 *Price* v. *the United Kingdom* [2001] no. 33394/96; *Muisel* v. *France* [2002] no. 67263/01; *Mubilanzila Mayeka and Kaniki Mitunga* v. *Belgium* [2006] no. 13178/03; *Huylu* v. *Turkey* [2006] no. 52955/99; *Mechenkov* v. *Russia* [2008] no. 35421/05; *Tastan* v. *Turkey* [2008] no. 63748/00; *Yeter* v. *Turkey* [2009] no. 33750/03; *Guvec* v. *Turkey* [2009] no. 70337/01; *Gagiu* v. *Romania* [2009] no. 63258/00; *Poghosyan* v. *Georgia* [2009] no. 9870/07; *S.D.* v. *Greece* [2009] no. 53541/07; *A.B.* v. *Russia* [2010] no. 1439/06. See case-law and materials cited in Chapter 2, notes 239–242.

3 See, e.g., *Molka* v. *Poland* (dec.) [2006] no. 56550/00: 'In respect of the applicant's allegation that he was deprived of his right to vote on account of his disability, the Court raised of its own motion a complaint under Article 8 of the Convention'; *Botta* v. *Italy* (dec.) [1996] no. 21439/93: 'The Commission considers that the complaints which the applicant has brought under Articles 3 and 5 of the Convention should be examined under Article 8 of the Convention alone.'; *Pentiacova and 48 Others* v. *Moldova* (dec.) [2005] no. 14462/03; *Guerra and Others* v. *Italy* [1998] no. 14967/89, para. 44.

4 See, e.g., the *Belgian Linguistic* case [1968] nos 1474/62,..., 2126/64, para. 7; *Marckx* v. *Belgium* [1979] no. 6833/74, para. 31; *Moreno Gomez* v. *Spain* [2004] no. 4143/02, para. 55; *Sorensen and Rasmussen* v. *Denmark* [2006] no. 52562/99; 52620/99, para. 57.

Article 3 entails a positive obligation on the part of the State to protect the individual from acute ill-treatment, whether physical or mental, whatever its source. Thus if the source is a naturally occurring illness, the treatment for which could involve the responsibility of the State, but is not forthcoming or patently inadequate, an issue may arise under this provision.[5]

Admittedly, such an expanded scope of the Convention can have wide implications, and it is not difficult to contemplate a floodgates effect that could result in impossible and impractical situations, especially in areas of overlap with social rights. However, even in circumstances in which there can be a genuine overlap between social and human rights, this does not change the fact that a human right can still be involved. Notable is the rush of states to label the applicants' claims as 'social' so that they are automatically rejected as manifestly ill-founded under Article 35.3–4.[6] But mere labelling does not answer the question of whether a human right issue is or is not engaged under the Convention, and whether, and to what extent, a positive obligation might be imposed in the circumstances concerned.

Because human rights are legal rights, albeit of a constitutional nature, the state's assistance in circumstances of personal vulnerability is not claimed as a charity, but as a right to which the individual is entitled by law. The critical detail in the case of human rights is that they are usually broadly framed and, as a result, they require further elaboration to determine their scope in concrete circumstances. At the European level, the European judge interprets human rights under a law-making plan that has long treated the Convention as a 'living instrument' in order to address new challenges to human rights and adapt to rapidly changing social perceptions of their fundamental significance.[7] Under the supranational deal of the Convention, the Court is conferred with power to determine minimum priorities for the states in the area of human rights and fundamental freedoms that cannot generally be compromised or neglected by

---

5 *L.* v. *Lithuania* [2007] no. 27527/03, para. 46, citing *D.* v. *the United Kingdom* [1997] no. 30240/96, paras 51–54 and *Pretty* v. *the United Kingdom* [2002] no. 2346/02, paras 49–52. See also *Larioshina* v. *Russia* (dec.) [2002] no. 56869/00: 'the Court considers that a complaint about a wholly insufficient amount of pension and the other social benefits may, in principle, raise an issue under Article 3 of the Convention which prohibits inhuman or degrading treatment.'

6 *Zehnalova and Zehnal* v. *the Czech Republic* (dec.) [2002] no. 38621/97: '[The government] argued that Article 8 of the Convention was not applicable in the instant case as the rights claimed by the applicants were social rights, the scope of which went beyond the legal obligation inherent in the concept of "respect" for "private life" within the meaning of paragraph 1 of Article 8 of the Convention.' See also *Botta* v. *Italy* [1998] no. 21439/93, para. 29.

7 See, e.g., *Tyrer* v. *the United Kingdom* [1978] no. 5856/72, para. 31; *Pretty* v. *the United Kingdom* [2002] no. 2346/02, para. 54.

majoritarian policies of the elected representatives of the day. Accordingly, the development and application of the Convention affirm a basic and permanent ground of human rights protection that does not have to be negotiated with the demos at every electoral occasion but it is assumed to exist as a constitutional contract.

It pays, however, to recall that the critical justification of constitutional human rights imposing minimum priorities for the state has always been based on the liberal perspective of there being an act of interference, actual or potential, that is causally attributed to the state or non-state actors, including also very special circumstances in which the state legitimately exercises advanced control of some individuals' lives (e.g. prisoners). As human rights protection now extends to active assistance in circumstances of personal vulnerability, the element of causation cannot be established in the absence of an act of interference. As a result, the courts' independence in imposing positive obligations on the state in a non-interference context calls for a renewed justification under the principle of the separation of powers, as clearly there is a fundamental difference between reacting to an act of interference (a causal link exists) and intervening directly in the legislator's agenda (a causal link is absent). In principle, what is opposed is not the protection of the vulnerable as such, but the distribution of the limited resources of states, especially when the financial cost involved is substantial. Such considerations are particularly pertinent at the European level, given the economic disparities that exist between member states.

Thus, in circumstances of non-interference, it can generally be said that when the cost of human rights protection of vulnerable individuals is likely to put an unnecessary or impractical burden on the state's resources, a democratic limit is imposed on the Convention vis-à-vis the budgetary choices of the elected representatives of the state. In most cases, the cost of protection is calculated by taking into account the number of all those individuals who have similar human rights needs with the isolated applicant and who can equally claim protection from the state. In these terms, the legitimacy for the Court to intervene and impose positive obligations may only arise when the financial burden on the state will not be great. In short, it is not the financial cost attached to human rights protection of a vulnerable individual that is precluded as such by the scope of the Convention,[8] but rather the size of that cost, which, if it is large (due to the

---

8 In *Airey* v. *Ireland* [1979] no. 6289/73, para. 26: the Court has made clear that '[w]hilst the Convention sets forth what are essentially civil and political rights, many of them have implications of a social or economic nature. The Court therefore considers, like the Commission, that the mere fact that an interpretation of the Convention may extend into the sphere of social and economic rights should not be a decisive factor against such an interpretation; there is no water-tight division separating that sphere from the field covered by the Convention. See also *Botta* v. *Italy* [1998] no. 21439/93, para. 28; *Stec and Others* v. *the United Kingdom* (dec.) [2005] nos 65731/01, 65900/01, para. 52.

large number of potential applicants), cannot legitimately be imposed by the non-elected judiciary.

The task of this chapter is to present and further discuss general principles that the Court has developed for the examination of the human rights claims of vulnerable individuals in circumstances where a prior act of interference is absent (section 3.1), and, subsequently, to analyse in more depth pertinent variables that can provide a more reasoned framework for an objective adjudication and management of such claims within the system of the Convention (section 3.2).

## 3.1  General principles

### 3.1.1  The state's margin of appreciation in striking a fair balance between competing interests

In dealing with the human rights claims of vulnerable individuals, the Court often examines whether a fair balance has been struck between the competing interests of the individual and of the community as a whole, and accords the state a margin of appreciation.[9] To mention but one example, the Court applied the balance test in the case of *O'Reilly and Others*, which concerned a joint application of various individuals complaining that their private life was being adversely affected by the almost unusable state of a communal road (i.e. a bus refused to drive on the road to collect a handicapped resident, some school children fell on the road, etc.). The Court reiterated that as far as the state's positive obligations are concerned:

> regard must be had to the fair balance that has to be struck between the competing interests of the individual and of the community as a whole and to the margin of appreciation enjoyed by states in determining the steps to be taken to ensure compliance with the Convention (Rees v. the United Kingdom judgment of 17 October 1986, Series A, no. 106, § 37).[10]

However, it should be remembered that the fair balance test has its origins and has extensively been applied in cases in which an act of interference can directly or indirectly be attributed to the state.[11] When this test is

---

9  *Botta* v. *Italy* [1998] no. 21439/93, para. 33; *Sentges* v. *the Netherlands* (dec.) [2003] no. 27677/02; *Molka* v. *Poland* (dec.) [2006] no. 56550/00; *Pentiacova and 48 Others* v. *Moldova* (dec.) [2005] no. 14462/03; *Zehnalova and Zehnal* v. *the Czech Republic* (dec.) [2002] no. 38621/97. Y. Arai-Takahashi, *The Margin of Appreciation Doctrine and the Principle of Proportionality in the Jurisprudence of the ECHR* (Antwerp: Intersentia, 2002); S. Greer, *The European Convention on Human Rights: Achievements, Problems and Prospects* (Cambridge: Cambridge University Press, 2006), pp. 222–230.

10  *O'Reilly and Others* v. *Ireland* (dec.) [2002] no. 54725/00.

11  For detailed discussion of the fair balance test, see Chapter 2, sections 2.1.1–3.

transposed to a different context in which the issue of interference cannot be said to be relevant in the human rights claims of vulnerable individuals, its conceptual and technical justifications have to be revisited.

Starting from the technical issue which is practically pertinent, it should be said that the state's margin of appreciation and the fair balance test have originally been connected to the legitimate aims of interference that are exhaustively listed in the second paragraph of Article 8, as seen for example in the case of *Rees* which is cited as an authority in the passage above.[12] Clearly, when there is no issue of interference, the legitimate aims of the second paragraph (i.e. the community's interests) cannot be applicable. It follows, as a result, that in the absence of specified community interests, the fair balance test is considered *in abstracto*. In addition, the state's margin of appreciation is never absolute, but is closely connected to the principle of proportionality.[13] However, since no legitimate counter-interests are specified in the examination of the human rights claims of vulnerable individuals, the principle of proportionality becomes disconnected from the operation of the state's margin of appreciation, a fact that adds to the uncertainty of the balance assessment.

It can thus be argued that the emphasis should not be on a fair balance test, which sits uneasily in contexts in which no prior acts of interference with human rights exist but, rather, on the democratic limit to the scope of the Convention that applies in such contexts. Accordingly, the pertinent question is whether the Court is able, having estimated the borders of this limit, to determine a legitimate scope for its intervention to impose positive obligations. This question is not confined to the circumstances of the individual applicant, but concerns, by virtue of the principle of equality, the overall management of analogous claims of other vulnerable individuals, not necessarily belonging to the same group.

The shift in emphasis on the justification of the Court's intervention, rather than on the absurd application of the state's margin, is more obvious when the protection of a vulnerable individual is examined in connection to the human rights interests of Articles 2 and 3, whose semi-absolute and absolute status, respectively, precludes the state's margin by definition. Thus, although a margin cannot arise for the state in relation to these two Articles, this does not automatically mean that positive obligations can be imposed by the European judge. This position is

---

12  *Rees* v. *the United Kingdom* [1986] no. 9532/81, para. 37. See also *Gaskin* v. *the United Kingdom* [1989] no. 10454/83, para. 42; *Hatton and Others* v. *the United Kingdom* [2003] no. 36022/97, para. 98. For informed criticism of the balance test, see C. Forder, 'Legal Protection under Article 8 ECHR: Marckx and Beyond' (1990) 37 (2) *NILR* 162–181, p. 179.

13  *Ruano Morcuende* v. *Spain* (dec.) [2005] no. 75287/01 (available in French only).

further reinforced by the fact that in most cases the examination of the claims of vulnerable individuals is exhausted at the admissibility level, which proves per se that the pertinent question is not the merits assessment of the fair balance test (which is exactly what the fair balance test is about in the established case-law), but rather to find and define the legitimate ground of the Court's intervention, starting from preliminary issues of the applicable scope of the Convention provisions (see discussion below, pp. 157–163).

The adversarial competition of the interests of an individual against those of the whole community, within which the balance test frames the examination of the human rights claims of vulnerable individuals, has also to be justified from a conceptual point of view, which is equally pertinent given that no legitimate aims are specified as community interests for which a balance is required. It is, therefore, asked how the individual and the community can ever be subjected to such a rigid division, as if the community is not an inclusive entity for all individuals. Does a vulnerable individual exist in isolation, or are there also other vulnerable individuals in the same or analogous circumstances? Are these individuals alone in the world or part of a nexus of a family that reveals additional individuals who are also affected? As the community is the whole set of individuals (conveniently illustrated as $A + \ldots + Z = AZ$), the 'fair' balance test regards, in essence, the interests of the vulnerable added together as $A + B + C\ldots$ ($A$, $B$ and $C$ being groups of various vulnerable individuals in need of human rights protection) against the interests of the rest $AZ - (A + B + C\ldots)$. A question, therefore, is addressed to the $[AZ - (A + B + C\ldots)]$ community of whether there can ever be an adversarial competition of interests in the protection of basic human rights. Of particular relevance to this question is the basic fact that human life is not static. A classic illustration of this starting point is the sphinx's riddle: 'What animal goes on four legs in the morning, two legs at noon, and three legs in the evening?' As Oedipus answered, that animal is man in various stages of age – in childhood crawling, in adulthood walking and in old age using a cane. Therefore, individuals from the $[AZ - (A + B + C\ldots)]$ community are unlikely to accept an actual competition with the interests of, say, disabled individuals, as disability comes also with age and illness or accident, and as a result a member of the $[AZ - (A + B + C\ldots)]$ community is very much a prospective member of the $(A + B + C\ldots)$ community. Also, informed individuals understand very well that various dramas and tragedies lie ahead during the course of life and, therefore, by not supporting the interests of the $(A + B + C\ldots)$ community, they would effectively undermine their own entitlement to basic human rights protection if they or their family members should come, whether it is likely or not, at some point to be classified among the minority part of the community. There is no need to say more on the conceptual justification of the balance test or the use in that test of the term 'community', which derives from the word 'common', describing the

essential characteristic of what a community is about, given that its technical merits have already been criticised above.

From the foregoing analysis, it can be concluded that it is not so much
a question that the state has a margin of appreciation in striking a balance
between 'competing' interests, but whether the Court is capable of estimating the borders of its democratic limit and determining accordingly
the exact point of its legitimate intervention to impose positive obligations
on the states vis-à-vis the human rights of vulnerable individuals.

### 3.1.2 The setting of a pan-European minimum

The human rights claim of one vulnerable individual usually reveals a
group of individuals with similar needs. Under the principle of equality, it
is expected that the European judge will contemplate the macro-level effect
of her/his decision before setting a precedent that could open the floodgates of litigation and impose a disproportionate burden on the states. The
Court has expressly anticipated such an effect in the case of *Sentges*, in
which a severely disabled individual complained of the state's refusal to
fund the cost for a sophisticated robotic arm. The same reasoning applied
in *Pentiacova and 48 Others*, in which a group of individuals suffering from
liver insufficiency claimed that the state should fund three, instead of two,
haemodialysis sessions per week. In both cases, the Court reflected that
'while it will apply the Convention to the concrete facts of this particular
case in accordance with Article 34, a decision issued in an individual case
will nevertheless at least to some extent establish a precedent.'[14]

Such anticipatory considerations can be traced as far back as the first case
on positive obligations in *Marckx*, in which the Court pointed out that 'it is
inevitable that the Court's decision will have effects extending beyond the
confines of this particular case', citing also the practice of the European
Court of Justice, which had recalled in its case-law that 'the practical consequences of any judicial decision must be carefully taken into account'.[15]

With regard to the retroactive effect of a Court's decision, the position
of the government deserves due attention. In particular, it was argued:

> if the Court were to find certain rules of Belgian law to be incompatible
> with the Convention, this would mean that these rules had been con-
> trary to the Convention since its entry into force in respect of Belgium
> (14 June 1955); the only way to escape such a conclusion would be to
> accept that the Convention's requirements had increased in the inter-
> vening period and to indicate the exact date of the change ...[16]

14 *Sentges* v. *the Netherlands* (dec.) [2003] no. 27677/02, and *Pentiacova and 48 Others* v.
 *Moldova* (dec.) [2005] no. 14462/03. See further discussion of these cases below.
15 *Marckx* v. *Belgium* [1979] no. 6833/74, para. 58.
16 Ibid.

If we apply this argument to the human rights claims of vulnerable individuals, the retroactive effect of the Court's decisions can be encountered in two instances: first, as additional or reinforced claims for harm (i.e. non-enjoyment of a human right) suffered prior to the new standards of law that often develop at the occasion of the applicant's case. Second, when claims concern lack of appropriate facilities in public or private buildings, a successful outcome could potentially require their alteration. In that regard, it is easy to note that the retroactivity of positive obligations further accentuates the quantitative element of the financial cost that already accrues from extending an isolated human right claim to those of a whole group of individuals, and which can suffice by itself as a ground for precluding positive obligations. Therefore, a clear and firm statement to 'indicate the exact date of the change' and the corresponding non-retroactivity of positive obligations may offer a pragmatic, forward-looking approach to controlling and managing the quantitative element so as to accommodate realistically, and hence legitimately, the protection of human rights of the vulnerable.

A parallel example of non-retroactivity when a positive obligation constitutes a development of the existing human rights standards has been seen in the case of *Goodwin*, in which the Court overruled its previous decision in *Rees*, opening the way for a new positive obligation of states to implement the recognition of gender change of post-operative transsexuals.[17] In examining the parallel claim for an award of damages under Article 41, the Court did not dispute that the applicant had suffered distress and anxiety in the past, but stressed that until that time similar issues were found to fall within the state's margin of appreciation. It went on to reason that the finding of violation, with the consequences which will ensue 'for the future', from introducing new European human rights standards at the very occasion of the applicant's case, constitutes in itself just satisfaction.[18] This insightful approach succeeds in reconciling the autonomous development of European human rights law that contemplates the future with the legitimate expectation of the state to understand the scope of its international liability in advance.

### 3.1.3  A multi-speed commitment of the states

In a supranational system such as that of the Convention, the uniform application of European human rights law is essential to its purpose. However, a slight (contextual) deviation from this prerequisite should be considered, as far as the positive obligations of the state towards the vulnerable are concerned. In such a context, and unlike any other, there is no question whether or not vulnerable individuals have to be protected.

17 As confirmed in *L.* v. *Lithuania* [2007] no. 27527/03, para. 56.
18 *Goodwin* v. *the United Kingdom* [2002] no. 28957/95, para. 120.

In practice, everything comes down to the limited availability of the state's resources, the prioritisation of their allocation and the financial disparities that exist between member states. Arguably, as no uniform standards can be imposed, it is difficult to see how a pan-European minimum of human rights protection can ever emerge.

To circumvent this reality, the Court considers uniform legal standards only in cases in which a general framework of protection has already been provided for at the domestic level. This has mostly been seen in the context of medical care whose relevance to human rights is established by the very nature of its business. The European judges may refrain from imposing a positive obligation on states to set up a healthcare system but, if such a system exists, they have shown themselves capable of reviewing minimum human rights standards therein. In that way, the initiative of allocating the state's resources remains with the representatives of the state but, subsequently, the judiciary is entitled to intervene to clarify human rights priorities.

Thus, although the Court starts from the point that it is unfortunate that in the contracting states many individuals do not have access to a full range of medical treatment because of lack of resources and, therefore, 'the Convention does not guarantee as such a right to free medical care', it leaves the possibility open when 'it is shown that the authorities of a Contracting State put an individual's life at risk through the denial of health care which they have undertaken to make available to the population generally.'[19] However, beyond this general position, there is an urgent need for specification and exactness under concrete principles that will shed more light on the human rights protection that can be afforded in such a context.

### 3.1.4 The existence of a direct and immediate link

In a number of cases, the Court has been called to determine the scope of Article 8, which accounts for the most positive obligations claims due to the broadness of the term 'private life', which has been connected, since early jurisprudence, to the development of one's personality.[20] In *Botta*, in

---

19 *Pentiacova and 48 Others* v. *Moldova* (dec.) [2005] no. 14462/03; *Nitecki* v. *Poland* (dec.) [2002] no. 65653/01; *Makuc and Others* v. *Slovenia* (dec.) [2007] no. 26828/06, para. 176; *Cyprus* v. *Turkey* [2001] no. 25781/94, para. 219; *Gheorghe* v. *Romania* (dec.) [2005] no. 19215/04. This statement is usually made under the heading of the right to life (Article 2 of the Convention), but also has a practical application under Article 8, whose 'private life' component has long been interpreted as covering a person's physical and psychological integrity, see, e.g., the parallel claim under Article 8 in *Pentiacova and 48 Others* v. *Moldova*.

20 For commentary and analysis of earlier case-law, see P. Duffy, 'The Protection of Privacy, Family Life and Other Rights under Article 8 of the European Convention on Human Rights' (1982) 2 *YbkEL* 191–238; L. Loucaides, *Essays on the Developing Law of Human Rights* (Dordrecht: Martinus Nijhoff, 1995), chapter 4: 'Personality and Privacy under the European Convention on Human Rights', pp. 83–107.

examining the disabled applicant's claim for access to a private beach at a holiday resort, the Court for the first time reasoned that 'a State has [positive] obligations of this type where it has found a direct and immediate link between the measures sought by an applicant and the latter's private and/ or family life.'[21] In applying this test to the facts of the case, it held that there was no violation of Article 8, because no such direct link could be deducted from 'interpersonal relations of such broad and indeterminate scope'.[22]

The 'direct and immediate link' has also been examined in subsequent cases involving disabled individuals,[23] but it remains unclear how much reliance is put on this test. Indeed, the finding of 'interpersonal relations of such broad and indeterminate scope' would suffice by itself to conclude that the applicant's claim could not fall within the scope of 'private life' under Article 8. A more informed explanation on the scope of Article 8 was given in *Zehnalova and Zehnal*, which concerned a disabled individual's claim (the first applicant) for access to a number of public and private buildings. The Court explained:

> Article 8 of the Convention cannot be taken to be generally applicable each time the first applicant's everyday life is disrupted; it applies only in exceptional cases where her lack of access to public buildings and buildings open to the public affects her life in such a way as to interfere with her right to personal development and her right to establish and develop relationships with other human beings and the outside world (see *Pretty* v. *the United Kingdom*, no. 2346/02, § 61, ECHR 2002-III).[24]

Accordingly, it might be better to rely first on the already established principles and conceptual understanding of the Convention provisions before inserting additional parameters that have yet to be clarified sufficiently.

Looked at more closely, the 'direct and immediate link' test emphasises calculating parameters of 'directness' and 'immediacy' that call for a careful evaluation and in-context application. It should be noted that the authorities cited in *Botta* to justify that test, namely *Airey*,[25] *X and Y*,[26] *Lopez Ostra*,[27] *Guerra and Others*,[28] concern circumstances in which there has been an act of interference by third parties for which the state is made indirectly

---

21 *Botta* v. *Italy* [1998] no. 21439/93, paras 33–34.
22 Ibid., para. 35.
23 See, e.g., *Marzari* v. *Italy* (dec.) [1999] no. 36448/97; *Maggiolini* v. *Italy* (dec.) [2000] no. 35800/97 (available in French only); *Sentges* v. *the Netherlands* (dec.) [2003] no. 27677/02; *Zehnalova and Zehnal* v. *the Czech Republic* (dec.) [2002] no. 38621/97; *Molka* v. *Poland* (dec.) [2006] no. 56550/00.
24 *Zehnalova and Zehnal* v. *the Czech Republic*, ibid.
25 *Airey* v. *Ireland* [1979] no. 6289/73.
26 *X and Y* v. *the Netherlands* [1985] no. 8978/80.
27 *Lopez Ostra* v. *Spain* [1994] no. 16798/90.
28 *Guerra and Others* v. *Italy* [1998] no. 14967/89.

responsible for not intervening to protect the injured party as required.[29] Clearly, when there is an issue of interference, the elements of 'directness' and/or 'immediacy' are usually established from the real consequences of that interference. As already stressed, the position is different when individuals claim assistance from the state due to their own personal vulnerability in order to be able to enjoy human rights.

The point that this sub-section intends to make is not against the application of the 'direct and immediate link' test as such, but about the exact context and stage of its judicial examination. An alternative (useful) application of that test could be in claims to protect the physical and psychological integrity of individuals under Article 8, including the right to life (Article 2). Such claims can be seen, for example, in the context of medical care, whose field involves by definition the physical and/or psychological integrity of individuals. Thus, in order to control the quantitative element involved in the number of potential claims, the European judge can use the 'direct and immediate link' test as an adjusting principle that manages the standard of remoteness so as to identify accordingly a legitimate scope for the Court's intervention.[30] This point is further explored below (p. 162).

### 3.1.5 The discrimination issue

The lack or insufficiency of protection of vulnerable individuals has always been argued as an indirect and, for some, direct form of discrimination that is tolerated in society. For the purposes of this study, which is exclusively concerned with the system of the Convention, the issue of discrimination will be approached from its legal and hence technical aspect, as the rights enshrined in the treaty give rise to real and binding results, albeit in the context of European international law. The discussion is restricted to concrete proposals, such as that made by Olivier De Schutter, who has argued that the anti-discriminatory right under Article 14 could be interpreted in such a way so that the requirement of non-discrimination includes an obligation to accommodate disabled people.[31] The commentator relies on the Court's decision in *Thlimmenos*, in which it was stated that '[t]he right not to be discriminated against in the enjoyment of the rights guaranteed under the Convention is also violated when States without an objective and reasonable justification fail to treat differently persons whose situations are significantly different.'[32] It is suggested that under that

---

29  *Botta* v. *Italy* [1998] no. 21439/93, para. 34.
30  See, e.g., the applicants' claims under Articles 2 and 8 in *Pentiacova and 48 Others* v. *Moldova* (dec.) [2005] no. 14462/03.
31  O. De Schutter, 'Reasonable Accommodations and Positive Obligations in the European Convention on Human Rights', in A. Lawson and C. Gooding (eds), *Disability Rights in Europe: From Theory to Practice* (Oxford: Hart, 2005), pp. 35–64, p. 52.
32  *Thlimmenos* v. *Greece* [2000] no. 34369/97, para. 44.

statement an apparently 'neutral measure' can now be seen as a disadvantage and therefore 'the failure to provide effective accommodation [of the needs of the disabled individuals] is a failure to create an exception.'[33]

Admittedly, this is a generous approach whose adoption has yet to be elaborated by judges and legal practitioners alike. However, some difficulties in the articulation of a more specific proposal have to be noted. First, it should be recalled that Article 14 is not free-standing but comes into play in conjunction with a substantive right.[34] This means in practice that if a positive obligation to protect a disabled individual cannot be imposed by a substantive right in the particular circumstances complained of, then the claim will be rejected as manifestly ill-founded under Article 35.3–4. Also, unlike the facts in *Thlimmenos*, we deal here with the question of the active protection of vulnerable individuals who are not able by themselves to enjoy human rights. In this respect, the existence of a prior act of interference, direct or indirect, that can be attributed to the state, as seen in that case, concerns an entirely different context (see discussion above, pp. 142–145). Accordingly, the Convention does not concern itself with 'neutral' measures but instead with issues of interference by a state or non-state actor, or with the non-enjoyment of human rights in circumstances of personal vulnerability. By way of example, where a railway station is built by the state without providing access for the disabled, the state cannot be said to have acted in order to interfere with the private life of disabled individuals. Equally, where the state's failure is seen as an omission, no issue of discrimination can arise if the state is not under a prior positive obligation to build appropriate access facilities for the disabled. This is also clear in the judgment of the case of *Zehnalova and Zehnal*, in which, in rejecting the applicants' Article 14 claim in conjunction with Article 8, the Court reiterated:

> Article 14 complements the other substantive provisions of the Convention and its Protocols. It has no independent existence, since it has effect solely in relation to the enjoyment of the rights and freedoms safeguarded by those provisions. Although the application of Article 14 does not presuppose a breach of those provisions – and to that extent it is autonomous – there can be no room for its application unless the facts of the case fall within the ambit of one or more of the latter (see, *mutatis mutandis*, *Botta*, ..., § 39).[35]

---

33 O. De Schutter, in A. Lawson and C. Gooding (eds), *Disability Rights in Europe: From Theory to Practice*, p. 53.

34 *Botta* v. *Italy* [1998] no. 21439/93, para. 39; *Thlimmenos* v. *Greece* [2000] no. 34369/97, para 40; *Zehnalova and Zehnal* v. *the Czech Republic* (dec.) [2002] no. 38621/97; *Molka* v. *Poland* (dec.) [2006] no. 56550/00.

35 *Zehnalova and Zehnal* v. *the Czech Republic*, ibid.; *Makuc and Others* v. *Slovenia* (dec.) [2007] no. 26828/06, paras 214–215; *Molka* v. *Poland*, ibid.

By contrast, the force of the discrimination argument is more pressing where it can be shown that the protection claimed has already been offered to other vulnerable individuals in similar contextual circumstances. In *Pentiacova and 48 Others*, a case arising in the context of medical care (discussed above, p. 149), it was additionally argued under Article 14 that other hospitals in the same city were better financed or that their patients received better treatment. The European judges showed themselves willing to consider this argument that was nevertheless rejected because the applicants failed to submit supporting evidence. This course of argumentation is promising and can either be transposed and added to the multi-speed commitment of the states, as discussed above (section 3.1.3), or be elaborated further under Article 14, given that this Article has an autonomous application irrespectively of whether there has been a breach of one of the substantive rights (provided, at least, that the facts of the case fall within its scope).[36] Having said that, it should be stressed that, in the examination of the state's positive obligations under a substantive right, the questions of what is a 'breach' and what is the 'scope' of that right, as seen in the passage quoted immediately above, are often two sides of the same coin. Thus, a better understanding of the underlying parameters that determine the imposition and extent of a positive obligation under the substantive rights will be valuable in appreciating the concurring potential of the anti-discriminatory provision of the Convention.

## 3.2 Moving towards an objective legal reasoning

Beyond the 'how often-cited' status of the general principles lie the details that determine the positive obligations of the state. The task in the following sections is to elaborate more on objective variables that already form part of the development of the relevant jurisprudence in order to make a coherent proposal for a workable framework within which the adjudication of the human rights claims of vulnerable individuals can be effectuated in a consistent and predictable manner.

### 3.2.1 *The positive obligation equation*

The positive obligations of the state to protect individuals who cannot enjoy human rights due to their own circumstances of personal vulnerability may only arise as an issue under paragraph 1 of the substantive rights of the Convention, whose provisions engage the active protection of human

---

36 *Botta* v. *Italy* [1998] no. 21439/93, paras 35 and 36. *Zehnalova and Zehnal* v. *the Czech Republic*, ibid.: 'unless the facts of the case fall within the ambit of one or more of the latter [Convention rights]', as quoted in the main text above and cited in note 35.

rights. Although most of the discussion revolves around the financial cost that is attached to implementing a positive obligation, it should be recalled that a financial cost for the protection of the Convention rights has always been presupposed.[37] Indeed, what is really debated is the size of that cost due to the underlying democratic limit of the Convention in circumstances where an act of interference by a private or public actor is absent (i.e. the non-interference context). Importantly, although the financial cost is a pertinent variable, it is not the only one or even the first to examine in the legal equation that determines the state's positive obligation. The calculation of a positive obligation under paragraph 1 of the Convention rights incorporates both qualitative and quantitative elements whose examination exhausts the former in priority. Thus, if we abbreviate for reasons of convenience – positive obligation (*po*), human right (*hr*) and financial cost (*fc*) – their combined effect can be reflected in a methodological equation that determines a positive obligation as follows:

$$po = \frac{hr}{fc}$$

In this equation, the qualitative element is the human right of the Convention that is relevant in the circumstances complained of, the quantitative element being the financial cost of the practical implementation of that right, which can vary from one claim to another, but is never *de minimis*. Although the quantitative element is a dominant variable, it is the qualitative element that reveals how pertinent the issue of human rights protection is or not under the circumstances; if it is not pertinent, the applicant's claim will not fall within the scope of a Convention right. As a human right cannot be engaged (*hr*=0), a positive obligation will not arise for the state, reflecting accordingly the equation that $po = 0/fc \Rightarrow po = 0$.

The qualitative element is assessed under its own quantified aspect, which is the degree of the negative consequences on the individual concerned. The examination of this element is pertinent on two levels: first, to determine the applicability of a human right (a threshold of severity of consequences operates), and, second, to reinforce the prospects of imposing a positive obligation with any increase in the measurement of the quantified unit (i.e. negative consequences) exceeding the actionable threshold. The latter is particularly pertinent when the applicant's claim will ultimately have to be compared with the meritorious claims of other vulnerable individuals and an informed decision will have to be made as to which interests should be protected. Accordingly, high thresholds of

---

37 See also note 8.

applicability of the Convention rights limit the flow of claims that will pass the admissibility stage, providing in that way a natural barrier that reduces the quantitative element of the financial cost that is associated with the number of potential applicants.

There are cases, however, in which the protection that one individual seeks from the state will also meet the needs of other vulnerable individuals without their having to pursue a separate action. In such a situation, the qualitative element does not solely concern the human right of one person/the applicant ($hr_1$), since there are other potential beneficiaries, whose needs ($hr_2$, $hr_3$, ..., $hr_n$) relate to the same human right interest ($hr_1 = hr_2 = ... = hr_n$). Such an instance will arise in a claim for disabled access to transport stations, which, although, in practical terms, is pursued by one disabled individual, the qualitative element can be evaluated by taking into account the same human rights needs of other individuals, given that their protection does not incur an extra financial cost. In such cases, the positive obligation equation $po = hr_1/fc_1$ reflects virtually $po = (hr_1 + hr_2 + ... + hr_n)/fc_1 = n\ hr/fc_1$.

The financial cost is a separate variable that merits additional examination in its own right, provided that the qualitative element has first been established (i.e. a human right can be engaged in the applicant's circumstances). In the positive obligation equation, the financial cost serves as the quantitative element that is set in inverse proportion ($1/fc$) as $po = hr/fc = hr \times 1/fc$ in order to reflect the democratic limit of the Convention and, conversely, its corresponding legitimacy to impose positive obligations when this cost is not disproportionate nor likely to impose an unrealistic and unnecessary burden on the state.

In the following, we analyse the qualitative and quantitative elements that determine the state's positive obligations with reference to specific examples from real claims, as pursued by various applicants before the Court.

### 3.2.1.1 The qualitative element

THE CONCEPTUAL QUESTION

It has already been discussed in the introductory chapter that the Convention rights can be given a holistic reading through the central concept of private life, which has been interpreted, since early jurisprudence, as the development of one's personality. Under this clarification, the scope of Article 8 targets the necessary conditions that allow the individual to develop their personality, or, put in negative terms (perhaps more accurately), those critical conditions without which the personality of an individual cannot develop. Such conditions have been recognised in Article 8 case-law as including 'the physical and psychological integrity' of a person and the possibility to 'develop relationships with other human beings'.[38] The former interest can additionally relate to Articles 2 and 3, whose scope involves higher degrees of negative consequences on one's physical and/or psychological integrity.

Before examining actionable degrees of negative consequences under Articles 2, 3 and 8, whose provisions are mostly relevant in the circumstances of vulnerable individuals, we should note that the holistic reading of these Articles offers a natural priority framework of human rights protection. Such a framework is best appreciated when applied to claims arising out of the same context. In the context of healthcare, for example, it can reasonably be maintained that the organisation of medical services has to adjust to the degree of seriousness of the patients' conditions. In addition, the higher the degree of consequences that reflects the scope of a Convention right, the smaller the number of potential applicants that can be implied in an isolated complaint, a fact that justifies a priority framework among the Convention rights from the angle of the quantitative variable also, that is the financial cost of protection which is calculated beyond the circumstances of the given applicant.

SETTING ACTIONABLE THRESHOLDS

Under the current structure of the Convention rights, the negative impact threshold of Articles 2 and 3 is higher than that of Article 8 because the preservation of life and freedom from torture and inhuman or degrading treatment reflect graver consequences for the person.[39] Aiming at some

38 See e.g., *Botta* v. *Italy* [1998] no. 21439/93; *Sentges* v. *the Netherlands* (dec.) [2003] no. 27677/02; *Molka* v. *Poland* (dec.) [2006] no. 56550/00; *Zehnalova and Zehnal* v. *the Czech Republic* (dec.) [2002] no. 38621/97; *Niemietz* v. *Germany* [1992] no. 13710/88. For commentary and analysis of early case-law, see Duffy, 'The Protection of Privacy, Family Life and Other Rights under Article 8 of the European Convention on Human Rights'; Loucaides, *Essays*. See also the submissions of both the government and the applicant in *Botta* v. *Italy* (dec.) [1996] no. 21439/93, which confirms the well-entrenched interpretation of 'private life' as the development of one's personality and the specification of the necessary condition to develop relationships with others, (a) per government: 'As to the substance of the case, the Government consider that the domain of private life is closely bound up with a person's emotional life. They emphasise that, according to the case-law of the Convention organs and academic opinion, the function of the protection of private life is to ensure that an individual has the opportunity to develop his own personality in relationships with other persons, without any external interference', (b) per applicant: 'According to the applicant, the heart of the concept is that the individual should have the opportunity to establish and develop relationships with other human beings, an opportunity which is essential for the development of personality'. In the judgment of *Botta* v. *Italy* [1998] no. 21439/93, para. 32, the Court provided a complete explanation that also includes the additional condition of one's physical and psychological integrity. See also discussion and the relevant quoted passage from the Court's judgment in Chapter 1, section 1.3.3, note 22.

39 *Soering* v. *United Kingdom* [1989] no. 14038/88, para. 88; *Pretty* v. *United Kingdom* [2002] no. 2346/02, paras 37, 49; *Estamirov and Others* v. *Russia* [2006] no. 60272/00, para. 98; *Salah Sheekh* v. *the Netherlands* [2007] no. 1948/04, para. 135; *Solomou and Others* v. *Turkey* [2008] no. 36832/97, para. 63.

general observations when various human rights claims are assessed within the same contextual situation, it can reasonably be said that the interconnected structure of Articles 2, 3 and 8 underlines a hierarchical relationship.[40] In practice, when an individual fails to engage Article 8, then higher claims under Articles 2 and 3 cannot possibly be pursued. A more in-depth look at the practice of the Court should be made in order to elaborate more on the scope of these Articles, whose applicability is organised through actionable thresholds reflecting respective degrees of the negative impact on the individuals. Article 8 should be examined first due to the lowest liability threshold involved.

ARTICLE 8

In the cases of *Botta, O'Reilly and Others* and *Zehnalova and Zehnal*, the disruption of private life and, as generously interpreted, one's development of personality did not reflect an impact that was of such severity as to bring the applicant's circumstances within the scope of Article 8. Although, admittedly, for the applicants such a response may sound legalistic since there was undeniably a negative impact on their circumstances (being 'unable to enjoy a normal social life' or 'to lead an active life while retaining her independence and dignity', as argued in *Botta* and *Zehnalova and Zehnal*, respectively), it is the function of law, and it is more so at the European level, to determine legal thresholds that correspond to various degrees of negative impact. For reasons of coherence, we note again the Court's clarification in *Zehnalova and Zehnal* that disruptions to personal life which affect the development of one's personality apply to exceptional circumstances.[41] Accordingly, the actionable degree of negative impact under Article 8 is assessed in negative terms, namely to identify the critical level at which an individual cannot develop their personality. Although this explanation entails a considerable degree of subjectivity, its value lies in securing an objective base upon which the parties' arguments will have to be placed and actionable thresholds can be flexibly fixed to adjust to the quantitative element also.

In *Marzari*, the Court has made clear that the claim of the severely disabled applicant for housing accommodation adequate to his condition has to be examined under an impact-based assessment. In particular, it considered that

---

40 Loucaides, *Essays*, chapter 9, sec. 3: 'Rights Subject to Special Protection', p. 182; F. Sudre, 'Droits Intangibles et/ou Droits Fondamentaux: Y a-t-il des Droits Prééminents dans la Convention Européenne des Droits de l'Homme?', in G. Cohen-Jonathan *et al.* (eds), *Liber Amicorum Marc-André Eissen* (Brussels: Bruylant, 1995), pp. 381–398; Greer, *The European Convention*, p. 266.

41 *Zehnalova and Zehnal* v. *the Czech Republic* (dec.) [2002] no. 38621/97. See the relevant passage from the Court's judgment quoted above, at page with note 24.

although Article 8 does not guarantee the right to have one's housing problem solved by the authorities, a refusal of the authorities to provide assistance in this respect to an individual suffering from a severe disease might in certain circumstances raise an issue under Article 8 of the Convention because of the impact of such refusal on the private life of the individual.[42]

In the absence of a negative impact of a rather high degree of severity, a prospective applicant will not manage to engage Article 8, meaning that their claim is not actionable in the eyes of law and, as a result, will be rejected as 'manifestly ill-founded' under Article 35.3–4. Otherwise, the general position is that stated by the Court in the *Makuc and Others* case that '[w]hile it is clearly desirable that every human being have a place where he or she can live in dignity and which he or she can call home, there are unfortunately in the Contracting States many persons who have no home'.[43]

By contrast, the situation is different when a homeless person becomes ill, as seen in the case of *O'Rourke*, in which the impact on the applicant from the alleged refusal of the state to offer accommodation had to be objectively assessed by medical experts in order to establish its severity.[44] Following a medical diagnosis that found the applicant with an asthmatic condition and chest infection, expert opinion advised for his urgent housing. However, the applicant's claim failed before the Court, as temporary accommodation had been made available, thereby discharging the state's positive obligations in these circumstances. Therefore, it can reasonably be said that a valid human rights claim for housing accommodation can be raised as long as the impact on the applicant's physical and/or psychological integrity has reached and maintains the level of severity contemplated by Article 8. The threshold of actionable level of severity under Article 8 can, of course, be flexibly set high, provided that it does not negate the very substance of that right and is lower than the applicable thresholds under Articles 2 and 3.

Importantly, it should be noted that in the cases of *Marzari* and *O'Rourke* the assessment of the level of severity in the applicants' circumstances has presupposed a core administrative process at the domestic level, which involves expert opinion in order to guarantee an objective base for the merits examination of various claims. In appropriate circumstances, the evidential proof also binds those claiming human rights protection. In *O'Reilly and Others* (discussed above, p. 146), the Court did not undertake an impact-based examination and merely observed the 'hardship and inconvenience' on the applicants. This kind of reasoning can be explained

---

42 *Marzari* v. *Italy* (dec.) [1999] no. 36448/97 (cited case omitted); *O'Rourke* v. *the United Kingdom* (dec.) [2001] no. 39022/97.
43 *Makuc and Others* v. *Slovenia* (dec.) [2007] no. 26828/06, para. 171 (cited case omitted).
44 *O'Rourke* v. *the United Kingdom* (dec.) [2001] no. 39022/97.

by the fact that the case concerned a joint application in which different people had submitted different claims, some of which cannot be said to concern the domain of human rights at all (e.g. some school children had to cease cycling to school because of the bad state of the communal road). As a result, little attention was paid to more worthwhile claims (e.g. the movement of disabled residents on that road). In *Zehnalova and Zehnal*, the burden of proving the negative impact from the lack of access to some buildings was passed on to the applicants, who, as the Court noted, failed to furnish persuasive evidence and give precise details of the alleged obstacles. Such a large number of buildings were cited that the Court particularly doubted the first applicant's need to visit them on a daily basis. This establishes a parallel link with *O'Reilly and Others* as to the imprecision and broadness of some claims that eventually undermine any effort to prima facie engage an arguable claim under Article 8.

ARTICLE 2

Claims under the right to life are usually straightforward, given the precision of its wording. Because of the irreversible consequences from the loss of human life and the basic truth that without life there can be no development of one's personality, the negative impact on individuals is undisputed in all circumstances. The role of expert opinion is equally vital here in assessing the seriousness of the applicant's condition, as can be seen for example in complaints about the suitability or adequacy of a medical treatment.[45]

The main difficulty with the Article 2 claims lies in the fact that a great range of events can ultimately have an impact on one's life, and hence the Court's pragmatism that 'the Convention does not guarantee as such a right to free medical care'.[46] In *Pentiacova and 48 Others*, the Court rejected the applicants' claim that the state was under a positive obligation to fund three haemodialysis sessions per week, not because the third haemodialysis was not required for their condition, which was already recognised as a 'very serious progressive disease', but due to the applicants' failure to adduce evidence that their lives had been put at risk. Because to suffer from a 'very serious progressive disease' establishes per se a risk to life without the need for further evidence, the other critical parameter is the 'progressiveness' of the disease that denotes a standard of remoteness. As suggested earlier above, it may be useful to insert the parameters of 'directness' and 'immediacy', explored elsewhere, in order to identify a manageable and hence legitimate scope for positive obligations in such a context.[47]

45 *Nitecki* v. *Poland* (dec.) [2002] no. 65653/01; *Pentiacova and 48 Others* v. *Moldova* (dec.) [2005] no. 14462/03; *Scialacqua* v. *Italy* (dec.) [1998] no. 34151/96.
46 *Makuc and Others* v. *Slovenia* (dec.) [2007] no. 26828/06, para. 177.
47 See discussion on the parameters of 'directness' and 'immediacy' at pages with notes 21–30 above.

If these parameters were considered in that case, the applicants would have to establish that their lives were put at an imminent risk.

Such underlying considerations can be seen in *Gheorghe*, in which a haemophiliac individual complained that the suspension of preventive medical treatment put his life at risk.[48] While recognising the gravity of the applicant's condition due to the irreversible nature of his illness, the Court, nevertheless, limited itself to a statement of regret about the lack of permanent and preventive medical treatment that could eventually slow down the disease. The parameter of an imminent risk to life clearly underlined the judicial decision, as the Court was satisfied that free medical treatment was available for bleeding incidents, which is the more advanced stage of the disease. According to the evidence submitted by the respondent state, the applicant had access to such treatment on the numerous occasions for which his hospitalisation was required.

From the case-law analysed above, it is clear that it is the quantitative element of financial cost, as reflected in the number of potential applicants, that restricts the scope of the state's positive obligations. It is suggested that the threshold of actionable level of severity under Article 2 is set high enough to cover the most severe impact whose determination can objectively be made by employing a standard of remoteness in examining the parameters of directness and immediacy of a risk to human life. In that way, the Court is able to control the number of potential applicants and identify accordingly a legitimate scope for its intervention in order to pronounce on the state's positive obligations.

ARTICLE 3

When a claim is brought under the heading of torture or inhuman and degrading treatment, as specified in Article 3, it must be shown that the negative impact involved in the applicant's circumstances reaches the requisite high degree of severity, as set by the Court due to the absolute nature of this provision. In *Zehnalova and Zehnal*, the Court has reiterated that 'ill-treatment must attain a minimum level of severity if it is to fall within the scope of Article 3 of the Convention',[49] that minimum being the high threshold of negative impact that has to be reached in the circumstances complained of and 'involves actual bodily injury or intense physical or mental suffering'.[50]

In order to secure an objective evaluation process, the Court takes into account various parameters, such as the duration of the treatment, its

---

48 *Gheorghe* v. *Romania* (dec.) [2005] no. 19215/04 (available in French only).
49 *Zehnalova and Zehnal* v. *the Czech Republic* (dec.) [2002] no. 38621/97. See, e.g., *L.* v. *Lithuania* [2007] no. 27527/03, para. 47; *Makuc and Others* v. *Slovenia* (dec.) [2007] no. 26828/06, para. 199; *O'Rourke* v. *the United Kingdom* (dec.) [2001] no. 39022/97.
50 *Pretty* v. *the United Kingdom* [2002] no. 2346/02, para. 52.

physical or mental effects and, in some cases, the sex, age and state of health of the applicant, etc.[51] The Article 3 jurisprudence suggests that the only successful complaints involving vulnerable individuals have been in cases in which an act of interference has, directly or indirectly, been attributed to the state, including special contexts in which individuals are legitimately put under the control of the state (e.g. in prisons, immigration centres).[52] An act of interference is in essence a prior 'treatment' within the meaning of Article 3, which is the basic determinative of the state's international liability under the Convention and, therefore, it amounts to a critical factor of considerable weight in assessing the threshold of impact under Article 3. Given that such a prior treatment is absent in the free-standing claims of vulnerable individuals for active assistance from the state, it is not difficult to see that Article 3 is likely to be engaged when extremely exceptional circumstances are present. A rare example from the jurisprudence is the euthanasia claim of the applicant in *Pretty*, which, nevertheless, failed due to conflict with Article 2.[53]

### 3.2.1.2 The quantitative element

In general, the financial cost of guaranteeing real, as opposed to theoretical, human rights has always been presupposed.[54] However, due to the limited availability of the state's resources, the economic disparity between member states and the democratic limit of the Convention in circumstances in which an act of interference is absent, the human rights protection of vulnerable individuals depends in inverse proportion on the financial cost involved.

The Court is particularly mindful of unwarranted implications of precedent that are likely to place a disproportionate burden on the states. As the individual who seizes the authority of the Court is just another member of a group of individuals with similar human rights needs, and that group is along with other groups, the vulnerable members of the society all having analogous claims for human rights protection, the judge has the arduous task of developing a reasoning of broad applicability due

---

51 *Makuc and Others* v. *Slovenia* (dec.) [2007] no. 26828/06, para. 199; *Costello-Roberts* v. *the United Kingdom* [1993] no. 13134/87, para. 30; *Ireland* v. *the United Kingdom* [1978] no. 5310/71, para. 162.

52 See, e.g., *Keenan* v. *the United Kingdom* [2001] no. 27229/95; *Price* v. *the United Kingdom* [2001] no. 33394/96; *Muisel* v. *France* [2002] no. 67263/01; *Farbtuhs* v. *Latvia* [2004] no. 4672/02; *Mubilanzila Mayeka and Kaniki Mitunga* v. *Belgium* [2006] no. 13178/03; *Mechenkov* v. *Russia* [2008] no. 35421/05. See also note 2 above and in Chapter 2, notes 239–242.

53 *Pretty* v. *the United Kingdom* [2002] no. 2346/02, para. 54.

54 See, e.g., *Botta* v. *Italy* [1998] no. 21439/93, para. 28: 'fulfilment by States of their domestic or international legislative or administrative obligations depended on a number of factors, in particular financial ones'. See also note 8.

to the principle of equality that binds the institution of justice. Accordingly, the financial cost involved can quantitatively be assessed by estimating the number of persons being in similar circumstances to the applicant.

It should be reiterated that the quantitative element is only examined when the qualitative element of the applicable scope of a human right can successfully be established in the applicant's circumstances. It has already been noted above (pp. 159–160) that the setting of actionable thresholds of human rights applicability leaves a degree of subjectivity that allows the judge some room for flexible adjustments that, consciously or unconsciously, involve quantitative calculations that may not be always expressly stated by reason of not undermining the parallel effort to establish the general conceptual understanding of a Convention right, which is of broad applicability and transcends context.

However, there comes a point that leaves no more room for manoeuvre in defining the scope of a human right without undermining its very substance or the certainty and coherence of the jurisprudence, and here the Court will have to make a separate statement on the scope of the state's positive obligation. As pointed out by the Court in *Zehnalova and Zehnal*, 'the sphere of State intervention [as protection] and the evolutive concept of private life do not always coincide with the more limited scope of the State's positive obligations.'[55] In that account, a wide margin of appreciation is accorded to the state to decide on the allocation of its limited resources and the assessment of the funds that are available to that group or other groups of vulnerable individuals.[56] The state's margin is, in essence, the manifestation of the democratic limit of the Convention when human rights protection (in the non-interference context) involves numbers that cannot legitimately be handled by the unelected judiciary, let alone the international judge. And, conversely, therefore, no such margin can be said to exist when a manageable number of individuals are involved.

In the following, we look at issues concerning human rights claims that correspond to small numbers of interested individuals, a possible exception to the democratic limit of the Convention, and the relevance of engaging private resources to cover the financial cost of protection.

## SMALL NUMBERS OF POTENTIAL APPLICANTS

When a small and/or otherwise manageable number of individuals are indirectly implied in the human rights claim of one isolated vulnerable individual (i.e. the pilot case), then the financial burden on the state from similar potential claims may not be disproportionate or impossible.

55  *Zehnalova and Zehnal* v. *the Czech Republic* (dec.) [2002] no. 38621/97.
56  *Sentges* v. *the Netherlands* (dec.) [2003] no. 27677/02; *Pentiacova and 48 Others* v. *Moldavia* (dec.) [2005] no. 14462/03; *Molka* v. *Poland* (dec.) [2006] no. 56550/00.

In such a case, the democratic limit does not apply, as small numbers of likely applicants preserve the legitimacy of the Convention, enabling the European judge to intervene and pronounce on the state's positive obligations.

In *L.*, the Court dealt with a complaint about the state's failure to guarantee a medical operation (i.e. gender-reassignment surgery) to a transsexual that would reflect his new sexual identity. Had such an operation been accessible to the applicant, he would be able to update his new sexual identity in the public certificates pursuant to the domestic law that applies to post-operative transsexuals and, thus, be spared the daily humiliation and the legal and social ostracism that have left him, as submitted, in a permanent state of depression with suicidal tendencies. Although it is established case-law under Article 8 that the new sexual identity of post-operative transsexuals must be recognised by the state,[57] the issue of funding the medical operation for a gender reassignment was dealt with in that case for the first time. Relying on the evidence before it, the Court found that, given the small number of potential applicants in similar conditions (some 50 people), the budgetary burden on the state would not be expected to be unduly heavy.[58] As a result, the Court was able to pronounce on the positive obligation of the state to guarantee the medical operation to the individual concerned. It also held that if this cannot be possible in view of the uncertainty of the medical expertise currently available at the domestic level, the positive obligation could be met by having the final stages of the necessary surgery performed abroad and financed, at least in part, by the state. The Court went as far as to make a conditional award of €40,000 in pecuniary damage if the state fails to discharge its positive obligation towards applicant, as defined in that judgment.[59]

Another point that needs particular attention is that, in order to evaluate the wider quantitative element involved, the Court relied on unofficial estimates pointing to some 50 people who are in similar circumstances. This information was held admissible due to the lack of counter-evidence from the state to challenge that number. It can reasonably be asserted, therefore, that the burden of evidential proof is always on the state, as it is the state that argues the disproportionate financial cost involved.[60]

57  *Goodwin* v. *the United Kingdom* [2002] no. 28957/95; *Van Kuck* v. *Germany* [2003] no. 35968/97; *Grant* v. *the United Kingdom* [2006] no. 32570/03; *L.* v. *Lithuania* [2007] no. 27527/03, para. 56.
58  *L.* v. *Lithuania*, ibid., para. 59.
59  Ibid., paras 58, 74.
60  A similar reasoning applied in *Goodwin* v. *the United Kingdom* [2002] no. 28957/95. In rejecting the state's margin of appreciation in that case, the Court noted that '[n]o concrete or substantial hardship or detriment to the public interest has indeed been demonstrated [by the state] as likely to flow from any change to the status of transsexuals', para. 91.

THE EXCEPTION TO THE DEMOCRATIC LIMIT

In the human rights claims of vulnerable individuals arising in a non-interference context, the democratic limit of the Convention that restricts the Court's intervention is subject to an exception when what is claimed is the very access to the democratic process or to the institution of justice that adjudicates on the applicable law of the state. From all claims for physical access to various buildings that the applicants pursued in *Zehnalova and Zehnal*, that regarding disabled access to a court is of particular importance, in that physical access to a court means basically access to legal rights. Unfortunately, this particular aspect of the applicants' complaint was not sufficiently stressed by their legal representation and it was largely buried by the unsuccessful effort to solve all problems of physical access of the disabled in one single petition.

The issue of physical access in such a context has recently been dealt with in the case of *Farcas*. The disabled applicant relied on Article 6, which guarantees effective access to a court, to claim that he had not been able to challenge by legal proceedings the termination of his employment contract and the official categorisation of his disability, because the court's entrance was not specially adapted to his needs. Unlike *Zehnalova and Zehnal*, the complaint about physical access to a court's building had been specific and separated from the other general claims. As a result, the Court was able to recognise that the impossibility of physical access to a court could constitute a hindrance in fact that was capable of contravening the Convention just like a legal impediment, unless effective access could be achieved by other means.[61] In the particular circumstances of the case, it was found that the right of access to a court had not been impaired, since national procedures allowed the initiation of court proceeding by post, a form of communication which the applicant had used in the past, including his petition before the European Court.

The exception to the democratic limit was equally pertinent in the case of *Molka*, in which the Court asked on its own initiative under the *jura novit curia* principle whether the lack of disabled access to a polling station during local elections (see the main claim under Article 3 of Protocol 1) was an issue within the scope of the concept of 'respect' for 'private life' set forth in Article 8. After a brief impact-based evaluation of the facts, the Court pointed to 'feelings of humiliation and distress capable of impinging on his personal autonomy, and thereby on the quality of his private life', reiterating also that 'the very essence of the Convention is respect for human dignity and human freedom'. In the end, the Court accorded a

---

61 *Farcas* v. *Romania* (dec.) [2010] no. 32596/04 (available in French only), paras 47 and 48, citing *Golder* v. *the United Kingdom* [1975] Series A, no. 18, para. 26. The Court also recognised that Article 8 (either alone or in combination with Article 14) may also be applicable in such circumstances, given the consequences that judicial decisions can have on the daily life of the applicant, para. 63.

wide margin of appreciation to the state in assessing the allocation of its limited resources. It failed, however, to make a direct connection to the least and most basic right of physical access to the democratic process, that is the very process from which the representatives of the people emerge, whose elected status entitles the state to a wide margin to appreciate and decide on the allocation of public funds for the protection of vulnerable individuals. Also, the point that the applicant's complaint concerned one isolated incident is not convincing if juxtaposed with the practical realities that the voting power of the demos is exercised after long intervals. Perhaps it would be more straightforward to reject the complaint on the same grounds as those reasoned under the examination of Article 3 of Protocol 1, in which it was found from the evidence submitted that the elections of the institutions in question did not form part of the respondent state's 'legislature' within the meaning of that Article and hence they were not the occasion that could qualify for an exception to the democratic limit of the Convention.[62]

## PASSING ON THE FINANCIAL COST TO PRIVATE PARTIES

Although a high financial cost associated with the active protection of vulnerable individuals may preclude positive obligations, the position is different where this cost is claimed from various private parties whose activities it is the responsibility of the state to regulate. In *Botta*, the positive obligation of the state was examined over its failure to implement and enforce a disabled access policy to seaside resorts that are administered by private companies. In *Zehnalova and Zehnal*, disabled access was also claimed in relation to some buildings in the private sector (e.g. cinemas, lawyers' offices, doctors' surgeries). It was argued that 'there were no budgetary implications for the State as the costs were borne by the owner.'[63] However, it should be pointed out that these arguments were never addressed because the Court had already found that the applicants' circumstances did not reach the applicable threshold of severity engaging a Convention right, that is the question of the qualitative element which arises in priority.

The possibility of enjoying human rights in venues controlled and administered by private interests is clearly legitimate, given that all activities form part of the organised society within which the individual interacts and develops their personality. However, although passing on the financial cost to private parties does not put a financial burden on the state, it may be unreasonable to expect that all private businesses have the financial resources to accommodate the human rights needs of vulnerable individuals. As pointed out above, a more realistic solution should be to restrict, as far as possible, the retroactive effect of any future decision of

62 *Molka v. Poland* (dec.) [2006] no. 56550/00.
63 *Zehnalova and Zehnal v. the Czech Republic* (dec.) [2002] no. 38621/97.

the Court which constitutes a development in the Convention's human rights standards.[64]

To elaborate further on which private businesses may be targeted, it can easily be recognised that, given the modern structures of urban environments, the use of public transport by persons with disabilities is necessary in order for them to establish relationships with other individuals and, by extension, to develop their personality. In many member states, public transport is controlled and administered by private interests. The main argument for the privatisation of public transport was to secure funding from private resources, rather than from the limited budget of the state. Within that policy framework, the financial burden on private companies that is incurred by making special access facilities available can be offset by passing on that cost to all customers using their services. Indeed, this may have been the underlying aim of the legislator in *Botta* and *Zehnalova and Zehnal* in enacting relevant law regulating disabled access standards in some activities of the private sector that, eventually, were not implemented in the end.[65] Therefore, it can reasonably be maintained that, incrementally at least, there is fair room for development to address the human rights interests of vulnerable individuals when the financial cost involved is borne by private parties.

### 3.2.2 The extent of human rights protection

A critical detail in the adjudication of claims of vulnerable individuals is that human rights protection is not often considered in absolute terms (whether to protect), but as to what extent protection has to be guaranteed to the individuals concerned (how much to protect). The issue of the extent of protection is present in those cases in which the state has already provided for the human rights of vulnerable individuals, either collectively by reference to the needs of a group of individuals or on a more narrow and personal basis. For example, in claims for medical treatment under Articles 2 or 8, as seen in *Pentiacova and 48 Others*, the state's assistance has already been provided, but not to the extent claimed by the applicants.[66] Expert opinion can be required to show whether what is claimed, or what is given, is what is required in the applicants' circumstances. It is also assumed, where appropriate, that income-based criteria are regulated by the state to assess the practical effect of vulnerability.

---

64 See discussion on the retroactive effect of newly developed human rights standards at page with note 17 above.

65 *Botta* v. *Italy* [1998] no. 21439/93, paras 17, 27; *Zehnalova and Zehnal* v. *the Czech Republic* (dec.) [2002] no. 38621/97, section B. 'Relevant domestic law', subsection 2, 'Building legislation'.

66 See also *Nitecki* v. *Poland* (dec.) [2002] no. 65653/01.

In *La Parola and Others*, the applicants (unemployed parents) claimed that the state had failed to guarantee their right to life and health in the form of assistance for the medical, housing and economic needs of their severely disabled child (the third applicant).[67] However, it was found in the examination of their claim under Article 8 (Article 2 held not relevant) that the applicants had already received economic assistance from the state in relation to the third applicant, and the amount offered was found to be of a level that effectively discharged the state's positive obligations under the minimum standards of the Convention.

Looked at more closely, it is argued that the claims of vulnerable individuals can be subjected to an objective assessment of evidential proof that can be required by all litigant parties. In *Sentges*, a severely disabled individual complained of the state's refusal to cover the cost of a robotic arm, but his claim failed because a wide margin of appreciation was accorded to the state to determine its budgetary priorities for the protection of disabled individuals as a whole. Beyond circular reasoning to the effect that the state should enjoy a margin of appreciation when it invokes its margin of appreciation in matters where a margin of appreciation is generally recognised, it is important to note that the Court relied also on the finding that the applicant had already received some assistance (i.e. an electric wheelchair with an adapted joystick) having met the applicable disability and income-based criteria. However, the Court's scrutiny could have been more intense in assessing whether the assistance offered was the protection required under the minimum requirements of the Convention. In that respect, evidential proof could be required from both parties in the dispute to substantiate their respective arguments. Thus, a question could be raised of whether the robotic arm claimed was the required protection in such circumstances. If we apply the positive obligation equation $po = hr/fc$ to this question, evidential proof is required to support the examination of both variables, namely the Convention right ($hr$) and the financial cost ($fc$) involved. As a human right (here, Article 8) entails a threshold of negative impact, the assistance already offered calls for a recalculation of the degree of severity that applies in the applicant's circumstances in order to assess the remaining impact. If that impact is still within the threshold of severity, and hence is still actionable, then the examination can continue to evaluate the financial cost that is attached to the human rights protection. From the expert evidence submitted by the applicant, it was shown that his dependence on the constant presence of carers would be reduced by at least one to three hours a day. In principle, it is for the Court to set the applicable thresholds of the Convention provisions and decide whether or not one to three hours' autonomy per day for a 100 per cent disabled individual is so critical for the development of his

---

67  *La Parola and Others* v. *Italy* (dec.) [2000] no. 39712/98 (available in French only).

personality, within the meaning of private life under Article 8.[68] If (and only if) this question can be answered in the affirmative, then the negative impact involved in the applicant's circumstances should be re-examined to subtract the assistance already offered, assessing anew whether the impact is still within the threshold of severity afforded by Article 8 so as to update the current status of the applicant.

In addition, the variable of the financial cost ( *fc*) needs also to be considered, and it is for the state to provide the requisite evidence to justify its margin of appreciation. From the information provided in the judicial decision, it appears in a report of the Health Care Insurance Board (*College voor zorgverzekeringen*) that between 150 and 400 persons a year might be eligible for a robotic arm whose individual cost would amount to €10,900 per year. As these numbers are clearly comparable to the 50 individuals and the conditional award of €40,000 for the cost of the medical operation that the Court considered in *L.*, it reasonably follows that it was the difference in the measurement of the quantified aspect of the qualitative element under Article 8, that is the negative impact exceeding the actionable threshold of severity under that Article, that justified the different outcome reached in *L.*

The emphasis upon an evidential base to guarantee an informed assessment of the human rights claims of vulnerable individuals is also evident in the Court's admissibility decision in *Marzari*. In examining the severely disabled applicant's claim for accommodation adequate to his disability, the Court found that the accommodation offered was dictated by expert opinion. Having evaluated the applicant's disability based on an impact assessment of his personal conditions, specific housing arrangements and alterations were made by the state's authorities in order to meet his needs. In that regard, the protection offered is not what is claimed but what is required according to the applicable thresholds of impact and the evaluation of objective evidence.

The difference between what is claimed, offered, required or can be required needs careful consideration by interested individuals who are contemplating bringing a complaint under the Convention's provisions. Claims with far-reaching implications upset both variables of the positive obligation equation, as seen in *Zehnalova and Zehnal* and *Molka* above. An informed approach could be to frame human rights claims more narrowly, targeting one public building, rather than all buildings, that could be specially designed to accommodate or coordinate the public service needs of vulnerable individuals. Alternative measures in the form of public service (including voting) through the Internet or postal service could also be argued.[69] In that way, a realistic claim of protection retains the legitimacy of the Court's review that guarantees a process to evaluate the direct (as opposed to

---

68 The young age of the applicant (17 years old) is one of the parameters against which the negative impact can be evaluated.

69 *Farcas* v. *Romania* (dec.) [2010] no. 32596/04, paras 50, 52.

broadly argued) negative impact on the applicant, thereby enabling the European judge to examine what the state has already offered or can offer, instead of rejecting the applicant's claim outright for reasons of impracticality and hence inadmissibility under the scope of the Convention's rights.

## 3.3 Conclusion

The adjudication of claims for state's assistance to those individuals who cannot actually enjoy certain human rights due to their own personal vulnerability reflects a growing recognition of human rights as freestanding constitutional imperatives. The broad scope of human rights in the system of the Convention requires a carefully crafted technical framework to provide a realistic, and hence legitimate, ground for the protection of the vulnerable.

The critical detail in the case of vulnerable individuals is that the protection of human rights often arises as an issue due to their own physical and/or mental conditions. As a result, their claims do not arise from acts of interference attributed directly or indirectly to the state, or from special circumstances in which individuals are legitimately put under the control of the state. Additionally, under the principle of equality, the protection of one vulnerable individual is viewed through its collective dimension to encompass all individuals having similar or analogous human rights needs. Cumulatively, the macro-level effect of one isolated human rights interest coupled with the absence of a causal link imposes a democratic limit on the Convention in relation to issues that can potentially put an unnecessary and impossible burden on the limited resources of the state. For this reason, the Convention accords the state a wide margin of appreciation to decide on such issues.

Conversely, the position is different when the human rights claims of vulnerable individuals will not impose a disproportionate burden on the state's resources. In that connection, the Court can legitimately intervene in order to define positive obligations for the state in appropriate circumstances. In these terms, the question of the human rights of the vulnerable is closely dependent on the legal methodology by which the Court can justify the legitimacy for its intervention.

A careful study of the relevant jurisprudence can reveal an added emphasis on the calculation of a whole string of closely interwoven parameters through which the state's margin is subjected to an objective assessment that is additionally supported by the inventive ability of the European judges to manage pan-European minima in areas in which the commitment of the contracting states cannot realistically be uniform. Building on this trend towards objectivity, a more sophisticated determination of the state's positive obligations can be guaranteed by carefully evaluating qualitative and quantitative elements that reflect the actionable thresholds engaging Convention rights and the corresponding financial cost that is attached to their practical realisation in concrete circum-stances. The combination of these elements allows flexible adjustments to be made between them, with the ultimate aim of securing an objective framework within which the human rights claims of vulnerable individuals can be examined. This aim is aided by, if not conditioned upon, a suffi-cient evidential proof that has to be provided by all parties in litigation to support their respective arguments. In short, what is proposed is a systemic approach to supersede ad hoc balances of competing interests that usually lead to uncertain results.

In spite of the fact that only a small number of cases are expected to succeed at the European level, the benefit of working with objective varia-bles lies in securing a methodological framework for intensified evidential proof within which the human rights claims of vulnerable individuals will have to be assessed. It is this process that locks the protection of human rights of the vulnerable as a permanent issue to be constantly examined through an evaluation system that the European judge can reasonably require to exist at the domestic level.

# 4 Access points of domestic implementation

The positive obligations of the state must produce a practical result.[1] This result is considered in relation to the subsidiary nature of the Convention, whose Article 35.1 requires that the aggrieved parties exhaust effective domestic remedies as a preliminary condition of admissibility.[2] Provided that the substantive content of positive obligations is reasonably certain, the direct result to which the whole system of the Convention is ultimately destined is the actual implementation of the state's obligations at the domestic level. For this purpose, an institutionalised procedural mechanism must be in place to provide access to interested individuals.

The Court's scrutiny necessarily extends to the state's procedural structures, which implement the substantive law of positive obligations. It is pertinent, therefore, to ask what the degree of this scrutiny should be. If 'the starting-point and subject matter of the international control is always the domestic proceedings', as reaffirmed by Wolfgang Strasser, then European scrutiny on procedural structures should be intensified accordingly.[3] A shift in emphasis on the domestic procedural mechanism will strengthen the subsidiary nature of the Convention and lead to a more effective management of its caseload.[4] However, this aim is undermined when the

---

1 *Airey* v. *Ireland* [1979] no. 6289/73, para. 24: 'The Convention is intended to guarantee not rights that are theoretical or illusory but rights that are practical and effective.'; *Marckx* v. *Belgium* [1979] no. 6833/74, para. 31; the *Belgian Linguistic* case [1968] nos 1474/62,..., 2126/64, paras 3 and 4; *Golder* v. *the United Kingdom* [1975] no. 4451/70, para. 35.

2 *Z and Others* v. *the United Kingdom* [2001] no. 29392/95, para. 103: 'It is fundamental to the machinery of protection established by the Convention that the national systems themselves provide redress for breaches of its provisions, the Court exerting its supervisory role subject to the principle of subsidiarity.'

3 W. Strasser, 'The Relationship Between Substantive and Procedural Rights Guaranteed by the European Convention on Human Rights', in F. Matscher and H. Petzold (eds), *Protecting Human Rights: The European Dimension, Studies in Honour of G.J. Wiarda* (Köln: Heymann, 1988), pp. 595–604, p. 595; R. Sapienza, 'Il Diritto ad un Ricorso Effettivo nella Convenzione Europea dei Diritti dell'Uomo' (2001) 2 *RDI* 271–297, p. 283: 'In general, it should be noted that the usual means of the international protection of rights are not the international recourse mechanism, but the recourse in the state's legal order.', (translation).

4 Strasser, ibid., pp. 603–604.

judicial control does not maintain the close relationship that exists between the substantive and procedural aspect of human rights protection. If procedural issues are not adequately addressed, how can 'a correct and just result' be achieved?[5] Strasser has proposed:

> all these difficulties could easily be avoided if the concentration on procedural issues was carried one step further and if it was made the primary field of examination in these cases, while the ruling on the substantive issue was reserved... [In this respect,] it would become necessary in each case to examine first of all whether the relevant procedural requirements had been met.[6]

This general proposal stresses the preliminary importance of the procedural aspect of human rights protection which has to be recognised accordingly in the order by which the judicial examination is structured. The need to intensify the review of procedural issues is also highlighted in the provisions of the new Protocol 14 and the various working papers and reports on the subject of the domestic implementation of the Convention's standards that are commissioned by the Council of Europe.[7]

Moving from general to specific applications, it is first expected that positive obligations should be reasonably certain as part of the substantive law of the Convention. Since the procedural aspect of human rights protection concerns procedural structures that implement the substantive law, the latter should exist and be clear in the first place. As already discussed in previous chapters, the substantive law of positive obligations involves a core content of protection where the applicant's circumstances relate to a wide context of private interactions in which known human rights issues exist. More specific measures of protection are also defined in the Convention's jurisprudence, taking account of comparative examples. The content of procedural structures can be examined in close relationship to the substantive content of protection that defines the duties of both private parties and public officials (in relation to the acts of the former). Where protection of human rights concerns direct assistance to vulnerable individuals, the substantive content of positive obligations develops incrementally, and hence the procedural issue may not, as yet, be pertinent, although a procedural framework for an objective evaluation of critical parameters is increasingly confirmed.

The task in this chapter is to identify and analyse domestic procedural structures that can serve as access points for the participation of interested

5  Ibid. p. 603.
6  Ibid.
7  See, e.g., Working Paper of the General Assembly of the Council of Europe, 'Implementation of Judgments of the European Court of Human Rights', AS/Jur (2005) 32 (9 June 2005).

individuals in the enforcement and implementation of positive obligations. What is looked at here is the European minimum procedural measure that is critical to the standard of effectiveness and, therefore, our analysis is not in principle affected by general statements on the state's margin of appreciation.[8] Preliminary issues have to be discussed first in relation to the general procedural framework of the Convention (section 4.1) and the basic working principles that are employed in the judicial examination (section 4.2). In recognition that the substantive law of positive obligations can ultimately be directed to the actual prevention of human rights violations, a first content of procedural structures concerns access points through which substantive positive obligations can be enforced before a violation occurs (section 4.3). In the event of a violation, such access should be provided to the victims in order to maintain a continuous and uniform compliance of the standards of human rights protection (section 4.4). For access points to be effective, the intermediate procedural stage of investigation must also exist, and be accessible and effective in its own right (section 4.5).

## 4.1 The general framework

### 4.1.1 Procedural rights of access

Procedural rights of access are mainly seen in the provisions of Articles 6 and 13.[9] Article 6 guarantees the right to a fair trial, while Article 13 requires an effective remedy in the event of a human rights violation, whether or not direct responsibility lies with a private or public actor. All procedural obligations fall within the scope of Article 13, which serves as *lex generalis*.[10] As a result, Article 13 is also examined in conjunction with Article 6 in claims for a violation of the latter.[11] The codification of a *lex specialis* in the form of Article 6 highlights access to a judicial tribunal as

---

8  See Sapienza, 'Il Diritto ad un Ricorso Effettivo nella Convenzione Europea dei Diritti dell'Uomo', p. 297, who points out that: '[p]robably, the idea ... according to which the states enjoy a margin of appreciation in the application of Article 13, does not practically make sense under the strict application of the doctrine. The interpretation of Article 13 can only be that of the Court due to the particular function of that Article.', (translation).

9  Procedural rights of a narrow contextual application also exist under Article 5.

10 Sapienza, 'Il Diritto ad un Ricorso Effettivo nella Convenzione Europea dei Diritti dell'Uomo', p. 281; J. Frowein, 'Art. 13 as a Growing Pillar of Convention Law', in P. Mahoney *et al.* (eds), *Protecting Human Rights: The European Perspective: Studies in Memory of Rolv Ryssdal* (Köln: Carl Heymanns Verlag, 2000), pp. 545–550, p. 550: 'Indeed, Art. 13 should be seen as one of the most important guarantees to make Convention law effective and real in the legal order of member states.'

11 See, e.g. *Kudla* v. *Poland* [2000] no. 30210/96; *Laghouati and Others* v. *Luxembourg* [2007] no. 33747/02 (industrial accidents) (available in French only). Sapienza, ibid., pp. 293–294.

the most fundamental remedy, for which specific standards of procedural fairness are prescribed.[12]

There are, however, important limits to the scope of Article 6, since its application is restricted to 'civil rights and obligations' that must *already* exist in the domestic legal system.[13] Although the right to a fair trial has an independent standing (i.e. not confined to human rights issues),[14] it only applies when there is a substantive base of a given right or obligation in the state's legal system. In *Z and Others*, the Court, in reversing its previous position in the *Osman* case, held that the failure of social care agents to protect children from abuse could not be challenged under Article 6. Whether or not the majority of judges have interpreted narrowly the substantive national law of liability in negligence, which binds all professionals but not, apparently, some civil servants, the Court's ruling has showed the limits of Article 6, at least, in relation to Article 13.[15] In the examination of Article 13, the Court reviewed the procedural standard of *ex post* compliance of positive obligations independently of the content of domestic law. The state was found in violation of Article 13 on the ground that the applicants did not have access to hold public officials accountable for their failure to implement the substantive content of positive obligations under the circumstances.

Because *ex post* compliance is an indispensable framework of law that is presupposed in all circumstances in which human rights standards are regulated, procedural guarantees are also examined under the substantive rights of the Convention.[16] The Court can examine the procedural aspect of the substantive right and may also repeat this examination under Article 13 (in conjunction with the substantive right) since the scope of Article 13 is 'broader',[17] or give a summary conclusion under Article 13 pointing to

12  C. Rouiller, 'L'Influence de l'Article 6 de la Convention Européenne des Droits de l'Homme sur les Procédures Nationales', in P. Mahoney *et al.* (eds), *Protecting Human Rights: The European Perspective: Studies in Memory of Rolv Ryssdal* (Köln: Carl Heymanns Verlag, 2000), pp. 1225–1233.

13  *Golder* v. *the United Kingdom* [1975] no. 4451/70.

14  See, e.g., *Le Compte, van Leuven and de Meyere* v. *Belgium* [1981] nos 6878/75; 7238/75; *Benthem* v. *Netherlands* [1985] no. 8848/80; *Deumeland* v. *Germany* [1986] no. 9384/81; *Editions Periscope* v. *France* [1992] no. 11760/85; *Menchinskaya* v. *Russia* [2009] no. 42454/02.

15  *Z and Others* v. *the United Kingdom* [2001] no. 29392/95, para. 103. See also the dissenting opinion of judge Rozakis joined by judge Palm and also the partly dissenting opinion of judge Thomassen joined by judges Casadevall and Kovler. For commentary, see A. Di Stefano, 'Public Authority Liability in Negligence e Diritto ad un Ricorso Effettivo nell' Ordinamento Britannico: Nota all Sentenza della Corte Europea dei Diritti dell'Uomo nel Caso Z e altri c. Regno Unito' (2003) 1 *RIDU* 97–127.

16  See, e.g., *Silih* v. *Slovenia* [2007] no. 71463/01, para. 103. D. Xenos, 'Asserting the Right to Life (Article 2, ECHR) in the Context of Industry' (2007) 8 *GLJ* 231–254, pp. 247–250; E. Dubout, 'La Proceduralisation des Obligations Relatives aux Droits Fondamentaux Substantiels par la Cour Européenne des Droits de l'Homme' (2007) 70 *RTDH* 397–425.

17  *Silih* v. *Slovenia*, ibid., para. 103; *Dink* v. *Turkey* [2010] nos 2668/07,…, 7124/09, para. 144.

the procedural examination under the substantive right.[18] Article 13 can also be examined in conjunction with a substantive right that has exclusively been found applicable under its procedural aspect for an *ex post* remedy (e.g. investigation).[19] Whether or not the applicant invokes Article 13 (or, where appropriate, Article 6), the Court can examine the procedural issue under the substantive right only.[20]

The examination and interpretation of procedural rights and obligations is not affected by the different meaning of the word '*recours*' and that of 'remedy' that appear in the French and English versions of Article 13, respectively, because procedural obligations are inherent in the structures of the institution of Law.[21]

The main question before us is how to connect the substantive law of the Convention that imposes specific positive obligations on the states with the procedural system of compliance at the domestic level.[22] In technical terms, this means that both the 'broad scope' of Article 13[23] and the inherent procedural aspects of the substantive rights have to be adjusted to the specific content of positive obligations.[24]

### 4.1.2 Actions against private parties and public officials (in relation to the acts of the former)

As with every provision of law, a positive obligation can only be a legal obligation if its content can be enforced by judicial action. Article 13 is the key

---

18  *M.C.* v. *Bulgaria* [2003] no. 9272/98.
19  *Menson and Others* v. *the United Kingdom* (dec.) [2003] no. 47916/99; *Dudnyk* v. *Ukraine* [2009] no. 17985/04. Cf. *Mantog* v. *Romania (No. 2)* [2007] no. 2893/02, para. 77.
20  *Makaratsis* v. *Greece* [2004] no. 50385/99; *Eugenia Lazar* v. *Romania* [2010] no. 32146/05.
21  P. Mertens, *Le Droit de Recours Effectif devant les Instances Nationales en cas de Violation d'un Droit de l'Homme* (Brussels: Editions de l'Université de Bruxelles, 1973), p. 68: 'In the strict sense, the term "recours" is understood as access to a right that constitutes an *action* (administrative or judicial), as opposed to an exception. The use of the term "*remedy*" in the English version indicates, however, that the word merits a broader interpretation.', (translation). Cf. J. Raymond, 'A Contribution to the Interpretation of Article 13 of the European Convention on Human Rights' (1980) 3 *HRR* 161–175, pp. 165–167.
22  W. Strasser, in F. Matscher and H. Petzold (eds), *Protecting Human Rights: The European Dimension, Studies in Honour of G.J. Wiarda*, who discusses the 'common aim and purpose' that links the procedural and substantive guarantees, p. 602.
23  See, e.g., *Mahmut Kaya* v. *Turkey* [2000] no. 22535/93, para. 126; *Kilinc and Others* v. *Turkey* [2005] no. 40145/98, para. 93; *Koku* v. *Turkey* [2005] no. 27305/95, para. 182; *Isayeva* v. *Russia* [2005] no. 57950/00, para. 227; *Musayev and Others* v. *Russia* [2007] nos 57941/00,..., 60403/00, para. 173.
24  Di Stefano, 'Public Authority Liability in Negligence e Diritto ad un Ricorso Effettivo nell' Ordinamento Britannico', p. 126. See also Sapienza, 'Il Diritto ad un Ricorso Effettivo nella Convenzione Europea dei Diritti dell'Uomo', p. 288, who points out: '[i]ndeed, the Court affirms that the interpretation of Article 13 should be in harmony with the rest of the Convention that has to be read as a whole.', (translation), commenting on the case of *Klass and Others* v. *Germany* [1978] no. 5029/71.

procedural provision that expressly requires the state to make available an effective remedy.[25] For a positive obligation to be guaranteed at the domestic level, this remedy should connect the Convention's substantive law of positive obligations to the possibility of challenging the direct and indirect responsibility of private parties and public officials, respectively. In particular, an action is expected to be available at the domestic level against:

1  The private party that directly causes the violation of a human right;[26] and/or
2  The public officials who are in charge of the actual implementation of the substantive positive obligations of the state in the given circumstances (e.g. against the acts of the private party).[27]

Early examples of such actions have been seen in the Article 13 jurisprudence on positive obligations, in the cases of *Plattform 'Arzte fur das Leben'*[28] and *Powell and Rayner*.[29] In the former case, the applicants challenged the effectiveness of the police officers' response to the threats of counter-demonstrators (the (2) type action). In the latter case, the applicants complained that the state did not provide access to challenge a private party, whose activities were causing continuous nuisance (the (1) type action).

Whether the aggrieved individual decides to pursue an action against the private party or the public officials, or both, it is necessary that their respective obligations are effectively regulated in advance. As seen in the discussion of known contexts of private interactions in Chapter 2, a substantive content of positive obligations must be implemented in the form of core administrative steps. Accordingly, an action to challenge the performance of public officials, who are in charge of the job of human rights protection, can only be possible or effective, if their negligent liability in

25  Article 13 is one of those provisions that justify positive obligations as 'inherent' in the system of the Convention. J. De Meyer, 'The Rights to Respect for Private and Family Life, Home and Communications in Relations Between Individuals, and the Resulting Obligations for States Parties to the Convention', in A.H. Robertson (ed.), *Privacy and Human Rights* (Manchester: Manchester University Press, 1973), pp. 255–275; Mertens, *Le Droit de Recours*; J. Frowein, in P. Mahoney *et al.* (eds), *Protecting Human Rights: The European Perspective: Studies in Memory of Rolv Ryssdal*, p. 546: 'It took unfortunately much too long until the importance of Art. 13 was recognised in Convention law.' See also discussion in Chapter 1, p. 21.

26  A public entity that is engaged in private activities (e.g. such as those of the private sector) is also a private party, a fact that is confirmed by the uniform regulation of standards of professional negligence. See, e.g., *Vo. v. France* [2004] no. 53924/00, para. 89; *Oneryildiz v. Turkey* [2004] no. 48939/99, para. 71; *Tatar v. Romania* [2009] no. 67021/01, para. 7 (available in French only); *Wojtas-Kaleta v. Poland* [2009] 20436/02, para. 42.

27  *Dink v. Turkey* [2010] nos 2668/07,…, 7124/09, para. 76 (available in French only).

28  *Plattform 'Arzte fur das Leben' v. Austria* [1988] no. 10126/82.

29  *Powell and Rayner v. the United Kingdom* [1990] no. 9310/81.

the state's law has previously been defined in connection to the administrative steps of which the substantive content of positive obligations consists.

Such a requirement has first been seen in the jurisprudence of negative obligations. In *Halford*, the Court had to deal with a complaint about the interception of telephone calls by state agents in the applicant's workplace. In such a setting, direct interference is attributed to state agents and has to be justified under the safeguards of paragraph 2 of Article 8. In that case, the state agents' interference could not be justified, because their practice had not been regulated 'in accordance with the law', as required by paragraph 2.[30] This conclusion reasonably influenced the examination of the parallel claim for an effective remedy. In finding a violation of Article 13, the Court reasoned that the applicant could not challenge the practice complained of or seek appropriate relief, since 'there was no provision in domestic law to regulate' the state agents' interference.[31]

Thus, whether public officials are involved in a direct interference or in the active protection of human rights, a remedy can only be possible if their conduct is subjected to prior regulations that define the practice and the standards of duty of care against which their liability can only arise. The same applies to the private parties that directly cause the violation of a human right.[32] Private parties can only be challenged if their human rights obligations and standards of conduct have been regulated in advance. In addition, in order for a remedy against private parties and public officials to be effective, it is necessary that the content of these regulations is linked to the substantive content of positive obligations in the circumstances concerned.

## 4.2 Basic working principles

### 4.2.1 Pursuing an 'arguable' human rights claim

The right to an effective remedy, within the meaning of Article 13, presupposes access to a legal claim as, without such access, no remedy can be guaranteed.[33] A critical parameter is the victim status, which is an

---

30  *Halford* v. *the United Kingdom* [1997] no. 20605/92, paras 50–51.

31  Ibid., para. 65; *Liberty and Others* v. *the United Kingdom* [2008] no. 58243/00, para. 73. See also discussion of *Makaratzis* v. *Greece* [2004] no. 50385/99 in Chapter 2, p. 124.

32  An exception to prior regulation may be considered in appropriate circumstances where the factual situation is (convincingly) argued as being entirely new (i.e. never seen before) and, therefore, a positive obligation may not arise if the element of knowledge of the need of protection cannot be established in the context concerned. See discussion in Chapter 2, p. 85, with reference to *Colak and Tsakiridis* v. *Germany* [2009] nos 77144/01 and 35493/05.

33  G. Malinverni, 'Variations sur un Thème encore Méconnu: l'Article 13 de la Convention Européenne des Droits de l'Homme' (1998) 33 *RTDH* 647–57, p. 650: 'No one can establish a violation before a national authority if he or she is not able to seize that authority in the first place.', (translation).

admissibility criterion at the European level (only). Under Article 34, petitions are accepted from an individual (including a collective body) who 'claims' to be a victim of a violation of a Convention right.[34] The Court has clarified that under Article 13 an effective remedy (e.g. access to court proceedings) must be made available at the domestic level to the individual who has an 'arguable' claim.[35] Because an 'arguable' human rights claim is not less open-ended, accessibility is reasonably dependent on the criteria qualifying a claim as arguable. In some cases, 'arguability' has been connected to the examination of whether a claim is manifestly ill-founded under Article 35.3–4 (former Article 27.2).[36] In the following, we analyse relevant jurisprudence in which Article 35.3–4 has been used to examine an arguable human rights claim.

In *Powell and Rayner* (arising from a complaint of nuisance, similar to that seen in *Hatton and Others*), the Court stated:

> [w]hatever threshold the Commission has set in its case-law for declaring claims "manifestly ill-founded" under [the former] Article 27 § 2 (art. 27–2) [current Article 35. 3–4], in principle it should set the same threshold in regard to the parallel notion of "arguability" under Article 13 (art. 13).[37]

At the admissibility stage, the Commission rejected the applicants' complaint under Article 8 after a merits evaluation of the facts, but allowed their claim for an effective remedy under Article 13. In examining Article 13 in conjunction with Article 8, the Court did not find a violation of Article 13, since no violation of Article 8 could be established after a detailed examination of the merits of the Article 8 claim under the

---

34  In appropriate circumstances, an individual can claim to be a potential victim of an act of interference, which has been initiated but has not caused any harm yet. See, e.g., *Klass and Others* v. *Germany* [1978] no. 5029/71; *Cambell and Cosans* v. *the United Kingdom* (dec.) [1980] Series B.42 (Commission's Report), p. 36; *Dudgeon* v. *the United Kingdom* [1981] no. 7525/76; *Norris* v. *Ireland* [1988] no. 10581/83; *Monnat* v. *Switzerland* [2006] no. 73604/01, para. 31.

35  See, e.g., *Boyle and Rice* v. *the United Kingdom* [1988] nos 9659/82, 9658/82, para. 54; *Powell and Rayner* v. *the United Kingdom* [1990] no. 9310/81, para. 31; *Z and Others* v. *the United Kingdom* [2001] no. 29392/95, para. 108; *Hatton and Others* v. *the United Kingdom* [2003] no. 36022/97, para. 137; *Gungor* v. *Turkey* [2005] no. 28290/95, para. 94. Sapienza, 'Il Diritto ad un Ricorso Effettivo nella Convenzione Europea dei Diritti dell'Uomo', pp. 290–293; Malinverni, 'Variations sur un Thème encore Méconnu: l'Article 13 de la Convention Européenne des Droits de l'Homme', p. 652; J. Frowein, in P. Mahoney *et al.* (eds), *Protecting Human Rights: The European Perspective: Studies in Memory of Rolv Ryssdal*, p. 546.

36  Frowein, ibid., p. 549.

37  *Powell and Rayner* v. *the United Kingdom* [1990] no. 9310/81, para. 33; *Boyle and Rice* v. *the United Kingdom* [1988] nos 9659/82, 9658/82, para. 54: 'on the ordinary meaning of the words, it is difficult to conceive how a claim that is "manifestly ill-founded" can nevertheless be "arguable", and vice versa'.

heading of Article 13. However, when access to an arguable human rights claim is conditioned on a merits evaluation of the facts, the following paradox applies: as a merits evaluation needs a process to evaluate the merits of the applicant's claim, how then can access to such an evaluation process be dependent on the prior evaluation of the merits involved?

The applicants' complaint for access to an action in nuisance against the private party – the private corporation controlling Heathrow airport – had revolved around the exclusionary effect of section 76(1) of the Civil Aviation Act 1982. The effect of that statutory law was addressed subsequently in the similar case of *Hatton and Others*. Unlike *Powell and Rayner*, the Court found a violation of Article 13, despite its opposite conclusion under Article 8. The issue of arguability was presumed by the mere fact that Article 8 was applicable for a merits evaluation. Applicability of Article 8 was grounded on the undisputed fact, by all litigant parties, that the applicants' private and family life was adversely affected when the private corporation extended its business activities during the night.

As discussed in Chapter 2, the state is under a positive obligation to regulate appropriate human rights standards in the operation of industrial activities. If interested individuals are not able to access a court in order to assert their human rights and, by extension, to challenge the current practices, then positive obligations exist only in the sphere of theory. To the extent that a core content of protection is already due for implementation, access to a legal claim to enforce that content is not excluded because of the occasional decision of the state agents to pursue a legitimate interference through the activities of a private party. In addition, acts of interference that are directly or indirectly attributed to the state, as seen in *Powell and Rayner* and *Hatton and Others*, can only be justified on the condition that the relevant criteria and safeguards of paragraph 2 limitations can be met. Therefore, can there ever be an argument that the evaluation process of justifying an interference is not open to a challenge by the party whose human rights interests are compromised?

From the foregoing analysis, it can reasonably be said that the arguability of a human rights claim that conditions access to a court to assert an effective remedy cannot be dependent on a prior merits evaluation for the purposes of Articles 13 and 35.3–4. This assertion conforms also to the new paragraph b) of Article 35.3, inserted by Protocol 14, which provides for a 'significant disadvantage' threshold as an additional criterion of admissibility, but expressly specifies also that 'no case may be rejected on this ground which has not been duly considered by a domestic tribunal.'

From this general position, an exception should be made where the examination of Article 35.3–4 concerns the determination of the very scope of a Convention right. In such a situation, the Court, before deciding whether the applicant's claim falls within the scope of a Convention right, has first to deal with the preliminary strategic issue of what the scope of that right should be. Such issues are expected to be more relevant in new claims, as opposed to well-known contexts of private interactions.[38] Examples include the totality of the cases discussed in Chapter 3 (direct assistance to vulnerable individuals),[39] unless the applicant's claim targets an entrenched process of evaluation of objective parameters that are pertinent to the examination of the scope of a Convention right.

### 4.2.2 Legal aid

Individuals increasingly claim legal aid as an intermediate procedural right to access the main human rights claim.[40] In this subsection, we highlight some cases which have successfully been asserted before the Court in order to include legal aid as one of the factors determining effective access to a remedy in appropriate circumstances.

In the text of the Convention, the right to legal aid is expressly guaranteed to those charged with a criminal offence (Article 6.3.(c)). The expansion of legal aid beyond this narrow context has been prompted by the case of *Airey*, in which the Court confirmed the inherent nature of the state's positive obligations in the system of the Convention (see also discussion in Chapter 1).[41] The applicant complained about the prohibitive cost of litigation that prevented her from petitioning for judicial separation against her abusive husband. In such a context, the state is under a positive obligation to regulate various aspects of private relationships that have human rights implications.[42] In order to ensure that the Convention does not contain rights that are theoretical or illusory but rights that are practical and effective, the content of positive obligations is examined in relation to those critical details that determine the standard of effectiveness.[43] In this respect, it is for the state to 'make this means [judicial separation] of protection effectively accessible, when appropriate, to anyone who may wish to have recourse thereto.'[44] In that case, although judicial separation was generally

---

38 In *Kontrova* v. *Slovakia* [2007] no. 7510/04, paras 43–44, 61, the Court found that the applicant rightly did not exhaust domestic remedies that could possibly develop the domestic law at the occasion of her very case. The European judges accepted the applicant's argument that her complaint should not be the occasion to achieve avant-garde interpretations. Clearly, the existence of a well-known context (violence against the person/protection from the police) has influenced the Court's decision in favour of the applicant. See also the admissibility decision of 13 June 2006, no. 7510/04.

39 See, e.g., *Zehnalova and Zehnal* v. *the Czech Republic* (dec.) [2002] no. 38621/97, in which the European judges, in rejecting the applicants' Article 13 claim, simply stated that 'the applicants have not raised any arguable grievances in the instant case as the Court has held that all their complaints are either incompatible *ratione materiae* with the provisions of the Convention or inadmissible as being manifestly ill-founded.'

40 M. Puéchavy, 'L'Accès Égal de Tous à la Justice' (2003) 19 *AtA* 743–765.

41 *Airey* v. *Ireland* [1979] no. 6289/73, para. 32.

42 Ibid., para. 25.

43 Ibid., para. 24; *Marckx* v. *Belgium* [1979] no. 6833/74, para. 31.

44 *Airey* v. *Ireland*, ibid., para 33.

available, it was not practically accessible to the applicant due to the high cost of litigation. Consequently, the state was found in a violation of its positive obligation under Article 8.

An additional violation was found under Article 6, which has a more expansive and independent application, since its scope is not confined to human rights issues. Although domestic law did not oblige an individual to be legally represented in such disputes, the Court found that a lay person could not have a fair trial due to the complexity of the legal issues that had to be examined.[45]

Another important case is *Steel and Morris*, in which there has been a violation of Articles 6 and 10 in circumstances where legal aid was not made available to defendants in defamation proceedings. The applicants had been sued by a powerful multinational corporation following the publication and distribution of a leaflet, which was highly critical of its practices. It is important to note that the applicants were, at the time, on part-time employment and had to rely on income-support benefits. The underlying consideration in that case was whether people of lower income have the right to free expression to criticise the practices of powerful corporations without being intimidated by litigation proceedings. In examining whether legal aid was necessary for a fair hearing (under Article 6), and by extension, for the effectiveness of the right to free expression (under Article 10), the Court looked at:

1   The importance of what is at stake for the applicant in the proceedings.
2   The complexity of the relevant law and procedure.[46]
3   The applicant's capacity to represent him or herself effectively.[47]

In general, the adjudication of defamation disputes is based on straight-forward rules of evidence of facts and/or value judgements. In that case, the Court found *inter alia* that '[t]he factual case which the applicants had to prove was highly complex, involving 40,000 pages of documentary evidence and 130 oral witnesses, including a number of experts dealing with a range of scientific questions, such as nutrition, diet, degenerative disease and food safety.'[48] As a result, the denial of legal aid had meant the applicants could not present their case effectively to the domestic court and had led to an unacceptable inequality of arms with the private corporation, in a violation of Article 6.1. A parallel violation was easily found under Article

45  Ibid., para. 24. See also the discrimination argument in the dissenting opinion of judge Evrigenis.
46  Cf. *Nicholas* v. *Cyprus* (dec.) [2000] no. 37371/97. Puéchavy, 'L'Accès Égal de Tous à la Justice', p. 756.
47  *Steel and Morris* v. *the United Kingdom* [2005] no. 68416/01, para. 61, citing, among other cases, *Airey* v. *Ireland* [1979] no. 6289/73, para. 26.
48  Ibid., paras 65–66.

10, as the right to free expression was inextricably linked to the fairness of legal proceedings.[49]

The context of freedom of expression needs particular attention, in that expression is infinite and, no matter how difficult the evidential proof may be, if there is no reasonable judgement in the expression complained of, clearly, general conclusions on legal aid are not readily obvious, as compared, for example, to divorce proceedings. To point *obiter* here, perhaps the focus of the legal examination in *Steel and Morris* should not have been on the issue of legal aid, but on the level of evidential burden that had to be discharged by ordinary members of the public before the domestic judge. The Court, having recognised that 'the limits of acceptable criticism are wider in the case of such companies', expressly stressed 'the legitimate and important role that campaign groups can play in stimulating public discussion' on the activities of powerful multinational companies.[50] In such contextual circumstances, it can be argued that individuals should not bear a high evidential burden at the domestic level, in which case the issue of legal aid becomes less pertinent when complexity is reduced or vanishes. In that respect, it may be more useful to prescribe a reasonable standard of evidential proof, rather than trying to impose legal aid to defend the indefensible.

### 4.2.3 Assessing the domestic standards

Access to a remedy or an arguable human rights claim is ultimately assessed against the standard of effectiveness.[51] It is argued that access can only be effective if the domestic judge applies the substance of law of the Convention. The domestic implementation of European human rights standards may be organised differently between states with a monist and dualist tradition to suit different presumptions of accommodating a state's sovereignty within the framework of international law. These issues, however, are mainly for domestic consumption and do not affect the technical analysis, since what counts in every case is the status of human rights and the level of their protection in the domestic legal order.[52]

The following discussion of the case-law aims to show that the effectiveness of access is closely dependent on the appreciation of the substantive law of the Convention at the domestic level.

49  Ibid., para. 95.
50  Ibid., paras 94–95.
51  Article 13: 'The right to an effective remedy'. The standard of effectiveness cuts across the whole spectrum of the Convention, see, e.g., *Artico* v. *Italy* [1980] no. 6694/74, para. 33; *Bendersky* v. *Ukraine* [2007] no. 22750/02, para. 42. Sapienza, 'Il Diritto ad un Ricorso Effettivo nella Convenzione Europea dei Diritti dell'Uomo', p. 297.
52  Sapienza, ibid., pp. 278–279.

### 4.2.3.1 Narrower scope of human rights

When access to a human rights claim is generally available at the domestic level, it pays to check whether the scope of the domestic human rights conforms to that of the rights enshrined in the Convention. The critical importance of this parameter has been seen in the case of *Lopez-Ostra*, in which the applicant complained under Article 8 that the state failed in its positive obligation to protect her private and family life from nuisance and environmental pollution caused by a nearby private plant. In the domestic court proceedings, it was found that the negative impact on the applicant's health was not so serious as to infringe the fundamental rights that were recognised in the state's constitution.[53] The different outcome reached by the Court in assessing the same impact meant that the applicable scope of the domestic right was more restrictive than that under Article 8. Thus, although access to a human rights claim was provided, the applicable narrower scope of the domestic right meant that such access could not be effective under the pan-European minimum standard of the Convention.

Another such case is *Kontrova*, where the applicant complained about the failure of the police to prevent the killing of her children. At the domestic level, the applicant did not claim compensation for non-monetary losses. In examining the state's preliminary objection under Article 35.1 for non-exhaustion of domestic remedies, the Court noted that the applicant's action would have to be brought under the heading of personal integrity, which was not sufficiently certain in both domestic theory and practice. Thus, a rejection of the state's preliminary objections under Article 35.1 reasonably influences the conclusion of violation of Article 13 for lack of an effective remedy at the domestic level.[54]

### 4.2.3.2 Less rigorous evaluative principles

The implementation of positive obligations is also dependent on the legal principles that the domestic court uses to evaluate the substantive content of positive obligations. If less rigorous evaluative principles are employed, then the institutional framework, through which the substantive law is determined and implemented in practice, is bound to conflict with the

---

53 *Lopez Ostra* v. *Spain* [1994] no. 16798/90, paras 11 and 15. See also *Gillan and Quinton* v. *the United Kingdom* [2010] no. 4158/05, para. 63; *Oluic* v. *Croatia* [2010] no. 61260/08, paras 39 and 62.

54 *Kontrova* v. Slovakia [2007] no. 7510/04, para. 65: 'From the above finding as regards the Government's preliminary objection [under Article 35.1], it follows that the action for protection of personal integrity provided her with no such remedy [under Article 13]. Accordingly, there has been a breach of Article 13 of the Convention, taken together with Article 2.' Cf. Raymond, 'A Contribution to the Interpretation of Article 13 of the European Convention on Human Rights', p. 167.

standards of the Convention.[55] Therefore, it is pertinent to ask, as did Strasser, 'how the substantive issue can be correctly assessed by the Convention organs without prior domestic proceedings having been conducted in accordance with the requirements of the Convention.'[56]

In the discussion of *Hatton and Others* in Chapter 2, we have seen that the Court closely examined the content and scope of various investigations and studies that the state authorities had undertaken in order to assess the negative impact on individuals from the expansion of activities of a private corporation. In the current chapter, we revisit this assessment process from the angle of Article 13. As noted above (p. 181), access to a remedy was not possible in that case, because of the wide scope of an exclusionary statutory provision. Although the exclusionary effect of the domestic law would suffice per se to find a violation of Article 13, the Court also examined the standards of judicial review that applied to the acts or omissions of the public administration (e.g. to grant permission for the extension of a private party's commercial activities). Under the standards of judicial review that applied at the time, an administrative practice with human rights implications would only be unlawful if it was unreasonable or irrational.[57] Since these standards did not conform with the lower threshold of liability of the Convention's proportionality principle, it meant that access to a remedy could not be effective, and therefore, there had been a violation of Article 13.

In addition, it should be recalled that there was a strong dissent by a considerable number of judges on the effectiveness of the actual investigations and studies that were carried out at the domestic level. Without counting the points of their criticism, it is only asked here how the balance between competing interests was found to be fair when the competent public administration did not assess the negative impact on individuals in accordance with the high threshold of necessity of the interference (i.e. pressing social need) so as to be proportionate, in both means and ends, to the legitimate aim pursued. Judicial review is not simply about access to a legal remedy. The evaluative principles and standards of judicial review are the alpha and omega of every administrative framework that educate public officials on how to carry out their duties and, therefore, they describe the standards of justification for public projects and the corresponding standards of professional negligence.

55 See Lord Steyn's opinion in *R.* v. *Secretary for Home Department ex parte Daly* [2001] UKHJ 26.
56 W. Strasser, in F. Matscher and H. Petzold (eds), *Protecting Human Rights: The European Dimension, Studies in Honour of G.J. Wiarda*, p. 603.
57 Following the Human Rights Act 1998 (which took effect in 2000), the principle of proportionality is used in the judicial review of human rights claims, see, e.g., *R* v. *Secretary of State for the Home Department ex parte Daly* [2001] UKHJ 26.

Moreover, it was argued by the government that the investigations and studies by the public authorities had taken account of the interests of the individuals concerned. In parallel with the analysis of *Lopez-Ostra* above, it is asked what were these interests against which the negative impact assessment was made at the domestic level, given that the right to respect for private and family life, within the meaning of Article 8, clearly did not exist in the state's legal system at the time (prior to the Human Rights Act 1998)? If Article 8 or another similar version of it were available, the first reaction of public officials would be to protect the human rights interests of the applicants. Thus, when a proposal for a legitimate interference is made, the public officials in charge of planning decisions (including the judges who become ultimately part of the process) should be able to understand the impact threshold of Article 8 and decide accordingly as to whether to accept or reject that proposal.[58]

Despite the deficiencies in the assessment of the negative impact by the public administration in *Hatton and Others*, the Grand Chamber did not find a violation of Article 8. It can be said that the Court took a pragmatic approach and, 'in substance', justice has been done in the end.[59] If this is a serious position, then we need to ask again whether the Court is a fourth instance forum or has a constitutional function of a subsidiary nature. If the latter applies, then Strasser's proposal that (critical) procedural issues need to be examined first can be extended, by conditioning the examination of the substantive issue on a prior finding of non-violation of the procedural aspect of the state's obligations. By no means do we argue that the Court's task was easy in that case, but there is an urgent need for a firm approach on procedural issues. It may be said that even if the domestic system had been in conformity with the procedural and substantive standards of the Convention, the examination of the particular facts could have reached the same outcome (i.e. non-violation of Article 8). There is, however, a fundamental difference between decisions made on ad hoc balances and those aiming at structural and procedural changes. An added emphasis on the latter puts pressure on the states to bring their systems in line with the standards of the Convention, thereby reducing substantially the need for international petition.

## 4.3 *Ex ante* accessibility

The substance of positive obligations regards the active protection of human rights. The content of the active protection is ultimately determined against the aim of the actual prevention of human rights violations.[60]

---

58 For the scope of private life under Article 8, see, e.g., *Lopez Ostra* v. *Spain* [1994] no. 16798/90, para. 51; *Fadeyeva* v. *Russia* [2006] no. 55723/00, para. 88. For the relevant quoted passages, see Chapter 2, note 151.

59 *Hatton and Others* v. *the United Kingdom* [2003] no. 36022/97, para. 129.

60 See discussion in Chapter 2, Section 2.3.2: 'The scope of protection: the underlying aim of prevention of human rights violations'.

In that respect, access to a legal claim to enforce the domestic implementation of positive obligations should be guaranteed before a violation of a human right occurs.

In examining the states' preliminary objection on the alleged failure of the applicant to exhaust domestic remedies, as required under Article 35.1,[61] the Court constantly stresses that

> the purpose of Article 35 is to afford the Contracting States the opportunity of preventing or putting right the violations alleged against them before those allegations are submitted to the Convention institutions... That rule is based on the assumption, reflected in Article 13 of the Convention – with which it has close affinity – that there is an effective remedy available in respect of the alleged breach in the domestic system.[62]

In the first sentence of that passage, it is noted that the state should be given 'the opportunity of *preventing*' an alleged violation. The combining effect of Articles 35 and 13, as is also emphasised in that passage, means that there should be access to enforce the standards of law before harm is sustained. In that respect, the requirement for an effective remedy under Article 13 should be examined in relation to the question of whether access to a claim to prevent a human rights violation was available before a national judge, even if the European review takes place *ex post facto* due to the admissibility criterion of victim status under Article 34.

Such access should be available against the private parties who have failed to comply with the regulated standards that condition the operation of their activities (i.e. the substantive content of positive obligations). In the civil law context, an action of prevention is not often possible if the applicant has not already suffered any damage. Therefore, interested individuals should be able to challenge the private parties through access to the decision-making process of the public administration that controls and supervises the private parties' activities. In addition, the professional duty of care of public officials, who are in charge of the specific tasks of control of private parties, should also be open to challenge.

---

61  Mertens, *Le Droit de Recours*, p. 90, with further references to the practice of international law in footnote 178.

62  *Selmouni* v. *France* [1999] no. 25803/94 paras 74–77; *D.* v. *the United Kingdom* [1997] no. 30240/96, para. 83; *Slimani* v. *France* [2004] no. 57671/00, para. 38; *Trocellier* v. *France* (dec.) [2006] no. 75725/01, para. 4; *Murillo Saldias and Others* v. *Spain* (dec.) [2006] no. 76973/01 (available in French only). When the effective remedy is examined as part of the procedural aspect of a substantive right, the close link between Articles 13 and 35.1 applies equally between the procedural aspect of the substantive right and Article 35.1. See, e.g., *Opuz* v. *Turkey* [2009] no. 33401/02, paras 150–152, 205.

Access to claim prevention of a human rights violation has also been facilitated by a relaxation of the victim criterion.[63] Notable is the case of the state's negative obligations, whose main application is an act of prior interference. In such a context, the *locus standi* of potential victims has long been recognised when an act of interference has been launched but has yet to cause any harm.[64] The relaxation of the victim criterion has reasonably been greater for positive obligations, since their substance concerns the active protection of human rights and, therefore, the state is required to step in within various contexts of private interactions in order to regulate and implement specific measures of protection.

The issue of access to claim prevention is particularly pressing when the physical and psychological integrity of individuals is at stake.[65] Before going on to discuss the exact stages at which such access should be available (i.e. the access points), we briefly note a case that reaffirms prevention as the underlying aim of positive obligations (see also discussion in Chapter 2, pp. 97–100). In *Kontrova*, the state was found in violation of Article 2 because of the failure of police officers to protect the applicant's children from being harmed from another individual (her husband). Although the public officials involved were criminally prosecuted at the domestic level in order to attribute their individual responsibility, this *ex post* remedy did not suffice to discharge the state's positive obligations under Article 2 or the requirements under Article 13. The same would apply even if the applicant were able to bring a parallel action against the private party who directly caused the human rights violation, since it was the reactive response of the state agents that was challenged before the Court. This case shows that the Court adopts a stricter approach to the state's positive obligations when there is a known context of private interactions (i.e. violence against the person) in which its agents are required to implement a core content of operational measures (entrenched in the jurisprudence) as obligations of means.[66]

---

63 *Monnat* v. *Switzerland* [2006] no. 73604/01, para. 31: 'the word "victim" in the context of Article 34 of the Convention denotes the person directly affected by the act or omission in issue, the existence of a violation of the Convention being conceivable even in the absence of prejudice [...]. An applicant cannot claim to be a "victim" within the meaning of Article 34 of the Convention unless he is or has been directly affected by the act or omission in question or runs the risk of being directly affected by it', (cited case omitted).

64 See, e.g., *Klass and Others* v. *Germany* [1978] no. 5029/71; *Dudgeon* v. *the United Kingdom.*

65 See, e.g., *Osman* v. *the United Kingdom* [1998] no. 23452/94, para. 115; *Guerra and Others* v. *Italy* [1998] no. 14967/89; *L.C.B.* v. *the United Kingdom* [1998] no. 23413/94, para. 36; *Z and Others* v. *United Kingdom* [2001] no. 29392/95; *Oneryildiz* v. *Turkey* [2004] no. 48939/99; *Bacila* v. *Romania* [2010] no. 19234/04 (available in French only).

66 *Kontrova* v. *Slovakia* [2007] no. 7510/04, paras 53, 61, 63, 65; *Hajduova* v. *Slovakia* [2010] no. 2660/03, para. 50.

In practical terms, the possibility of access can more clearly be seen in circumstances where the issue of human rights protection is not as spontane-
ous and immediate as in the cases of violence against the person. By way of
example, in the activities of industry, systematic failures in human rights
standards are regularly observed. Access to claim prevention of a human
rights violation has been seen in the pre-emptive action of the applicants in
the case of *Taskin and Others*. It should be remembered from previous discussion that the case concerned the decision of the state authorities to allow
the operation of a private gold mine, despite evidence of expert opinion
pointing to serious risks to the health and safety of the local population in
the future. In examining a prevention claim under Article 8, the Court has
reiterated the state's positive obligations in the form of a 'decision-making
process [that] must firstly involve appropriate investigations and studies in
order to allow them [public authorities] to predict and evaluate in advance
the effects of those activities'.[67] 'Appropriate investigations' and 'studies' are
core administrative steps that define the substantive content of the state's
positive obligations in the context of industry. Since it is these steps that
guarantee the practical issue of prevention, their individual standards of
effectiveness should be safeguarded by a complementary procedural framework that provides access to enforce their implementation.[68] As the Court
pointed out: 'the individuals concerned must also be able to appeal to the
[domestic] courts against any decision, act or omission where they consider
that their interests or their comments have not been given sufficient weight
in the decision-making process'.[69]

Accordingly, whether or not the state's procedural obligations under a
substantive Convention right (taken alone or in conjunction with Article
13) are reviewed at the European level *ex post facto*,[70] or pre-emptively for
pragmatic reasons (i.e. in defiance of the victim criterion, as in *Taskin and
Others*),[71] their content and standards of effectiveness can be evaluated
against the underlying aim of prevention of human rights violations.
In that respect, the state's liability is defined by the possibility of access
to challenge at the domestic level, before an actual violation occurs, the

---

67  *Taskin and Others* v. *Turkey* [2004] no. 46117/99, para. 116.
68  Xenos, 'Asserting the Right to Life (Article 2, ECHR) in the Context of Industry', pp.
    252–253.
69  *Taskin and Others* v. *Turkey* [2004] no. 46117/99, para. 116 (cited case omitted). See also
    *Tatar* v. *Romania* [2009] no. 67021/01, paras 20–23, 88, 101.
70  See also *Alekseyev* v. *Russia* [2010] nos 4916/07,…, 14599/09, para. 99 (concerning a
    counter-demonstration), in which the Court found a violation of Article 13 on the ground
    that it was 'not persuaded that the judicial remedy available to the applicant [at the
    domestic level] in the present case, which was of a *post-hoc* character, could have provided
    adequate redress in respect of the alleged violations of the Convention.'
71  See also *Ockan and Others* v. *Turkey* [2006] no. 46771/99 (available in French only); *Lemke*
    v. *Turkey* [2007] no. 17381/02 (available in French only). Cf. the government's submis-
    sion in *Taskin and Others* [2004] no. 46117/99, para. 104.

activities of private parties, as well as the performance of public officials during the core stages of administrative control of which the substantive content of the state's positive obligations consists in the context concerned.

## 4.4 *Ex post* accessibility

The absolute minimum form of access to enforce the substance of positive obligations concerns the *ex post* remedial action. In the system of the Convention, the *ex post* enforcement of human rights standards is expressly required as an effective remedy under Article 13 or implied under the provisions of the substantive rights.[72] A remedy to the aggrieved party is often synonymous to a sanction that is imposed on the private parties and public officials for their responsibility in the human rights violation. The task in this section is to discuss the principal forms of the *ex post* remedy that is required in various contexts of private interactions.

### 4.4.1 *Compensation*

Compensation is the most basic remedy and, very often, the only available when a human rights violation occurs. Complaints usually find their way before the Court, because an award of compensation could not effectively be claimed or agreed at the domestic level.[73] Compensation serves both as a remedy and as a sanction in the *ex post* procedural system of the state's positive obligations.

A claim for compensation will usually target the private party that is directly responsible for the human rights violation, especially in narrow circumstances that go beyond the regulatory and supervisory power of the state. Such will be the case when a violation of a human right is caused by medical negligence. The Court clarified in *Powell* that a contracting state cannot be called to account for its positive obligations where high professional standards have been regulated in the context of medical care.[74] An error of judgement on the part of a health professional, or even a negligent co-ordination among health professionals in the treatment of a patient, does not give rise to the responsibility of the state authorities.[75] In that case, the applicant was able to obtain compensation through a civil law action in which professional negligence could be established. Accordingly, the substantive positive obligation of the state to regulate professional standards of duty of care in a known context of private interactions

---

72  See, e.g., *Osman* v. *the United Kingdom* [1998] no. 23452/94, para. 115; *Oneryildiz* v. *Turkey* [2002] (Chamber) no. 48939/99, para. 91.

73  *Kyriakides* v. *Cyprus* [2008] no. 39058/05; *Biruk* v. *Lithuania* [2008] no. 23373/03; *Oyal* v. *Turkey* [2010] no. 4864/05. See also the separate opinion of judge Sajó.

74  *Powell* v. *the United Kingdom* (dec.) [2000] 45305/99.

75  See also *Byrzykowski* v. *Poland* [2006] no. 11562/05, para. 104.

is implemented (and accordingly discharged) by making available an *ex post* procedure to enforce the regulated standards. A finding of negligence in the execution of a duty of care gives rise to a right to compensation, which constitutes a remedy under the *ex post* framework of implementation of the state's positive obligations.

An additional claim for compensation will have to be available against the failures of public officials in circumstances where their involvement is expected to be more active and direct. In *Z and Others*, the state was found in violation of Article 3 because of various failures of its social services department to prevent the abuse of children of whom its agents have assumed supervision (discussed in Chapter 2, p. 113). In that case, compensation was claimed for the negligence (acts and omissions) of public officials, whose duty of care was assessed against obligations of means. It was, therefore, insufficient that the applicants were free to sue the third party (i.e. the perpetrator) or to obtain some general form of compensation from the Criminal Injuries Compensation Scheme.[76] A similar issue arose in *Kontrova*, in which the applicant petitioned before the Court because compensation was not available against the failure of the police to perform well-established duties of protection when her family members were threatened by another individual.

### 4.4.2 Sanctions

In some circumstances, compensation may not suffice by itself to implement effectively the state's positive obligations.[77] For this reason, there should be in addition adequate sanctions, which must be regulated in advance and made accessible to the victims of human rights violations or be pursued by the state's authorities on their own motion. In the following, we examine the type and intensity of sanctions in relation to the appropriate deterrent effect that has to be guaranteed in various contexts of private interactions.

#### 4.4.2.1 Violence against the person

The regulation of sanctions in the context of violence against the person must guarantee an appropriate deterrent effect, which has to be commensurate with the severity of consequences involved. For this reason, criminal law exists as a specific branch of law that is aided by a criminal

---

76 *Z and Others* v. *the United Kingdom* [2001] no. 29392/95, para. 111. Di Stefano, 'Public Authority Liability in Negligence e Diritto ad un Ricorso Effettivo nell' Ordinamento Britannico', p. 113. See also *Osman* v. *the United Kingdom* [1998] no. 23452/94, paras 145, 153.

77 *Oneryildiz* v. *Turkey* [2004] no. 48939/99, para. 147: 'The nature of the right at stake has implications for the type of remedy which the State is required to provide under Article 13. Where violations of the rights enshrined in Article 2 are alleged, compensation for pecuniary and non-pecuniary damage should in principle be possible as part of the range of redress available', (cited cases omitted).

justice system for the management of criminal (jailed) sentences. In the Court's jurisprudence, the intensity of sanctions has mainly been examined in relation to Articles 2, 3 and 8 whose scope reflects different degrees of negative impact on the physical integrity of the person.

In the introduction of this study, we have particularly noted the case of *X and Y* from the early period of application of positive obligations. In that case, the main question of the state's positive obligations towards the victim of a rape was whether criminal law sanctions had been regulated and enforcement procedures were made available to the applicants. Starting from the general (non-context-related) point that under Article 8 '[r]ecourse to the criminal law is not necessarily the only answer',[78] the Court specified that as far as cases where fundamental values and essential aspects of private life are at stake (i.e. higher degrees of negative impact), protection by the civil law is insufficient. It reasoned that '[e]ffective deterrence is indispensable in this area and it can be achieved only by criminal-law provisions'.[79] In short, in the context of violence against the person, it is hardly argued that criminal law sanctions are not the appropriate remedy.

Equally pertinent is the question of sanctions on public officials, whose salaried task is to actively protect individuals from threats of violence of which they have knowledge, as seen in the cases of *Osman* and *Z and Others*. In both these cases, the intensity of sanctions on public officials was not considered, as all energy was consumed on the basic question of whether the public officials, implementing the state's positive obligations on the ground, should be subjected to standards of professional negligence.[80] Subsequently, in *Kontrova*, it was no longer disputed that police officers could be liable for failing to protect, within the scope of

---

78  *X and Y* v. *the Netherlands* [1985] no. 8978/80, para. 24.

79  Ibid., para. 27. See also *M.C.* v. *Bulgaria* [2003] no. 9272/98, para. 153: 'the Court considers that States have a positive obligation inherent in Articles 3 and 8 of the Convention to enact criminal-law provisions effectively punishing rape and to apply them in practice through effective investigation and prosecution.' See also *Jankovic* v. *Croatia* [2009] no. 38478/05, para. 47.

80  In *Z and Others* v. *the United Kingdom* [2001] no. 29392/95, para. 106, the applicants' lawyers argued: 'accountability of public officials, central to both Articles 3 and 13, required a right of access to a court whereby the individual could hold the responsible officials to account in adversarial proceedings and obtain an enforceable order for compensation if the claim was substantiated. The wording of Article 13 also prohibited the creation of immunities for public officials and any such immunity must be regarded as contrary to the object and purpose of the Convention.' Di Stefano, 'Public Authority Liability in Negligence e Diritto ad un Ricorso Effettivo nell' Ordinamento Britannico', p. 113. For a study of the domestic standards of liability in negligence that apply to public officials following the judgments of *Osman* v. *the United Kingdom* and *Z and Others* v. *the United Kingdom*, see J. Wright, *Tort Law and Human Rights: The Impact of the ECHR on English Law* (Oxford: Hart, 2001); R. Drabble, J. Maurci, and T. Buley, *Local Authorities and Human Rights* (Oxford: Oxford University Press, 2004).

their powers, the applicant's children. In that case, criminal proceedings against the officers involved were still pending at the domestic level. As a result, the applicant's effort to target the state's response with regard to the individual responsibility of police officers was held premature under Article 35.1.[81]

In some circumstances, the question of the appropriate deterrent effect that expresses the pan-European minimum standard may also relate to lower sanctions than those prescribed in domestic law. Such an issue may arise indirectly in cases of extradition of suspects or convicted criminals to states in which the standards of human rights do not conform to those of the Convention.[82] In the case of *Soering*, the state was found in violation of Article 3 for its decision to extradite (stayed awaiting the Court's ruling) the applicant in a non-Council of Europe country in order to face criminal charges of a death penalty potential. It was held that the death-row phenomenon associated with these proceedings would expose the applicant to a real risk of treatment whose negative impact reaches the threshold of Article 3. As the status of Article 3 under the Convention is absolute, the deterrent effect of that treatment cannot be justified.[83] Within the geopolitical area of the Council of Europe, such issues are confined to a very small number of member states that have still not abolished the death penalty in peacetime.[84]

### 4.4.2.2 Medical negligence

Due to the special nature of its business, the entire context of medical care is subject to judicial scrutiny for violations of human rights.[85] Whether or not the state is under an obligation to set up a healthcare system to protect individuals in circumstances of personal vulnerability, as discussed in Chapter 3, it is expected that, as a minimum, the state should go beyond the ethical

81  *Kontrova* v. *Slovakia* (dec.) [2006] no. 7510/04.
82  *Sellem* v. *Italy* [2009] no. 12584/08.
83  *Soering* v. *the United Kingdom* [1989] no. 14038/88. P. Vegleris, ' "Twenty Years" experience of the Convention and Future Prospects', in A.H. Robertson (ed.), *Privacy and Human Rights* (Manchester: Manchester University Press, 1973), pp. 341–412, p. 350; P. van Dijk, ' "Positive Obligations" Implied in the European Convention on Human Rights: Are the States Still the "Masters" of the Convention?', in M. Castermans-Holleman *et al.* (eds), *The Role of the Nation-State in the 21st Century: Human Rights, International Organisations and Foreign Policy: Essays in Honour of Peter Baehr* (The Hague: Kluwer Law International, 1998), pp. 17–33, p. 27. *Al–Saadoon & Mufdhi* v. *the United Kingdom* [2010] no. 61498/08, para. 120.
84  *Ocalan* v. *Turkey* [2005] no. 46221/99. See also the partly concurring, partly dissenting opinion of judge Garlicki and the reference to international developments, especially those of the International Criminal Court, para. 6 of his opinion.
85  *Bendersky* v. *Ukraine* [2007] no. 22750/02, para. 59: 'Consequently, any assault of a medical nature, even minor, on the physical integrity constitutes an interference with the right to respect for private life' (translation), (available in French only).

demands of the Hippocratic oath to regulate professional standards of competence and due diligence in the law of negligence.[86] Such standards are expected to apply uniformly to practitioners of both the public and private sector.[87] Where a medical practitioner breaches their duty of care, as defined in the regulated standards, the determination of the appropriate level of sanctions is influenced by the degree of negative impact involved (i.e. the harm sustained by the patient or the loss of chance to be cured), the degree of medical negligence, and the unintentional nature of the act or omission complained of (to distinguish from intentional violence against the person).

In the case of *Calvelli and Ciglio*, the Court had to decide whether involuntary homicide that resulted from medical error should attract criminal charges. It was held that the minimum deterrent effect for the *ex post* procedural implementation of positive obligations is not that of criminal sanctions due to the involuntary character of the offence.[88] The majority of the European judges were satisfied that a civil action was available to the victim from which a friendly settlement was reached. As a result, the applicants could no longer claim to be 'victims' within the meaning of Article 34.[89] In such circumstances, due weight is given to the fact that the violation of a human right is often caused by an error of professional judgement in circumstances of pressure.[90] Also, as a matter of general policy, the over-regulation of the medical care system could perceivably lead to defensive practices that may run counter to the purpose of the whole system. By contrast, where a standardised medical procedure is involved that leaves no margin for error, the breach in the duty of care will be regarded as *gross* negligence. In such a case, a greater sanction than compensation or disciplinary measure should be envisaged in order to ensure due compliance of professional standards through a punishment of an appropriate deterrent effect.

In addition, it has been argued that civil action may not have the appropriate technical resources to evaluate any higher degree of negligence that may been involved under the circumstances. As pointed out in the dissenting opinion of judge Rozakis, joined by judge Bonello in *Calvelli and Ciglio*:

> it is difficult for one to accept that respect for the right to life, as provided for by Article 2, can, in principle, be satisfied by proceedings,

86  *Powell* v. *the United Kingdom* (dec.) [2000] 45305/99; *Calvelli and Ciglio* v. *Italy* [2002] no. 32967/96, paras 48–51; *Vo.* v. *France* [2004] no. 53924/00, paras 89–90; *Byrzykowski* v. *Poland* [2006] no. 11562/05, paras 104–105; *G.N. and Others v. Italy* [2009] no. 43134/05, paras 80–81.

87  *Powell* v. *the United Kingdom*, ibid.; *Calvelli and Ciglio* v. *Italy*, ibid., para. 49; *Dvoracek and Dvorackova* v. *Slovakia* [2009] no. 30754/04, para. 65.

88  *Calvelli and Ciglio* v. *Italy*, ibid., para. 51.

89  Ibid., paras 54–55.

90  *Byrzykowski* v. *Poland* [2006] no. 11562/05, para. 104.

which by their nature, are not designed to … establish any liability through a thorough examination of the circumstances which led to the death. Criminal proceedings contain exactly these safeguards.[91]

Such considerations were also relevant in the case of *Powell*, in which the Court was satisfied that an alternative and more rigorous course of action (i.e. in criminal law) was also available to the applicant.[92]

The development of the Court's jurisprudence in relation to the intensity of sanctions in the medical care context has seen a setback in the cases of *Maurice* and *Draon*.[93] In both cases, the Court found acceptable that the liability of medical professionals can outright be excluded when negligence occurs in pre-natal detection. It was only judge Bonello who stood for the Convention's well-established standards, pointing out, in his separate opinion, that

[t]he internationally accepted norm remains the principle of liability. Every person who has, through malice or negligence, caused harm to others is bound to make good all damage occasioned… Immunity, detestable by nature, appears doubly so when wielded to maim fundamental rights.[94]

The only other thing that is worth adding here is that the Court based its conclusion on the fact that the immunity from professional negligence was decided by the legislator after 'a comprehensive debate in Parliament' in the course of which account was taken of the 'general-interest considerations' of '*égalité*' and '*solidarité*' that the state's policy was pursuing 'in this difficult social sphere' for a 'fair treatment for all disabled persons'.[95] It failed, however, to distinguish that, unlike disabled individuals at large (as discussed in Chapter 3), in the present cases there was an express act (also in the form of omission) of interference that was causally attributed to a third party (i.e. the medical practitioner). This critical detail suffices per se to find the state in breach of its primary positive obligation to regulate standards of negligence and corresponding deterrent sanctions with regard to a professional activity, which is by nature connected to human rights.

Going back to the general discussion, it should be said that actions targeting public officials for their failure to prevent a human rights violation are hardly encountered, since the issue of protection is closely

---

91  *Calvelli and Ciglio* v. *Italy* [2002] no. 32967/96. See also the opinion of the dissenting judge Ress in *Vo.* v. *France* [2004] no. 53924/00.
92  See also *Silih* v. *Slovenia* [2007] no. 71463/01, para. 126.
93  *Maurice* v. *France* [2005] no. 11810/03; *Draon* v. *France* [2005] no. 1513/03.
94  Ibid., paras 6–7 of the separate opinion of judge Bonello.
95  *Maurice* v. *France*, ibid., paras 121–125; *Draon* v. *France*, ibid., paras 112–115.

linked to the duty care of the medical practitioner and/or the health condition of the patient. An action against public officials is more likely when they are involved in the handling of complaints between private individuals.[96]

### 4.4.2.3 Industrial activities

The state is under a positive obligation to control the activities of industry and commerce (be it public or private) in order to protect the human rights interests of identifiable individuals (i.e. workers, local population, consumers of a product or service). As already discussed in Chapter 2, the substantive content of positive obligations concerns the regulation of human rights standards in the activities of industry. In addition, public officials are required to assume the supervision and control of these activities in order to ensure the implementation of the regulated standards. In the *ex post* enforcement of positive obligations, the level of sanctions is expected to be commensurate to the degree of negligence and the gravity of consequences.

In *Oneryildiz*, which concerned a fatal industrial accident (discussed in Chapter 2), the Court laid down core administrative steps for the control of dangerous industrial activities. Accordingly, the victims of a human rights violation should be able to challenge the public officials to whom the specific tasks of control have been assigned. In examining the procedural aspect of the state's positive obligations as an integral part of the substantive right (Article 2), the Court found that the negligence of the state officials went beyond an error of judgement or carelessness (distinguishing case-law on medical negligence). Of importance was also the fact that the competent public officials had fully realised the negative consequences on individuals' physical integrity. It should be recalled from previous discussion that knowledge of the risks from a dangerous industrial activity is established by the public officials' own work. Therefore, when a systematic failure is detected, a criminal sanction should be imposed to deter future malpractice.[97] A sanction is not enough to carry the label 'criminal' but should have a sufficient deterrent effect, as judged by the standard of effectiveness.[98]

A remedy against the private party who controls and administers the industrial activity should also be available to the victims of human rights violations. If the private party has failed to implement the human rights standards that condition its activity, then the intensity of sanctions should reflect the degree of negligence involved.

---

96 *Powell v. the United Kingdom* (dec.) [2000] 45305/99; *Thilgen and Thonus v. Luxemburg* (dec.) [2008] no. 2196/05.
97 *Oneryildiz v. Turkey* [2004] no. 48939/99, paras 93, 112, 116–117.
98 Ibid., paras 116–117.

The level of sanctions is also determined in accordance with the degree of severity of consequences that have ensued from an industrial accident. Fatal incidents usually attract a criminal investigation by the competent state authorities (e.g. corporate manslaughter charges). Where there is incriminating evidence that establishes a causal link between the breach in the duty of care and the death of innocent individuals, the state authorities may be required to take an action against the third party and/or the public officials on their own motion.[99]

## 4.5 The investigation process: the intermediate determinative

The effectiveness of the implementation of positive obligations depends on the intermediate stage of investigation. Due to its indispensable role, the state's investigatory mechanism is examined separately by the Court, either as the procedural aspect of a human right or under Article 13. This means that an intermediate procedural safeguard has been recognised as being determinative of the whole issue of human rights protection and, therefore, it is examined in its own right. Accordingly, the issue of access to implement positive obligations also concerns access to challenge the standards of the investigation process.

The relevance and content of the investigation process can be seen in the case-law. In Chapter 2, we have seen that, in *Gungor*, the Court could not find that the state was under a positive obligation to protect the physical integrity of the applicant's son, because the police officers were not aware of any threat of violence against him (i.e. the element of knowledge).[100] However, when the examination turns to the *ex post* framework, what is looked at is the procedural obligation of state authorities to initiate an investigation in order to identify those responsible. It is through this process that the regulatory framework of criminal law can be implemented *ex post*.[101] In that case, the Court found that the investigation of the competent authorities did not meet the standards of effectiveness, due to their

---

99 *Pereira Henriques* v. *Luxembourg* [2006] no. 60255/00, para. 90: 'The mere fact that the authorities have been informed of the death will give rise *ipso facto* to an obligation under Article 2 of the Convention to carry out an effective investigation into the circumstances in which it occurred' (translation), (cited case omitted) (available in French only). See also *Menson and Others* v. *the United Kingdom* (dec.) [2003] no. 47916/99; *M.C.* v. *Bulgaria* [2003] no. 9272/98, paras 151, 153; *Filip* v. *Romania* [2006] no. 41124/02, para. 47 (investigation under Article 3); *Al Fayed* v. *France* (dec.) [2007] no. 38501/02, para. 73.

100 See discussion of *Gungor* v. *Turkey* [2005] no. 28290/95 in Chapter 2, p. 89.

101 *Gungor* v. *Turkey*, ibid., para. 67, 'The essential aim of such an investigation is to ensure the effective implementation of domestic laws that protect the right to life.', (translation), (available in French only); *Menson and Others* v. *the United Kingdom* (dec.) [2003] no. 47916/99; *Pereira Henriques* v. *Luxembourg* [2006] no. 60255/00, para. 56; *Mantog* v. *Romania (No. 2)* [2007] no. 2893/02, para. 64.

failure *inter alia* to follow important leads, summon appropriate witnesses or ensure that those summoned have testified before the police.[102]

The indispensable and free-standing value of investigation is highlighted in cases in which the applicant's complaint under a substantive human right is held admissible under its procedural aspect only. In such cases, what is examined is whether there have been any failures of the investigating authorities to determine the liability of third parties and/or that of public officials in relation to the acts of the former.[103]

A substantial body of case-law dealing with the standards of the investigation concerns complaints of disappearance in circumstances in which a disappearance phenomenon is widely observed.[104] On one hand, the investigation is relevant in order to examine whether state agents were directly involved in the interference complained of or, seen from the state's perspective, to substantiate its defence that its agents did not interfere. On the other hand, the state is under a positive obligation to take operational steps (an investigation) to trace missing persons and apprehend those responsible, that is the substantive positive obligation in *ex ante* circumstances.[105] In the *ex post* procedural framework, access to challenge the investigation process will have to be available in whichever stage an investigation has been required.[106]

The exact evaluation of the investigation process is made in accordance with the standard of effectiveness. In an often-cited statement, the Court reiterates that '[a]ny deficiency in the investigation which undermines its

---

102  *Gungor* v. *Turkey*, ibid. The deficiencies in the investigation are summarised in paragraph 89 of the judgment.

103  *Menson and Others* v. *the United Kingdom* (dec ) [2003] no. 47916/99 (investigation of violence against the person); *Pereira Henriques* v *Luxembourg* [2006] no. 60255/00 (investigation of a work-related accident); *Al Fayed* v. *France* (dec.) [2007] no. 38501/02 (investigation of a car accident); *Mantog* v. *Romania (No. 2)* [2007] no. 2893/02 (investigation of violence against the person); *L.Z.* v. *Romania* [2009] no. 22383/03 (investigation of a rape in prison) (available in French only); *Voiculescu* v. *Romania* [2009] no. 5325/03 (investigation of a car accident).

104  A. Reidy, F. Hampson, K. Boyle, 'Gross Violations of Human Rights: Invoking the European Convention on Human Rights in the Case of Turkey' (1997) *NQHR* 15(2) 161–173; C. Buckley, 'The European Convention on Human Rights and the Right to Life in Turkey' (2001) 1(1) *HRLR* 35–65. See, e.g., *Ulku Ekinci* v. *Turkey* [2002] no. 27602/95; *Tepe* v. *Turkey* [2003] no. 27244/95; *Tekdag* v. *Turkey* [2004] no. 27699/95; *Nuray Sen* v. *Turkey (No. 2)* [2004] no. 25354/94; *Celikbilek* v. *Turkey* [2005] no. 27693/95; *Mentese and Others* v. *Turkey* [2005] no. 36217/97; *Koku* v. *Turkey* [2005] no. 27305/95; *Gongadze* v. *Ukraine* [2005] no. 34056/02; *Osmanoglu* v. *Turkey* [2008] no. 48804/99; *Enzile Ozdemir* v. *Turkey* [2008] no. 54169/00; *Asadulayeva and Others* v. *Russia* [2009] no. 15569/06; *Varnava and Others* v. *Turkey* [2009] nos 16064/90,…, 16073/90.

105  For the substantive content of positive obligations in the form of investigation, see, generally, *Osman* v. *the United Kingdom* [1998] no. 23452/94; *Opuz* v. *Turkey* [2009] no. 33401/02.

106  *Gungor* v. *Turkey* [2005] no. 28290/95.

ability to establish the cause of death or the person responsible will risk falling foul of this standard [of effectiveness]'.[107]

In examining 'any deficiency' in the investigation that affects its effectiveness, the European judge is able to determine objectively and in great lengths the critical steps (and their own standards therein) that the investigating authority has to implement under the circumstances. Due to the nature and broad relevance of the investigation process, the standards of effectiveness have developed in the jurisprudence of both positive and negative obligations. Such standards include the promptness[108] and independence[109] of the investigation whose applicability transcends context.

A crucial stage of the investigation is the trial proceedings. At that stage, the trial judge can address any deficiencies in the investigation process. In some cases, a problem in the investigation may arise from a misapplication or under-evaluation of its findings at the trial stage. In the case of *M.C.*, the Court found that, although a regulatory framework for incidents of rape and sexual abuse has been provided by the state, as required by its positive obligations under Articles 3 and 8, the applicable judicial principles on the scope of the investigation undermined the effect of the domestic law. In estimating the required scope of the investigations under the circumstances, the Court relied on the practices of the member states and other international documents suggesting that incidents of rape and physical abuse occur also when the victim does not or cannot physically resist. It held that since the trial judge did not require the public investigator and prosecutor to expand beyond evidence of physical resistance, the state failed to satisfy its positive obligations under both Articles 3 and 8.[110] In *Oneryildiz*, the Court found the state in violation of Article 2 (its proced-

---

107  *McKerr* v. *the United Kingdom* [2001] no. 28883/95, para. 113; *Pereira Henriques* v. *Luxembourg* [2006] no. 60255/00, para. 57; *Gungor* v. *Turkey*, ibid., para. 69; *Al Fayed* v. *France* (dec.) [2007] no. 38501/02, para. 75.

108  *Ergi* v. *Turkey* [1998] paras 83–84; *Ogur* v. *Turkey* [1999] no. 21594/93, paras 91–92; *Kelly and Others* v. *the United Kingdom* [2001] no. 30054/96, para. 114; *Gungor* v. *Turkey*, ibid., para. 70; *Al Fayed* v. *France*, ibid., para. 75; *Opuz* v. *Turkey* [2009] no. 33401/02, paras 150–151; *Yeter* v. *Turkey* [2009] no. 33750/03, para. 65; *Dvoracek and Dvorackova* v. *Slovakia* [2009] no. 30754/04, paras 65–66; *Korogodina* v. *Russia* [2010] no. 33512/04, para. 60.

109  *Hugh Jordan* v. *the United Kingdom* [2001] no. 24746/94, paras 108, 136–140; *Menson and Others* v. *the United Kingdom* (dec.) [2003] no. 47916/99; *Gungor* v. *Turkey*, ibid., para. 68; *Mantog* v. *Romania (No. 2)* [2007] no. 2893/02, paras 69–70; *Kolevi* v. *Bulgaria* [2009] no. 1108/02, paras 193–194. The standard of independence is also connected to the standard of promptness; see the high-profile case of *Dink* v. *Turkey* [2010] nos 2668/07,…, 7124/09, para. 79: 'the opening of a prompt investigation by state authorities is generally seen as crucial in maintaining public confidence and adherence to the rule of law and in preventing any appearance of tolerance or collusion in unlawful acts' (translation), (cited case omitted) (available in French only). See also press coverage, 'Turquie: Les Images de Policiers Posant aux Côtés du Tueur de Hrant Dink Font Scandale', *Le Monde* (20 March 2007).

110  *M.C.* v. *Bulgaria* [2003] no. 9272/98, paras 153, 182–185.

ural aspect) on the ground *inter alia* that the life-endangering aspect of the public officials' negligence was not examined by the investigating authorities and this deficiency was not corrected by the trial judge.[111]

Similar issues have also been seen in cases that concern disputes between private parties in the context of medical negligence. In *Bendersky*, the state was found in violation of Article 6 because the domestic courts did not address one of the applicant's arguments pointing to additional evidence of medical expert opinion. Although this evidence was not decisive, it was important for the trial court's own investigation and assessment of the medical negligence complained of.[112] In addition, it has been discussed above that where involuntary homicide is caused by medical negligence, criminal sanctions may not be the European minimum standard. However, the scope of investigation can have a criminal law potential to ensure that the full degree of negligence can be exposed.[113] Thus, where serious consequences have ensued, a high degree of negligence calls for high compensation, or an action in criminal law if this option is available domestically.

In all circumstances, it is expected that the European review of the scope and content of the investigation process should be reasonably linked to the substantive content of the state's positive obligations. An illustration of this point can be seen in the examination of the investigation process in *Bone*. In that case, the applicant complained about the state's failure to ensure safety standards in the operation of rail services. The Court found first that the state satisfied its positive obligations under Article 2 by regulating specific precautionary measures against the activities of the rail operators. In examining the procedural issue, the Court held that the competent authorities launched an investigation following the accidental death of the applicant's son whose scope covered the rail operator's compliance with the regulated safety measures.[114] Therefore, when it is the investigation that is challenged, due to its vital role in the procedural implementation of human rights protection, the examination of its content and scope should at least include those steps of which the substantive law of positive obligations consists in the particular circumstances concerned.

---

111 *Oneryildiz* v. *Turkey* [2002] no. 48939/99, para. 109; *Oneryildiz* v. *Turkey* [2004] (Grand Chamber), paras 115–116. See also *Budayeva and Others* v. *Russia* [2008] nos 15339/02,..., 15343/02, para. 143.

112 *Bendersky* v. *Ukraine* [2007] no. 22750/02, para. 46.

113 See the dissenting opinion of judge Rozakis joined by judge Bonello in *Calvelli and Ciglio* v. *Italy* [2002] no. 32967/96, as quoted on page with note 91 above. See, similarly, under Article 13, *Oneryildiz* v. *Turkey* [2004] no. 48939/99, para. 148: 'In other words, there was a close procedural and practical relationship between the criminal investigation and the remedies available to those applicants in the legal system as a whole', (cited case omitted); *Gungor* v. *Turkey* [2005] no. 28290/95, para. 97.

114 *Bone* v. *France* (dec.) [2005] no. 69869/01 (available in French only). See also *Budayeva and Others* v. *Russia* [2008] nos 15339/02,..., 15343/02, para. 162; *Kalender* v. *Turkey* [2009] 4314/02, paras 49 and 58 (available in French only).

## 4.6  Conclusion

Positive obligations produce a practical result when the protection of human rights can directly be asserted at the domestic level. For this purpose, institutional access points should be in place to enable interested individuals to participate in the implementation and enforcement of the state's positive obligations.

Domestic access is essential to guarantee the subsidiary nature of the Convention and its own effectiveness. At the European level, the Court is first expected to determine the substantive content of the state's positive obligations in various contexts in which private individuals interact. When the substantive law is reasonably certain, then the following task is to target the state's procedural system that implements the content of protection at the domestic level. Proposals for a priority examination of procedural issues are particularly pertinent in the current phase of development of the jurisprudence, in which the substantive content of positive obligations is increasingly defined in the form of a proceduralised framework of core administrative steps.

The procedural implementation of the state's positive obligations depends on (1) whether individuals can have access to challenge those who have specific human rights obligations and (2) whether the effectiveness of such access is guaranteed by parallel procedural safeguards.

At first, an action should be available to challenge the private parties whose activities involve threats to human rights. For such an action to be possible, the standards of duty of care should be regulated in advance. In many circumstances, the substance of positive obligations regards an administrative framework (i.e. the corollary to the regulatory framework), which supervises the activities of private parties in order to realise the aim of prevention of human rights violations. Administrative steps that are core to the issue of prevention can be marked as access points for the participation of interested individuals in the enforcement of human rights standards before a violation occurs. For this purpose, the performance of public officials should be challenged during the supervision and control of the activities of private parties so as to guarantee the effectiveness of the administrative framework. Individuals should also be able to have access to the critical stages of the decision-making process of the public administration in order to challenge the practices of private parties against the regulated human rights standards.

Where there has been a violation of a human right, the *ex post* implementation of the substantive content of positive obligations is secured by a procedural framework that allows the victim access to a remedy. To this aim, sanctions should be prescribed and imposed whenever the regulated standards are breached. The intensity of these sanctions should reasonably correspond to the degree of negligence and the severity of consequences involved. Individuals should be able to seek a remedy against the private parties that have directly caused the violation of a human right. Where a causal link can be established between the acts (or omissions) of private parties and the breach of a duty of care of the public officials during the control and supervision of the activities of the former, access to challenge the negligence of public officials should also be available.

All access points of the procedural framework of implementation of positive obligations in both *ex ante* and *ex post* circumstances depend on the intermediate stage of investigation. Since the process of investigation is crucial for the effectiveness of the individuals' accessibility and, by extension, for the whole system of human rights protection, a parallel access should also exist in order to challenge the investigation's own effectiveness. Accordingly, the evaluation process opens to all those parameters and standards that are critical to the effectiveness of the investigation. It has been argued that, as a minimum, the scope and content of the investigation should be evaluated in relation to the substantive law of the state's positive obligations that defines the duty of care of both private parties and public officials in the circumstances concerned.

# 5 Summing up

## 5.1 The general message of positive obligations

Positive obligations were initially developed in the system of the Convention to render the states indirectly responsible for violations of human rights by private parties. The growing social pressure, as expressed by a new generation of human rights complaints and the writings of insightful scholars in the 1960s and 1970s, culminated in the judgments of *Marckx* and *Airey* in 1979 in which positive obligations were recognised as 'inherent' in the system of the Convention. To the generation of Alexandra Marckx (the child of the applicant from the homonymous case) – that is, all of us who have been brought up taking the state's positive obligations for granted and the Convention as a common European space and culture – positive obligations mean something more. Following the popular perception that human rights have to be enjoyed in a wide range of circumstances, rather than simply not violated, European individuals are increasingly asserting positive obligations across the board. This new reality has been reflected in the first application of positive obligations in *Marckx*, in which the issue of human rights protection did not involve an interference by a private party.

The first message of positive obligations is the existence of the Convention as the institutional forum in which the individual can initiate a human rights claim. The second message of positive obligations is the active protection of human rights by the state. The source of the threat (i.e. the activities of private parties, including state-funded businesses) against which the state's protection has initially been directed no longer appears in the second message of positive obligations due to the concurring reading of the first message. Once an independent forum has been secured and the active protection of human rights has been recognised as inherent in the Convention law, the general message of positive obligations has been stated.

When the individual is able to directly access the supranational system of the Convention in order to question where and how human rights have to be protected under the state's positive obligations, the initiative of the constitutional balance of human rights passes from the legislator to the people. The participatory ability of the ordinary individual should be evaluated through the reach of the Convention, which has long been established as an international regulator of human rights standards. There is no precedent in the political history of humankind in which the participation of the individual (not only the citizen) in both the domestic and international levels of power has been possible in such an open-ended range of circumstances and in such a direct, simple, and yet most influential way. If we depart from the millennia-old assertion that man is a political animal, then it is the individual's participation in the affairs of the polis that satisfies her/him most. In that respect, European individuals are 'united' around the common effort of building a supranational institution to control peace through an advanced control of the states by the individuals residing within their jurisdiction.[1]

It is important, however, that the opportunity of the active protection of human rights has a practical effect. Positive obligations can only be taken seriously if a legal expertise is developed to manage their open-ended scope. It is also observed that, due to a fashionable excitement or deliberate choice, positive obligations are often used as a buzzword for every measure of compliance with human rights standards, a fact that leads gradually to their dilution. Therefore, a technical expertise has first to secure the *distinctive nature* of positive obligations from which any meaningful *content* can subsequently be determined.

## 5.2  The distinctive nature of positive obligations

The binding effect of positive obligations is imposed by virtue of paragraph 1 of the Convention rights, which require the state to organise the protection of human rights in advance. In principle, therefore, the positive obligations of the state to actively protect human rights can be directed to the aim of prevention of human rights violations. In this regard, it is reasonably expected that the judicial examination of the state's response should follow the hierarchical structure of the Convention rights (from paragraph 1 to paragraph 2) that reflects the logical organisation of human rights protection. In most of the Court's case-law, however, the positive obligations of the state have not clearly been distinguished from its negative obligations, which arise under paragraph 2 of the Convention rights. This situation is exacerbated by the growing tendency to label every measure of human rights compliance as a positive obligation.

In the case-law, positive and negative obligations are often merged through the so-called 'fair balance' between the interests of the individual

---

1  W. Friedmann, *The Changing Structure of International Law* (London: Stevens & Sons, 1964): p. 191: 'The individuals of a state are counted in millions, whereas there are only about sixty states [sic] in the world; and these individuals by and large have the same basic interests, personal and proprietary, whereas the interests of states are almost infinitely unique.'

and those of the community. The Court has regularly reiterated that the legitimate aims of a state's interference, as listed in paragraph 2 of the Convention rights (where applicable), may be of a 'certain' relevance in striking this balance. Under this approach, the judicial examination concentrates on ad hoc balances for which the state has a margin of appreciation. Consequently, it is not easy to define the European minimum standard that guides both the right-holders and the state in their respective rights and obligations in future instances. More seriously, when positive obligations are confined to the examination of paragraph 2, the obligation of the active protection of human rights appears as an incidental and indirect issue.

Positive obligations are recognised as 'inherent' in the system of the Convention under paragraph 1 of the Convention rights, because the issue of the active protection of human rights is different from that of direct interference by the state or the process of its possible justification (i.e. negative obligations). In technical terms, this means that the distinctive nature of positive obligations has to be recognised accordingly in the order by which the judicial examination is structured. For this purpose, three conditions are particularly important.

1   When the state upholds the act (or omission) of a private party that interferes with a human right, direct responsibility for the ensuing violation of that right lies with the state, because it is the laws of the state that have allowed that act. In such circumstances, the state is under a clear negative obligation to abstain from interfering (i.e. from upholding the act complained of) without meeting the exhaustively listed aims and criteria of paragraph 2 provisions. In other words, the distinctiveness of positive obligations passes from the distinctiveness of negative obligations for which the paragraph 2 legitimate aims of interference do not have a 'certain' relevance but are categorical criteria for strict observance.

2   An act of interference on the part of the state establishes the element of knowledge of the need for human rights protection, for which ground, clearly, the obligation to abstain from an unjustified interference becomes essential. Analogously, it is the element of knowledge that can establish the state's 'involvement' in the wide range of circumstances in which the active protection of human rights may be required as a positive obligation. The existence of this objective element conditions the application of positive obligations and proves a manageable scope of the state's liability. The element of knowledge will be implied in circumstances where known human rights issues exist.

3   Positive obligations arise in relation to paragraph 1 of the Convention rights which are the only provisions relevant to the issue of the active protection of human rights. In these provisions, the Convention contains the necessary normative resources to target directly the

improvement of the domestic legal principles and procedures that guarantee the effectiveness and implementation of human rights protection. Due to this directness, positive obligations often involve a core content of protection which is not affected by the optional choice of a state authority to pursue a justifiable interference.

## 5.3 The content of positive obligations

The general content of positive obligations involves the substantive law of the active protection of human rights and the procedural guarantees that implement it in the state's legal order. In many circumstances, in order for the protection of human rights to be effective, a series of interdependent measures have to be taken in various stages. In that respect, positive obligations are determined as a multilevel structure, whose organisation points to a whole system of protection. Such an organised structure can clearly be defined when the content of positive obligations is evaluated in relation to the wide context of activities of private parties to which the applicant's circumstances relate.

Both the general and detailed content of positive obligations are guided by the standard of effectiveness. This standard is evaluated against the aim of prevention of human rights violations that constitutes the practical meaning of the active protection of human rights. A continuous review of the effectiveness of protection is expected in order to adapt the content of positive obligations to the ever-changing socio-political circumstances.

### 5.3.1 The substantive content

The substantive content of positive obligations is organised as a system of active protection that aims ultimately at the prevention of human rights violations. Due to the wide scope of the active protection, European standards can only prescribe a manageable content of positive obligations.

As a starting point, the liability of the state for violations of human rights, which are not directly caused by its agents, is conditioned on the objective element of knowledge of the need of human rights protection that establishes the state's involvement in the circumstances concerned. In that respect, a *core content* of positive obligation includes, first, those measures establishing the element of knowledge in the various stages in which the active protection of human rights is required.

Of preliminary importance is also the fact that positive obligations can only arise in relation to the specific rights that are enshrined in the Convention. It is pertinent, therefore, to estimate what the applicable scope of a human right is. In addition, inherent limits of practicality have also to be recognised due to the limited resources of the member states and the economic disparities between them. Although, technically speaking, the questions of *scope* and *limits* may be examined separately, their individual determination requires mutual adjustments so as to manage the application of positive obligations accordingly.

Moving beyond the basics of a manageable scope of positive obligations, their more specific content is determined in relation to the particular requirements of protection and the contextual differences involved. Where the state authorities decide to uphold directly or tacitly an act of interference of a private party, including situations of competing human rights interests, the distinctiveness and priority of the active protection of human rights is preserved by a *synthesis* of the state's positive and negative obligations.

### 5.3.1.1 *Defining the scope of the Convention rights*

Positive obligations, or any kind of obligations, can only be imposed on the state as long as a Convention right is engaged in an applicant's circumstances. It is necessary, therefore, to have a prior understanding of the applicable scope of the Convention rights. In technical terms, the question of the scope of a Convention right involves: (1) the conceptual aspect of the human right concerned and (2) its quantified aspect in the form of the actionable degree of the negative impact on the individual. It is expected that the European judges should set the threshold of negative impact reasonably high in order to accommodate the issue of protection to the practical realities of the Convention's capabilities and those of the member states, and also to maintain the constitutional status of human rights in the hierarchy of norms. In that way, it is made clear that the business of the Convention is open for the adjudication of important human rights issues.

### 5.3.1.2 *Limits*

Inherent limits on positive obligations are implied in the provisions of paragraph 1 of the Convention rights due to the limited availability of the state's resources.

In most circumstances, positive obligations arise where there is a causal link between the activity of a private party and the violation of a human right. The limits of the state's positive obligations are determined differently depending on whether the act complained of is taken (1) in accordance with the laws of the state (e.g. lower human rights standards apply domestically) or (2) in defiance of the state's legal standards.

The imposition of limits is not particularly extensive when the main financial burden of protection is borne of the funds of the private party whose lawful activities threaten human rights. By contrast, when the active protection of human rights is examined in relation to unlawful acts, limits are more easily justified due to the frequency or unpredictability of such acts. As with other technical issues, limits are evaluated against the standard of effectiveness, which provides an objective base to determine the minimum content of protection.

Limits can reasonably be imposed to a far greater extent when the active protection of human rights is examined in circumstances where the causal element of a prior interference from a state or non-state actor is absent. When positive obligations are claimed by individuals who cannot enjoy human rights due to their own circumstances of personal vulnerability (i.e. physical and/or mental conditions), limits are determined in conjunction with the scope of the Convention rights and the actionable thresholds of negative impact. In such a context, the financial cost of protection reasonably influences the setting of the actionable threshold that determines the applicability of a Convention right. In that respect, the question of limits is directly connected to the justifiability of positive obligations over the preliminary question of the scope of a Convention right which may well be elaborated at the very occasion of the applicant's claim.

### 5.3.1.3 Core and ad hoc measures

The positive obligations of the state to actively protect human rights often involve reactive measures to address a given threat on human rights. Reactive measures are closely dependent on a core content of regulatory and administrative measures in order for protection to be practically effective. Due to the preliminary importance of the core measures of protection, it is expected that their implementation should be guaranteed in priority, something that should be reflected accordingly in the structure of the judicial examination. Viewed also from the point of the economy of process, upon which the Convention's own effectiveness depends, a core content of positive obligations can be directly targeted as a comprehensive system of protection.

This approach is supported by the element of knowledge of the need of human rights protection which conditions the state's liability at whichever level and stage the content of positive obligations is examined. In that connection, the basic responsibility of the state's agents to react upon a specific threat to human rights will often arise if core measures have previously been implemented to establish the requisite evidence (knowledge) of that threat.

If the prevention of human rights violations is the ultimate aim, the content of positive obligations can be defined as a comprehensive system of human rights protection which comprises (1) a legislative/regulatory framework, (2) an administrative framework and (3) practical measures for ad hoc application.

In such a system, the effectiveness of protection depends on the individual effectiveness of core critical structures due to their interaction with the practical measures of the specific response. By way of example, when one of the practical measures of protection that is required in the applicant's circumstances is to warn about the dangers of some activities of private parties, it is reasonably presupposed that a core administrative practice must previously be implemented in order to establish the exact content of that information. In that way, both the ad hoc measure concerned (e.g. warning information) and the attached administrative practice (and the standards therein) that establishes it form part of the content of positive obligation that the state has to regulate in advance. Regulations are expected to be constantly updated following knowledge of the efficiency results of the current practices, or of qualitative and widely accepted international standards.

In appropriate circumstances, specific measures and practices of an administrative nature can also be regulated against the private parties whose activities directly threaten human rights, provided that the state authorities retain a supervisory control through the independent functioning of public administration.

### 5.3.1.4 A synthesis of human rights protection

When a violation of a human right is caused by a private party acting lawfully within the domestic legal order, the state may seek to justify the act complained of in pursuit of one of the legitimate aims of interference (where applicable) to limit the scope of a human right and, by extension, its positive obligations. In the post-*Hatton and Others* landscape of the jurisprudence, the examination of the standard of proportionality, as required under paragraph 2 of some Convention rights, involves an assessment of the negative impact on the individuals concerned. To guarantee the objectivity of the process, the judicial examination can extend to the administrative measures (i.e. to conduct a research) that provide the requisite evidence. Administrative measures are also required as core and direct positive obligations under paragraph 1 of the Convention rights. However, at the proportionality stage of paragraph 2, similar measures have only an indirect procedural relevance. Consequently, their determination is not made with the intensity and depth of the paragraph 1 examination. As was confirmed also in the Grand Chamber judgment of *Hatton and Others*, ad hoc balances of overall justice still prevail in paragraph 2.

Accordingly, there are two pertinent issues that have to be addressed: First, the protection of human rights is a permanent obligation under paragraph 1 of the Convention rights which has already arisen before the optional choice of the state to pursue a legitimate interference. Second, under paragraph 1, the examination of the content of positive obligations (i.e. core administrative practices) involves a detailed and comprehensive evaluation and definition of the critical parameters that guarantee the effectiveness of protection.

It is proposed that in order to maintain the priority and depth of positive obligations when a legitimate limitation to a human right is attempted, instead of merging the state's negative and positive obligations through the perspective of the former (i.e. a prior interference, directly or indirectly, attributed to the state), a synthesis of human rights protection can be realised from the distinctive nature of the state's dual obligations. The point of synthesis can be found in the first criterion of paragraph 2 which concerns the 'quality' of legal safeguards that the state is under an obligation to 'prescribe by law' before an interference is attempted. To the extent that core measures of human rights protection have already been required as positive obligations of the state, they amount to those legal safeguards that the law of the state must 'prescribe' and its authorities must implement in practice, before any legitimate limitation to the scope of a human right is attempted or considered.

Such a synthesis is also applicable where individuals are legitimately placed under the control of the state authorities (i.e. prisons, mental institutions, immigrations centres, military service, etc.). In such circumstances, a legitimate limitation to the human rights of these individuals (i.e. liberty, personal life) can have additional human rights implications (i.e. health and safety issues), which are already *known* before and at the time of the initial interference. In that respect, the additional positive obligations, which arise for the state, become part of the legal safeguards that the law has to 'prescribe' when the legitimacy of the interference is examined, reviewed or actually imposed.

A natural synthesis is observed in circumstances where opposing positive obligations arise for the protection of individuals whose human rights conflict with those of another (e.g. custody of children, defamation of one's reputation, counter-demonstrations, etc.). In such situations, the implementation of a positive obligation constitutes an act of interference that engages the provisions of paragraph 2. The distinctive nature, however, of positive obligations is still maintained, because that interference (as protection) does not have the optional imperative of the legitimate aims of paragraph 2 provisions. In such special circumstances, the synthesis of human rights protection requires a tailor-made approach to define a general prioritisation of the human rights interests involved and a due process, whose standards can be entrenched at the 'prescribed by law' level.

### 5.3.2 *Access points of domestic implementation*

Positive obligations produce a practical result when an enforcement framework exists at the domestic level to guarantee the implementation of their substantive content. In essence, the positive obligations of the state to actively protect human rights has one meaning – the prevention of their violations – and two levels of enforcement: (1) the *ex post* imposition of deterring sanctions, which are regulated in advance, and (2) the possibility to challenge *ex ante* the non-compliance of human rights standards. These two levels of action should be directed against both the private parties that directly cause the violation of a human right and the public officials in charge of control of the acts of the former. In order to secure the participation of the individual, as the directly affected party, in the implementation of positive obligations, various institutional access points should be available in relation to both levels of action. The effectiveness of such access depends on the intermediate procedural stage of investigation whose own effectiveness is guaranteed by parallel procedural safeguards.

1   At the *ex post* level, the enforcement of positive obligations is organised through deterring sanctions (e.g. civil compensation, criminal sentences), which are imposed on the private parties that have directly caused the violation of a human right. In that way, the regulated human rights standards, which condition the lawful operation of the activities of private parties, are implemented by a mechanism of sanctions that is set in motion when the victim has access to claim the prescribed sanction as a remedy. In appropriate circumstances, *ex post* enforcement is guaranteed by the initiative of public officials, provided that the victim is given access to the investigation process.

    Similar access points in *ex post* circumstances should also be made available in relation to the individual responsibility of public officials, who are in charge of the positive duties of protection of human rights. In that regard, a parallel framework of sanctions and professional standards (against which sanctions are assessed) should be arranged against the specific tasks of public officials, as defined by the substantive law of positive obligations.

    Being the absolute minimum level of enforcement, the *ex post* framework must be guaranteed in all circumstances where the substantive law of positive obligations is reasonably certain.

2   The enforcement of positive obligations can also be made before an actual violation of a human right occurs. An *ex ante* course of action is more feasible when the substantive content of positive obligation concerns a system of human rights protection that has been defined in relation to a known context of private interactions. The critical administrative stages of which such a system consists can serve as access points for the participation of the individual in the enforcement of the prescribed human rights standards. The main aim is to challenge directly the private parties through the public administration that controls their activities, including an action to challenge state officials for any deficiency during the execution of that control. The specific tasks of public administration can be enforced if they are open to a challenge (e.g. through judicial review) by interested individuals in the corresponding stages at which the administrative control of the activities of private parties is exercised.

The imposition by the Convention of the *ex ante* level of enforcement of positive obligations finds an apparent difficulty due to the admissibility criterion of victim status under Article 34. However, it should be remembered that this criterion applies at the European level only. There is nothing to prevent the Court, in its *ex post* judicial examination, from requiring that the state's administrative tasks of control be open to challenge prior to a violation of a human right, as the effective domestic remedy under Article 13, which is taken in conjunction with the substantive right under which these tasks are imposed (as the substantive law of positive obligations). In circumstances where the physical integrity of individuals is at stake, the Court has showed itself willing to admit complaints prior to an actual violation of a human right and require that interested individuals should have access to challenge entrenched tasks of administrative control, as an indispensable procedural corollary of positive obligations under the substantive right (i.e. Articles 2, 3, 8) (taken alone).

3   Institutional access for the implementation of positive obligations in the form of direct assistance to vulnerable individuals, where an act of interference is absent, is reasonably very limited. In such circumstances, the substantive content of positive obligations has yet to be determined through the preliminary questions of the legitimacy for the Court's intervention and the scope of the Convention rights. However, a certain tangible ground increasingly emerges in relation to the procedures, which guarantee the objective assessment of evidence in the examination of these preliminary questions. In that respect, access points can be required to enable individuals to challenge the procedural tasks through which an 'arguable' human rights claim is examined at the domestic level.

## 5.4 Conclusion

Positive obligations mark the emergence of the ordinary individual as the atomic unit in the control of peace through the advanced control of the state in the wide range of circumstances in which the active protection of human rights is required. This opportunity is made possible by the direct access of the individual to the supranational system of the Convention, which unites European people in the common project of building a European public order in the area of human rights and fundamental freedoms.

The expansion of positive obligations reflects the growing social movements of European individuals who press for their human rights in every circumstance in which they are relevant. It is important, however, to remember that, although social pressure comes from the domestic level, the beginning and binding effect of positive obligations lies in the common European space of the Convention.

In order to secure a manageable application of the wide scope of positive obligations, the Convention is required to adopt a comprehensive methodological framework that gives due weight to preliminary questions and contextual differences, including a corresponding categorisation of practical limitations. If such a technical framework is provided, the active protection of human rights is not only maintained as the distinctive meaning of positive obligations but can specifically be directed to the prevention of human rights violations. Setting prevention as the ultimate aim, the substantive content of positive obligations expands beyond ad hoc responses to target a multilevel structure of measures as a system of human rights protection. To ensure an objective application and development of the standards of protection, a core content of positive obligations can easily concern a range of administrative measures. Due to their procedural function, administrative measures can also serve as institutional access points for the participation of interested individuals in the domestic implementation of positive obligations. It is the possibility of access of the ordinary individual to the key levels of implementation of positive obligations that guarantees the constant vigilance and improvement of the standards of human rights protection, reminding the state of its basic constitutional priorities.

Continuing from the phrase of Jan De Meyer that '[w]ithout the text of the Convention having to be amended or a new protocol drafted', it is argued, in addition, that, whatever the number of petitions can be, positive obligations can be managed by shifting the focus of judicial examination on appropriate access points to allow the participation of the individual in the development and implementation of the active protection of human rights at the domestic level. The role of the Convention, as a non-living space, is to set human rights standards for the domestic systems. Once these standards have been set, repetitive cases raise only an issue of 'execution', for which political pressure is required under the peer political body of the Committee of Ministers.[2]

Positive obligations present one of the biggest opportunities ever. As with other worthwhile projects in the past, the opportunity of positive obligations can be lost through a trivial and ever-available use. In the current crucial juncture of development of positive obligations, the main challenge is to prove scientifically that the open-ended scope of positive obligations can be legally managed and controlled. It is the methodological result that preserves the potential of positive obligations and the continuous progress in the protection of human rights. The current work is an invitation and a contribution to this challenge.

---

2 L. Wildhaber, 'A Constitutional Future for the European Court of Human Rights?' (2002) 23 (5–7) *HRLJ* 161–165, pp. 162, 163.

# Bibliography

Αλιβιζάτος Ν., 'Οι «Ελληνικές» Υποθέσεις στο Στρασβούργο' (2002) ΤοΣ 1.

Alkema Albert, 'The Third-Party Applicability or "Drittwirkung" of the European Convention on Human Rights', in F. Matscher and H. Petzold (eds), *Protecting Human Rights: The European Dimension, Studies in Honour of G.J. Wiarda* (Köln: Heymann, 2nd edn, 1990), pp. 33–45.

Alston P. and Weiler J., 'An "Ever Closer Union" in Need of a Human Rights Policy: The European Union and Human Rights' (Harvard: Jean Monnet Working Paper No. 1, 1999), available at www.jeanmonnetprogram.org/papers/99/990101.html (accessed January 2011).

Arai-Takahashi Y., *The Margin of Appreciation Doctrine and the Principle of Proportionality in the Jurisprudence of the ECHR* (Antwerp: Intersentia, 2002).

Benson P., 'Equality of Opportunity and Private Law', in D. Friedmann and D. Barak-Erez (eds), *Human Rights in Private Law* (Oxford: Hart, 2001), pp. 201–243.

Berenstein A., 'Economic and Social Rights: Their Inclusion in the European Convention on Human Rights, Problems of Formulation and Interpretation' (1981) 2(3–4) *HRLJ* 257–280.

Bird C., *The Myth of Liberal Individualism* (Cambridge: Cambridge University Press, 1999).

Βογιατζής Π., 'Το 11ο Πρωτόκολλο της Ευρωπαϊκής Σύμβασης Δικαιωμάτων του Ανθρώπου-Προς την Δημιουργία ενός Ευρωπαϊκού Δικαίου' (1996) ΤοΣ 579.

Bomhoff J., 'Lüth's 50th Anniversary: Some Comparative Observations on the German Foundations of Judicial Balancing' (2008) 9 *GLJ* 121–124.

Bown A., 'Fundamental Rights in Private Law' (2000) *S.T.L.* 157–161.

Bowring, B., 'What is Realism in International Law and Human Rights?', in J. Joseph and C. Wight (eds), *Scientific Realism and International Relations* (Basingstoke: Palgrave and Macmillan, 2010), pp. 101–114.

Boyle K. and Hannum H., 'Individual Applications under the European Convention on Human Rights and the Concept of Administrative Practice: the Donnelly Case' (1974) 68 *AJIL* 440–453.

Buckley C., 'The European Convention on Human Rights and the Right to Life in Turkey' (2001) 1(1) *HRLR* 35–65.

Buquicchio de Boer M., 'Children and the European Convention on Human Rights: A Survey of Case-law of the European Commission and Court of Human Rights', in F. Matscher and H. Petzold (eds), *Protecting Human Rights: The European Dimension, Studies in Honour of G.J. Wiarda* (Köln: Heymann, 1988), pp. 73–89.

Caflisch L., 'The Reform of the European Court of Human Rights: Protocol No. 14 and Beyond' (2006) 6 *HRLR* 403–415.

Cançado Trindade A., *The Application of the Rule of Exhaustion of Local Remedies in International Law: Its Rationale in the International Protection of Individual Rights* (Cambridge: Cambridge University Press, 1983).

Champion M., 'Court Faults Turkey Over Editor's Murder', *The Wall Street Journal* (14 September 2010).

Cherednychenko O., 'Towards the Control of Private Acts by the European Court of Human Rights?' (2006) 13(2) *MJ* 195–218.

Chinkin C., 'A Critique of the Public/Private Dimension' (1999) 10 *EJIL* 387–395.

Clack A., 'Heathrow Case Challenged', *Guardian* (23 May 2005).

Clapham A., 'The Privatization of European Human Rights' (DPhil thesis, European University Institute, 1991).

Clapham A., *Human Rights in the Private Sphere* (Oxford: Oxford/Clarendon Press, 1993).

Clements L. and Read J., 'The Dog That Didn't Bark: The Issue of Access to Rights under the European Convention on Human Rights by Disabled People', in A. Lawson and C. Gooding (eds), *Disability Rights in Europe: From Theory to Practice* (Oxford: Hart, 2005), pp. 21–34.

Clements L. and Young J., 'Human Rights: Changing the Culture' (1999) 26(1) *JLS* 1–5.

Connelly A., 'The Protection of the Rights of Others' (1980) 5(2) *HRR* 117–140.

Connelly A., 'Problems of Interpretation of Article 8 of the European Convention on Human Rights' (1986) 35(3) *ICLQ* 567–593.

Cook K., 'Environmental Rights as Human Rights' (2002) 2 *EHRLR* 196–215.

Costa J.-P., 'La Liberté d'Expression selon la Jurisprudence de la Cour Européenne des Droits de l'Homme' (2002) 15 *ΔτΑ* 671–676.

Crawshaw R, 'International Standards on the Right to Life and the Use of Force by Police' (1999) 3(4) *IJHR* 67–91.

Cullen H., '*Siliadin v France*: Positive Obligations under Article 4 of the European Convention on Human Rights' (2006) 6 *HRLR* 585–592.

Cullet P., 'Definition of an Environmental Right in a Human Rights Context' (1995) 13(1) *NQHR* 25–40.

de Blois M., 'The Fundamental Freedom of the European Court of Human Rights', in R. Lawson and M. de Blois (eds), *The Dynamics of the Protection of Human Rights in Europe: Essays in Honour of H.G. Schermers* (Dordrecht: Martinus Nijhoff, 1994), pp. 35–59.

de Fontbressin P., 'L'Effet Horizontal de Convention Européenne des Droits de l'Homme et l'Avenir du Droit des Obligations', in G. Cohen-Jonathan, J.-F. Flauss and P. Lambert (eds), *Liber Amicorum Marc-André Eissen* (Brussels: Bruylant, 1995), pp. 157–164.

de la Rasilla del Moral I., 'The Increasing Marginal Appreciation of the Margin-of-Appreciation Doctrine' (2006) 7(6) *GLJ* 611–624.

Demerieux M., 'Deriving Environmental Rights from the European Convention for the Protection of Human Rights and Fundamental Freedoms' (2001) 21 *OJLS* 521–561.

De Meyer J., 'The Right to Respect for Private and Family Life, Home and Communications in Relations Between Individuals, and the Resulting Obligations for States Parties to the Convention', in A.H. Robertson (ed.), *Privacy and Human*

*Rights* (Reports and Communications Presented at the Third International Colloquy about the European Convention on Human Rights, 30 September–3 October 1970) (Manchester: Manchester University Press, 1973), pp. 255–275.

De Salvia M., 'Ambiente e Convenzione Europea dei Diritti dell'Uomo' (1997) 10(1) *RIDU* 78–83.

De Salvia M., 'Illustration et Défense du Système Européen de Protection Judicaire des Droits de l'Homme: Des Règles Précises pour des Obligations Claires et Partagées par les Etats' (2007) 69 *RTDH* 135–151.

De Sanctis F., 'What Duties Do States Have with Regard to the Rules of Engagement and the Training of Security Forces under Article 2 of the European Convention on Human Rights?' (2006) 10(1) *ILHR* 31–44.

De Schutter O., 'Reasonable Accommodations and Positive Obligations in the European Convention on Human Rights', in A. Lawson and C. Gooding (eds), *Disability Rights in Europe: From Theory to Practice* (Oxford: Hart, 2005), pp. 35–64.

Di Stefano A., 'Public Authority Liability in Negligence e Diritto ad un Ricorso Effettivo nell' Ordinamento Britannico: Nota all Sentenza della Corte Europea dei Diritti dell'Uomo nel Caso Z e altri c. Regno Unito' (2003) 1 *RIDU* 97–127.

Done K., 'Farborough Faced to Turned Away Business', *Financial Times* (11 February 2008).

Donner A., 'Transition', in F. Matscher and H. Petzold (eds), *Protecting Human Rights: The European Dimension: Studies in Honour of G.J. Wiarda* (Köln: Heymann, 1988), pp. 145–148.

Drabble R., Maurici J. and Buley T., *Local Authorities and Human Rights* (Oxford: Oxford University Press, 2004).

Drögue C., *Positive Verpflichtungen der Staaten in der Europaischen Menschenrechtskonvention* (Heidelberg: Springer, 2003).

Drost P., *The Crime of State: Penal Protection for Fundamental Freedoms of Persons and Peoples*, Book I: *Humanicide* (Leyden: A.W. Sijthoff, 1959).

Drost P., *Human Rights as Legal Rights: The Realization of Individual Human Rights in Positive International Law* (Leyden: A.W. Sijthoff, 2nd edn, 1965).

Drzemczewski A., 'The European Human Rights Convention and Relations Between Private Parties' (1979) 26(2) *NILR* 163–181.

Drzemczewski A., 'Το Έργο της Διεύρηνσης των Δικαιωμάτων του Ανθρώπου του Συμβουλίου της Ευρώπης' (1991) *EEEυρΔ* 685.

Dubout E., 'La Proceduralisation des Obligations Relatives aux Droits Fondamentaux Substantiels par la Cour Européenne des Droits de l'Homme' (2007) 70 *RTDH* 397–425.

Duffy P., 'The Case of Klass and Others: Secret Surveillance of Communications and the European Convention on Human Rights' (1979) 4(1) *HRR* 20–41.

Duffy P., 'The Sunday Times Case: Freedom of Expression, Contempt of Court and the European Convention on Human Rights' (1980) 5(1) *HRR* 17–53.

Duffy P., 'The Protection of Privacy, Family Life and Other Rights under Article 8 of the European Convention on Human Rights' (1982) 2 *YbkEL* 191–238.

Eissen M.-A., 'La Convention Européenne des Droits de l'Homme et les Obligations de l'Individu: une Mise à Jour', in *Amicorum Discipulorumque Liber René Cassin III: Protection des Droits de l'Homme dans les Rapports Entre Personnes Privées* (Paris: Pédone, 1971), pp. 151–162.

Eissen M.-A., 'Το Ευρωπαϊκό Δικαστήριο Δικαιωμάτων του Ανθρώπου' (1983) *EEEυρΔ* 499.

Eissen M.-A., 'L'Avocat devant la Cour Européenne des Droits de l'Homme', in F. Matscher and H. Petzold (eds), *Protecting Human Rights: The European Dimension, Studies in Honour of G.J. Wiarda* (Köln: Heymann, 1988), pp. 159–169.

Engle K., 'After the Collapse of the Public/Private Distinction: Strategizing Women's Rights', in D. Dollmeyer (ed.), *Reconceiving Reality: Women and International Law* (Washington, DC: American Society of International Law, 1993), pp. 143–155.

Evans R. and Boseley S., ' "Drug Firms" Lobby Tactics Revealed', *Guardian* (28 September 2006).

Ewing D., 'The Human Rights Act and Labour Law' (1998) 27(4) *ILJ* 275–292.

Feingold C., 'The Little Red Schoolbook and the European Convention on Human Rights' (1978) 3(1) *HRR* 21–47.

Feldman D., 'The Developing Scope of Article 8 of the European Convention on Human Rights' (1997) *EHRLR* 265–274.

Feldman D., 'Privacy-Related Rights and their Social Value', in P. Birks (ed.), *Privacy and Loyalty* (Oxford: Oxford/Clarendon Press, 1997), pp. 15–50.

Fenwick H., 'Clashing Rights, the Welfare of the Child and the Human Rights Act' (2004) 67 *MLR* 889.

Fierens J., *Droit et Pauvreté* (Brussels: Bruylant, 1992).

Flogaitis S., 'La Notion de Principe de Légalité' (1998) 10 *ERPL* 665–681.

Flogaitis S. and Petrou Ch., 'Les Avancés du Principe de Précaution en Droit Public Grec' (2006) 59 *RHDI* 449–470.

Forder C., 'Legal Protection under Article 8 ECHR: *Marckx* and Beyond' (1990) 37(2) *NILR* 162–181.

Frantz L., 'The First Amendment in the Balance' (1962) 71 *YLJ* 1424.

Fredman S., *Human Rights Transformed: Positive Rights and Positive Duties* (Oxford: Oxford University Press, 2008).

Friedmann W., *The Changing Structure of International Law* (London: Stevens & Sons, 1964).

Frowein J., 'Art. 13 as a Growing Pillar of Convention Law', in P. Mahoney, F. Matscher, H. Petzold and L. Wildhaber (eds), *Protecting Human Rights: The European Perspective: Studies in Memory of Rolv Ryssdal* (Köln: Carl Heymanns Verlag, 2000), pp. 545–550.

Giddens A., 'Foreword', in M. Glasius, M. Kaldor and H. Anheier (eds), *Global Civil Society* (Oxford: Oxford University Press, 2002).

Gohin O., 'La Responsabilité de l'État en tant que Législateur' (1998) 2 *RIDC* 595–610.

Gostin L., 'Beyond Moral Claims: A Human Rights Approach in Mental Health' (2001) 10 *Camb Q Healthc Ethics* 264–274.

Goulbourne S., 'Airport Noise and the Right to Family Life: A Legitimate Application of Article 8 of the European Convention?' (2002) 24 *LLR* 227–236.

Gray C., 'Remedies for Individuals under the European Convention on Human Rights' (1981) 5(3) *HRR* 153–117.

Greer S., 'The Exceptions to Articles 8 to 11 of the European Convention on Human Rights' (Council of Europe: Human Rights Files No. 15, 1997).

Greer S., *The European Convention on Human Rights: Achievements, Problems and Prospects* (Cambridge: Cambridge University Press, 2006).

Harmsen R., 'The European Convention on Human Rights after Enlargement' (2001) 5(4) *IJHR* 18–43.

Hélaoui S., 'Respecting Human Rights Abroad? On the Extraterritorial Application of the European Convention on Human Rights' (MPhil thesis, University of Lund 2005).

Helfer L., 'Redesigning the European Court of Human Rights: Embeddedness as a Deep Structural Principle of the European Human Rights Regime (2008) 19(1) *EJIL* 125–159.

Hickley M., 'Negligence Over Soldier Son's Death in Iraq', *Daily Mail* (19 August 2008).

Hofstötter B., 'European Court of Human Rights: Positive Obligations in E. and others v. United Kingdom' (2004) 2(3) *I·CON* 525–560.

Hunt M., '"The Horizontal Effect" of the Human Rights Act: Moving Beyond the Public–Private Distinction', in J. Jowell and J. Cooper (eds), *Understanding Human Rights Principles* (Oxford: Hart, 2001), pp. 161–178.

Jacobs F., 'The Extension of the European Convention on Human Rights to Include Economic, Social and Cultural Rights' (1978) 5(3) *HRR* 166–178.

Jarvis F. and Sherlock A., 'The European Convention on Human Rights and the Environment' (1999) 24 *ELR* SUPP (Human Rights) 15–29.

Joseph S., 'Denouement of the Deaths on the Rock: The Right to Life of Terrorists' (1996) 14(1) *NQHR* 5–22.

Kadelbach S., 'Nuclear Testing and Human Rights' (1996) 4 *NQHR* 389–400.

Keylor W., *The Twentieth-Century World: An International History* (Oxford: Oxford University Press, 3rd edn, 1996).

Kilkelly U., *The Child and the European Convention on Human Rights* (Aldershot: Ashgate, 1999).

Koch I., 'Dichotomies, Trichotomies or Waves of Duties' (2005) 5(1) *HRLR* 81–103.

Kumm M., 'Who is Afraid of the Total Constitution? Constitutional Rights as Principles and the Constitutionalization of Private Law' (2006) 7 *GLJ* 341–370.

Lavender N., 'The Problem of the Margin of Appreciation' (1997) 4 *EHRLR* 380–390.

Lawson R., 'Human Rights: The Best is Yet to Come' (2005) 1 *ECLR* 27–37.

Leach P., 'Positive Obligations from Strasbourg – Where do the Boundaries Lie?', available at www.londonmet.ac.uk/EHRAC (accessed July 2009).

Lippmann W., 'The Reconstruction of Liberalism', in C.H. McIlwain (ed.), *Constitutionalism & The Changing World* (Cambridge: Cambridge University Press, 1939), pp. 283–293.

Lord Lester of Herne Hill, 'Universality Versus Subsidiarity: A Reply' (1998) *EHRLR* 73–81.

Loucaides L., *Essays on the Developing Law of Human Rights* (Dordrecht: Martinus Nijhoff, 1995).

Lucas O., 'La Convention Européenne des Droits de l'Homme et les Fondements de la Responsabilité Civile' (2002) 6(6) *JCP* 286–290.

McBride J., 'Protecting Life: A Positive Obligation to Help' (1999) 24 *ELR* (SUPP HR) 43–54.

Mahoney P., 'Universality Versus Subsidiarity in the Strasbourg Case Law on Free Speech: Explaining Some Recent Judgments' (1997) *EHRLR* 364–379.

Malinverni G., 'Les Fonctions des Droits Fondamentaux dans la Jurisprudence de la Commission et la Cour Européennes des Droits de l'Homme', in W. Haller, A. Kölz, G. Müller and D. Thürer (eds), *Im Dienst an der Gemeinschaft* (Basel: Helbing & Lichtenhahn, 1989), pp. 539–560.

Malinverni G., 'Variations sur un Thème encore Méconnu: l'Article 13 de la Convention Européenne des Droits de l'Homme' (1998) 33 *RTDH* 647–657.

Maljean-Dubois S., 'La Convention Européenne des Droits de l'Homme et le Droit a l'Information en Matière d'Environnement: A propos de l'Arrêt rendu par la CEDH le 19 fevrier 1998 en l'affaire Anna Maria Guerra et 39 autres c. Italie' (1998) 4 *RGDIP* 995–1022.

Markesinis B. and Enchelmaier S., 'The Applicability of Human Rights as Between Individuals under German Constitutional Law', in B. Markesinis (ed.), *Protecting Privacy* (Oxford: Oxford University Press, 1999), pp. 191–243.

Masterman R., 'Determinative in the Abstract? Article 6(1) and the Separation of Powers' (2005) 6 *EHRLR* 628–648.

Mertens P., *Le Droit de Recours Effectif devant les Instances Nationales en cas de Violation d'un Droit de l'Homme* (Brussels: Editions de l'Université de Bruxelles, 1973).

Miller C., 'Environmental Rights in a Welfare State? A Comment on Demerieux' (2003) 23(1) *OJLS* 111–125.

Mitsopoulos G., '"Τριτενέργεια" και "Αναλογικότητα" ως Διατάξεις του Αναθεωρηθέντος Συντάγματος/"Drittwirkung" et "proportionnalité" dans la Constitution Hellénique Révisée en 2001' (2002) 15 *ΔτΑ* 641–663.

Mole N., 'Z and Others v UK and TP and KM v UK' (2001) *IFLJ* 117–123.

Mowbray A., *The Development of Positive Obligations under the European Convention on Human Rights by the European Court of Human Rights* (Oxford: Hart, 2004).

Muchlinski P., 'Mental Health Patients' Rights and the European Human Rights Convention' (1980) 5(2) *HRR* 90–116.

Mundlak G., 'Human Rights and the Employment Relationship', in D. Friedmann and D. Barak-Erez (eds), *Human Rights in Private Law* (Oxford: Hart, 2001), pp. 297–328.

Murdoch J., 'A Survey of Recent Case Law under Article 5 ECHR' (1998) 23 *ELR* (SUPP HR) 31–48.

Ni Aolain F. 'The Evolving Jurisprudence of the European Convention Concerning the Right to Life' (2001) 1 *NQHR* 21–42.

Norton-Taylor R., 'Sending Troops into Battle Without Proper Equipment Could Breach Rights, Says Judge', *Guardian* (12 April 2008).

Oliver D., *Common Values and the Public–Private Divide* (London: Butterworths, 1999).

Opsahl T., 'The Convention and the Right to Respect for Family Life Particularly as Regards the Unity of the Family and the Protection of the Rights of Parents and Guardians in the Education of Children', in A.H. Robertson (ed.), *Privacy and Human Rights* (Reports and Communications Presented at the Third International Colloquy about the European Convention on Human Rights, 30 September–3 October 1970), (Manchester: Manchester University Press, 1973), pp. 255–275.

Opsahl T., 'The Right to Life', in R. St. J. Macdonald, F. Matscher and H. Petzol (eds), *The European System for the Protection of Human Rights* (Dordrecht: Martinus Nijhoff, 1993), pp. 207–223.

Orakhelashvili A., 'Restrictive Interpretation of Human Rights Treaties in the Recent Jurisprudence of the European Court of Human Rights' (2003) 14 *EJIL* 529–568.

Palme O., Statement of the Prime Minister of Sweden before the UN General Assembly on the Occasion of the Commemoration of the Fortieth Anniversary of the United Nations (21 October 1985), available at www.olofpalme.org.

Παραράς, Π., 'Το Κεκτημένο του Ευρωπαϊκού Συνταγματικού Πολιτισμού' (2001) 10 *ΔτΑ* 543.

Παρασκευόπουλος Ν. και Φυτράκη Ε., 'Η «Αυστηροποίηση» και οι Άδειες των Κρατουμένων', *Ελευθεροτυπία* (16 November 2007).

Partsch K., 'Written Communication', in A.H. Robertson (ed.), *Privacy and Human Rights* (Reports and Communications Presented at the Third International Colloquy about the European Convention on Human Rights, 30 September–3 October 1970), (Manchester: Manchester University Press, 1973), pp. 275–282.

Περράκης Σ, 'Η Προστασία των Δικαιωμάτων του Ανθρώπου στα Σχέδια της Ευρωπαϊκής Ενοποιήσεως', σε *Σύμμεικτα Βεγλερή*, τόμος II, 585 (Athens: Αντ.Ν. Σάκκουλα, 1988).

Perrin G., 'Le Problème de la Faute dans la Responsabilité Internationale de l'Etat', in W. Haller, A. Kölz, G. Müller and D. Thürer (eds), *Im Dienst an der Gemeinschaft* (Basel: Helbing & Lichtenhahn, 1989), pp. 127–133.

Petersmann E.-U., 'On "Indivisibility" of Human Rights' (2003) 14 *EJIL* 381–385.

Petersmann E.-U, 'State Sovereignty, Popular Sovereignty and Individual Sovereignty: From Constitutional Nationalism to Multilevel Constitutionalism in International Economic Law?' (Florence: European Union Institute Working Paper Law No. 45, 2006), available at http://cadmus.iue.it/dspace/bitstream/1814/6446/3/LAW%202006-45.pdf (accessed January 2011).

Πινακίδης Γ., 'Η Συνταγματική Υφή της Ευρωπαϊκής Σύμβασης Δικαιωμάτων του Ανθρώπου' (2007) 33 *ΔτΑ* 71–95.

Post H., '*Hatton and Others*: Further Clarifications of the "Indirect" Individual Right to a Healthy Environment' (2002) 2 *N-SAIL* 259–277.

Puéchavy M., 'L'Accès Égal de Tous à la Justice' (2003) 19 *ΔτΑ* 743–765.

Raday F., 'The Constitutionalization of Labour Law', in R. Blanpain and M. Weiss (eds), *The Changing Face of Labour Law and Industrial Relations, Liber Amicorum for Clyde W. Summers* (Baden-Baden: Nomos, 1993), pp. 83–108.

Raymond J., 'A Contribution to the Interpretation of Article 13 of the European Convention on Human Rights' (1980) 3 *HRR* 161–175.

Reichman A., 'Property Rights, Public Policy and the Limits of the Legal Power to Discriminate', in D. Friedmann and D. Barak-Erez (eds), *Human Rights in Private Law* (Oxford: Hart, 2001), pp. 245–280.

Reidy A., Hampson F. and Boyle K., 'Gross Violations of Human Rights: Invoking the European Convention on Human Rights in the Case of Turkey' (1997) *NQHR* 15(2) 161–173.

Rivero J., 'La Protection des Droits de l'Homme dans les Rapports entre Personnes Privées', in *Amicorum Discipulorumque Liber René Cassin III: Protection des Droits de l'Homme dans les Rapports Entre Personnes Privées* (Paris: Pédone, 1971), pp. 311–322.

Rogers H. and Tomlinson H., 'Privacy and Expression: Convention Rights and Interim Injunctions' (2003) *EHLR* (SPI) 37–53.

Rogers J., 'Applying the Doctrine of Positive Obligations in the European Convention on Human Rights to Domestic Substantive Criminal Law in Domestic Proceedings' (2003) *CrimLR* 690–708.

Rouiller C., 'L'Influence de l'Article 6 de la Convention Européenne des Droits de l'Homme sur les Procédures Nationales', in P. Mahoney, F. Matscher, H. Petzold and L. Wildhaber (eds), *Protecting Human Rights: The European Perspective: Studies in Memory of Rolv Ryssdal* (Köln: Carl Heymanns Verlag, 2000), pp. 1225–1233.

(Roukounas E.) Ρούκουνας Ε., Διεθνές Δίκαιο (Athens: Α.Σ. Σάκκουλα, 3rd edn, 2004).

(Rozakis Ch.) Ροζάκης Χ., Η Προστασία των Ανθρωπίνων Δικαιωμάτων σε μία Μεταβαλλόμενη Ευρώπη (Athens: Αντ.Ν. Σάκκουλα, 1994).

Rozakis Ch., 'The Particular Role of the Strasbourg Case-Law in the Development of Human Rights in Europe' (2010), Νομικό Βήμα (Special Issue: European Court of Human Rights: 50 years), pp. 20–30, available at www.dsanet.gr/ NOMIKO_VIMA_50_YEARS.PDF (accessed January 2011).

Sadurski W., 'Constitutional Courts in the Process of Articulating Constitutional Rights in the Post-Communist States of Central and Eastern Europe, Part I: Social and Economic Rights' (Florence: European Union Institute, Working Paper Law No. 14, 2002), available at http://cadmus.iue.it/dspace/ handle/1814/3//items-by-author?author=SADURSKI%2C+Wojciech (accessed January 2011).

Sands P., 'Human Rights, Environment and the Lopez-Ostra Case: Context and Consequences' (1996) EHRLR 557–618.

Sapienza R., 'Il Diritto ad un Ricorso Effettivo nella Convenzione Europea dei Diritti dell'Uomo' (2001) 2 RDI 271–297.

Savarese E., 'Il Protocollo N. 14 all Convenzione Europea dei Diritti dell'Unomo' (2004) RDI 714–729.

Scheuner U., 'Fundamental Rights and the Protection of the Individual Against Social Groups and Powers in the Constitutional System of the Federal Republic of Germany', in Amicorum Discipulorumque Liber René Cassin III: Protection des Droits de l'Homme dans les Rapports Entre Personnes Privées (Paris: Pédone, 1971), pp. 253–268.

Shue H., 'The Interdependence of Duties', in P. Alston and K. Tomaševski (eds), The Right to Food (Utrecht: Martinus Nijhoff, 1984), pp. 83–95.

Simitis S. 'The Rediscovery of the Individual in Labour Law', in R. Rogowski and T. Wilthagen (eds), Reflexive Labour Law (Deventer: Kluwer, 1994), pp. 183–205.

Simitis S. and Lyon-Caen A., 'Community Labour Law: A Critical Introduction to its History', in P. Davies, A. Lyon-Caen, S. Sciarra and S. Simitis (eds), European Community Labour Law: Principles and Perspectives, Liber Amicorum Lord Wedderburn of Charlton (Oxford: Oxford/Clarendon Press, 1996), pp. 1–22.

Simitis S., 'Reconsidering the Premises of Labour Law: Prolegomena to an EU Regulation on the Protection of the Employees' Personal Data' (1999) 5(1) ELJ 45–62.

Simpson B., Human Rights and the End of the Empire (Oxford: Oxford University Press, 2001).

Singh R., Hunt M. and Demetriou M., 'Is There a Role for the "Margin of Appreciation" in National Law after the Human Rights Act?' (1999) 1 EHRLR 15–22.

Σισιλιάνος Λ., Ἡ Προστασία του Περιβάλλοντος και η Ευρωπαϊκή Σύμβαση Δικαιωμάτων του Ανθρώπου – Η Εξέλιξη της Νομολογίας ως την Υπόθεση Λόπεζ Οστρα' (1996) Νόμος και Φύση 33.

Smith R., 'The Public is Being Regularly Deceived by the Drug Trials Funded by Pharmaceutical Companies, Loaded to Generate the Results they Need', Guardian (14 January 2004).

Snellgrove L., Suffragettes and Votes for Women (London: Longmans, 1964).

Spielmann D., 'L'Effet Potentiel de la Convention Européenne des Droits de l'Homme entre Personnes Privées' (Brussels: Nemesis/Bruylant, 1995).

Spielmann D., 'Obligations Positives et Effet Horizontal des Dispositions de la Convention', in F. Sudre (ed.), *L'Interprétation de la Convention Européenne des Droits de l'Homme* (Brussels: Nemesis/Bruylant, 1998), pp. 133–174.

Starmer K., 'Positive Rights under the Convention', in J. Jowell and J. Cooper (eds), *Understanding Human Rights Principles* (Oxford: Hart Publishing, 2001), pp. 139–159.

Strasser W., 'The Relationship between Substantive and Procedural Rights Guaranteed by the European Convention on Human Rights', in F. Matscher and H. Petzold (eds), *Protecting Human Rights: The European Dimension, Studies in Honour of G.J. Wiarda* (Köln: Heymann, 1988), pp. 595–604.

Sudre F., 'Droits Intangibles et/ou Droits Fondamentaux: Y a-t-il des Droits Prééminents dans la Convention Européenne des Droits de l'Homme?', in G. Cohen-Jonathan, J.-F. Flauss and P. Lambert (eds), *Liber Amicorum Marc-André Eissen* (Brussels: Bruylant, 1995), pp. 381–398.

Sudre F., 'Les "Obligations Positives" dans la Jurisprudence Européenne des Droits de l'Homme', in P. Mahoney, F. Matscher, H. Petzold and L. Wildhaber (eds), *Protecting Human Rights: The European Perspective: Studies in Memory of Rolv Ryssdal* (Köln: Carl Heymanns Verlag, 2000), pp. 1359–1376.

Taylor N., 'Policing, Privacy and Proportionality' (2003) *EHRLR* (SPI: Priv) 86–100.

Ténékidès C., 'La Cité d'Athènes et les Droits de l'Homme', in F. Matscher and H. Petzold (eds), *Protecting Human Rights: The European Dimension, Studies in Honour of G.J. Wiarda* (Köln: Heymann, 1988), pp. 605–637.

Thompson E., *The Making of the English Working Class* (London: Penguin, new edn, 1991).

Tomuschat C., '"What is a Breach" of the European Convention on Human Rights?', in R. Lawson and M. de Blois (eds), *The Dynamics of the Protection of Human Rights in Europe: Essays in Honour of H.G. Schermers* (Dordrecht: Martinus Nijhoff, 1994), pp. 315–337.

Trouwborst A., *Evolution and Status of the Precautionary Principle in International Law* (The Hague: Kluwer Law International, 2002).

Τσεβρένης Β. and Καράκωστας Ι., 'Η Προστασία του Περιβάλλοντος κατά το Ιδιωτικό Δίκαιο' (2005) *ΧρΙΔΕ* 577–588.

Tulkens F., 'Human Rights, Rhetoric or Reality?' (2001) 9(2) *ER* 125–134.

Tulkens F. and Van Drooghenbroeck S., 'L'Évolution des Droits Garantis et l'Interprétation Jurisprudentielle de la CEDH' (Lecture at the University of Grenoble on 27 September 2002), available at http://webu2.upmf-grenoble.fr/espace-europe/acad2002/textes/tulkens.htm (accessed October 2010).

Tushnet M., 'The Issue of State Action/Horizontal Effect in Comparative Constitutional Law' (2003) 1(1) *I-CON* 79–98.

van Dijk P., 'Asylum Law and Policy in the Netherlands', in R. Lawson and M. de Blois (eds), *The Dynamics of the Protection of Human Rights in Europe: Essays in Honour of H.G. Schermers* (Dordrecht: Martinus Nijhoff, 1994), pp. 123–155.

van Dijk P., '"Positive Obligations" Implied in the European Convention on Human Rights: Are the States Still the "Masters" of the Convention?', in M. Castermans-Holleman, F. Van Hoof and J. Smith (eds), *The Role of the Nation-State in the 21st Century: Human Rights, International Organisations and Foreign Policy: Essays in Honour of Peter Baehr* (The Hague: Kluwer Law International, 1998), pp. 17–33.

Vegleris P., ' "Twenty Years" Experience of the Convention and Future Prospects', in A.H. Robertson (ed.), *Privacy and Human Rights* (Reports and Communications Presented at the Third International Colloquy about the European Convention on Human Rights, 30 September–3 October 1970), (Manchester: Manchester University Press, 1973), pp. 341–412.

(Vegleris ·P.) Βεγλέρης Φ., 'Η Σύμβαση των Δικαιωμάτων του Ανθρώπου και το Σύνταγμα' (1976) *ΤοΣ* 385.

Velu J., 'The European Convention on Human Rights and the Right to Respect for Private Life, the Home and Communications', in A.H. Robertson (ed.), *Privacy and Human Rights* (Reports and Communications Presented at the Third International Colloquy about the European Convention on Human Rights, 30 September–3 October 1970), (Manchester: Manchester University Press, 1973), pp. 12–95.

Warbrick C., 'The European Convention on Human Rights and the Prevention of Terrorism' (1983) 32 *ICLQ* 82–119.

Warbrick C., 'The Structure of Article 8' (1998) 1 *EHRLR* 32–44.

Warbrick C., 'Economic and Social Interests and the European Convention on Human Rights', in M. Baderin and R. McCorquodale (eds), *Economic, Social, and Cultural Rights in Action* (Oxford: Oxford University Press, 2007), pp. 241–256.

Warbrick C., 'Constitutionalism and European Court of Human Rights' (Lecture at the University of Leeds on 14 March 2007), available at www.law.leeds.ac.uk/leedslaw/webdocs/leedslaw/uploadeddocuments/cfig-warbrick.doc   (accessed October 2010).

Wildhaber L., 'A Constitutional Future for the European Court of Human Rights?' (2002) 23(5–7) *HRLJ* 161–165.

Wildhaber L., 'The European Court of Human Rights in Action' (2004) 21 *RLR* 83–92.

Williams K., 'Medical Samaritans: Is There a Duty to Treat?' (2001) 21 *OJLS* 393–413.

Wright J., *Tort Law and Human Rights: The Impact of the ECHR on English Law* (Oxford: Hart, 2001).

Xenos D., 'Asserting the Right to Life (Article 2, ECHR) in the Context of Industry' (2007) 8 *GLJ* 231–254.

Xenos D., 'The Human Rights of the Vulnerable' (2009) 13 (4) *IJHR* 591–614.

Yee A., 'Wreckers in Deep Water: The Largest Ship Breaking Site in the World is Fuelled by Lax Standards: But Times are Changing', *Financial Times* (Special Report—Waste & the Environment) (18 April 2007).

Zierlein K.-G., 'Functions and Tasks of Constitutional Courts', in P. Mahoney, F. Matscher, H. Petzold and L. Wildhaber (eds), *Protecting Human Rights: The European Perspective: Studies in Memory of Rolv Ryssdal* (Köln: Carl Heymanns Verlag, 2000), pp. 1553–1562.

Zwart T., *The Admissibility of Human Rights Petitions: The Case Law of the European Commission of Human Rights and the Human Rights Committee* (Dordrecht: Martinus Nijhoff, 1994).

## Miscellaneous

Activity Report: Reform of the European Convention on Human Rights of the Steering Committee for Human Rights (CDDH), CDDH (2006) 008, 7 April 2006.

Buttarelli Report on Protection of Personal Data with Regard to Surveillance, The [CJ-PD (2001)11 rev.], Council of Europe (for the Project Group on Data Protection).

Explanatory Report of Protocol No. 14 to the Convention for the Protection of Human Rights and Fundamental Freedoms, amending the control system of the Convention (Protocol 14 Explanatory Report) (CETS No. 194).

Issue Paper of the Commissioner for Human Rights of the Council of Europe, 'Children and Juvenile Justice: Proposals for Improvements', 19 June 2009, CommDH/IssuePaper (2009)1.

Memorandum by the European Court of Human Rights from the Third Summit of the Council of Europe, available at www.echr.coe.int/eng/Press/2005/April/SummitCourtMemo.htm (accessed June 2010).

Practical Guide on Admissibility Criteria, available at www.echr.coe.int/NR/rdonlyres/91AEEEBC-B90F-4913-ABCC-E181A44B75AD/0/Practical_Guide_on_Admissibility_Criteria.pdf (accessed January 2011).

Recommendation *Rec1327(1997)* of the Parliamentary Assembly of the Council of Europe on the Protection and Reinforcement of the Human Rights of Refugees and Asylum-Seekers in Europe, adopted 24 April 1997.

Recommendation *Rec1606(2003)* of the Parliamentary Assembly of the Council of Europe on Areas where the European Convention on Human Rights Cannot be Implemented', adopted on 23 June 2003.

Recommendation *Rec(2006)2* of the Committee of Ministers of the Council of Europe on the European Prison Rules (amending *Rec(1987)3)*, adopted 11 January 2006.

Report ECtHR, 'Analysis of Statistics 2010', available at www.echr.coe.int (Reports section).

Resolution *Res(2004)3* of the Committee of Ministers on Judgment Revealing an Underlying Systemic Problem (adopted 12 May 2004).

Working Document of the General Assembly of the Council of Europe, 'The Effectiveness of the European Convention on Human Rights at National Level', AS/Jur (2007) 35 rev, available at http://humanrightsdoctorate.blogspot.com/2007/08/european-convention-at-national-level.html (accessed January 2011).

Working Paper of the General Assembly of the Council of Europe, 'Implementation of Judgments of the European Court of Human Rights', AS/Jur (2005) 32 (9 June 2005).

# Index

Printed in Great Britain
by Amazon

79866102R00156